PAINTING THANGKAS ON
THE TIBETAN PLATEAU

STUDIES ON ETHNIC GROUPS IN CHINA

Stevan Harrell, Editor

PAINTING THANGKAS ON THE TIBETAN PLATEAU

BUDDHIST ART MAKING IN TRANSITION

XUE MING

UNIVERSITY OF WASHINGTON PRESS

Seattle

Painting Thangkas on the Tibetan Plateau was supported by a grant from the McLellan Endowed Series Fund, established through the generosity of Martha McCleary McLellan and Mary McLellan Williams.

This book will be made open access within three years of publication thanks to Path to Open, a program developed to bring about equitable access and impact for the entire scholarly community, including authors, researchers, libraries, and university presses around the world. Learn more at https://about.jstor.org/path-to-open/.

Acknowledgments for previously published materials appear on p. xv, which should be considered an extension of the copyright page.

Design by Katrina Noble   Composed in Calluna

Photographs and maps by the author unless otherwise noted.

UNIVERSITY OF WASHINGTON PRESS
uwapress.uw.edu

Cataloging information is available from the Library of Congress

LIBRARY OF CONGRESS CONTROL NUMBERS 2025022970
ISBN 9780295754581 (hardcover)
ISBN 9780295754130 (paperback)
ISBN 9780295754147 (ebook)

♾ This paper meets the requirements of ANSI/NISO Z39.48-1992 (Permanence of Paper).

For my teachers

When we paint thangkas, we think about others.

*—Tashi Gyatso and Chodrak, brothers
and Rebgong thangka painters*

CONTENTS

FOREWORD

STEVAN HARRELL

I once curated a small exhibit featuring a few selections from the extensive collection of thangkas, or Tibetan devotional paintings, at the University of Washington's Burke Museum. I invited a local lama to lead a sutra recitation and make some remarks at the exhibit opening. He pointed out that thangkas have many meanings. Foremost is their religious or devotional meaning—they embody the presence of Buddhas, bodhisattvas, arhats, and renowned lamas and serve as aids to both group ritual and individual devotion. But their sacred nature, the lama added, does not preclude our appreciating them in other ways. Thangkas are works of art, elements of a cultural tradition, material artifacts of the Tibetan diaspora, objects in museum collections. Each aspect of their being can teach us something without detracting from the paintings' primary religious significance.

Xue Ming's *Painting Thangkas on the Tibetan Plateau* introduces us to an important facet of thangkas' being: the people who paint them. Specifically, Xue introduces us to the artists who live and work in the villages around the valley of Rebgong in Amdo, or northeastern Tibet, now administered as part of Qinghai Province. Rebgong has long been a center of thangka painting and the subject of writings in many languages about the paintings, their meaning, and their artistic value. But the painters themselves have received less attention.

Dr. Xue lived with painters' families in several Rebgong villages during research sessions extending from 2009 through 2024, and she takes readers into the lives and work of local artists. We learn how the painters mastered their craft, through rigorous, years-long apprenticeships in the studios of senior artists, progressing from the study of proper geometric proportions

for each sacred portrait to filling in colors to adding ornamentation and finally
to designing and executing their own paintings. We learn about the painters'
ideas of creativity—the changing limits of proper artistic portrayal of venerable religious figures.

We learn, importantly, how painters make a living at their art. Nowadays,
monasteries and monks still commission thangkas for strictly devotional purposes, comprising an "internal market" for the paintings. But in today's interconnected world, there is also an "external market" of collectors, dealers, and
museum curators who buy thangkas for their artistic or even their speculatory
value. Xue is careful to point out, however, that paintings entering the external market do not, for the artists at least, lose their religious value—contrary
to what anthropologists of art have observed in other places, a thangka that
goes to a shop in Shanghai or Manhattan is no different in form from one
that hangs in the sutra hall of a monastery in Rebgong or elsewhere in Tibet.
And in today's China, non-Tibetans (often rich Han Chinese businesspeople)
who follow the teachings of Tibetan Buddhist teachers and purchase thangkas
make up an "intermediate market" consisting of outside devotees.

Beyond all of these markets, thangkas also exist in a local context of gender, family, and community. Strikingly, in recent decades women have begun
to take up the painter's art—some masters take on their daughters or other
talented young women as disciples, and many of them continue painting into
marriage and adulthood, persisting in their artistic vocations even as they are
expected to take on the married women's extra burdens of housework and
childcare. Xue tells us the story of Lutso, an exceptional woman who has not
only made a respectable living off of her own paintings but has also established
a studio where she trains both female and male apprentices. A highlight of
her story comes when one of her most important works is collected at the
American Museum of Natural History, where Xue works.

Yet another context of Rebgong thangkas is political. The current Chinese
government, despite its repressive policies toward many facets of Tibetan
culture and religion, is nevertheless eager to burnish its multicultural credentials. It has actively promoted thangka painting as an ethnic art and as
an element of cultural heritage, even sponsoring the creation of *The Great
Thangka*, a six-hundred-meter-long scroll painted by over three hundred artists, in a successful attempt to set the Guinness World Record for the world's
longest thangka. Again, Xue's focus here is on the painters and how they both
maneuver to be named cultural heritage inheritors and resist designation as

mere craftspeople, since they and their community know that they are both artists and important participants in local religion.

Through all these cultural, economic, and political permutations, however, Rebgong thangkas remain, as the lama reminded us that evening, ultimately icons with religious significance. The last chapter of *Painting Thangkas* takes us back to this primary meaning as it describes the creation and use of memorial thangkas, created for families' devotions to their recently deceased relatives and destined for display in increasingly elaborate family shrines in their own houses.

We invite readers of *Painting Thangkas* to contemplate thangka painters' complex reality, in which religious artists also pursue economic opportunities, in which an officially atheist government promotes religious art as evidence of its multicultural policies, and in which, most importantly, a centuries-old art form and the artists who create it persist in a brave, new, increasingly globalized world. Their persistence is due to the creativity and adaptability but also the devotion and skill of the Rebgong thangka painters who come alive in Xue Ming's book. We are proud to present *Painting Thangkas on the Tibetan Plateau* as the twenty-seventh volume of Studies on Ethnic Groups in China.

ACKNOWLEDGMENTS

"Learning by yourself can only get you so far," said Tashi Gyatso, a renowned thangka painter in Rebgong, as he explained to me what he considered most essential in learning thangka painting, "One needs teachers for guidance, to correct his mistakes, to share their accumulated knowledge, and to encourage his breakthroughs." The same principle certainly applies to doing anthropology—this book has been produced with an enormous debt to many teachers I have had over the years.

My deepest gratitude goes to my teachers (or *ge gen* in Tibetan) in Rebgong—thangka painters, local scholars, art school owners, and government officials, who have helped my research throughout the years, although it is regretful that I have to acknowledge some of them by pseudonyms. I am particularly indebted to Jampa, Drolma and Ama, Lutso and her family, Namgyal, Tsering Gyal, Norbu, Leshe, Rinchen, Tsomo, Lhamo, Pema Tso, and Thondup. I am very grateful to my teachers from Rebgong Nagarjuna Art School, in particular Tashi Gyatso, Chodrak, Wande Gyatso, Tamgrin Tsering, and Fan Qingji, for their support of my various research projects and for generously sharing their artworks with me in this book. I thank Mela and Kalsang for helping me interpret interviews and review translations. I could not ask for better teachers than Chamba and Dargye, who patiently answered my questions and corrected my mistakes without hesitation. I hope this book meets the expectations of my *ge gen*, who have taught me so much and always encouraged me to go further.

I also benefited greatly from my teachers in the American Museum of Natural History (AMNH), in particular Laurel Kendall, who shared with me her insights of material culture and material religion, broadened my view with her substantial cross-cultural research experiences, and sharpened my thoughts with intriguing questions. With the patience and support that one would expect from a fairy godmother, Laurel was there for me during the entire book writing process, with its ups and downs. Laila Williamson, with her valuable experience working with the Tibetan collection in the AMNH, was always enthusiastic about my research and provided helpful feedback on the early drafts of several chapters. I am blessed to have learned from them. I thank Peter Whiteley for encouraging me to share my Rebgong research at the department lecture series, where I met new teachers, including Serinity Young, Mark Norell, and Paul Beelitz. I am grateful to Mourrice Papi and Barry Landua, who prepared the image of Lutso's thangka painting to be included in the book.

My training at UCLA and subsequent fieldwork play a crucial part in the current ethnography. For this I thank my mentors and other teachers at UCLA, including Joan Silk, Alan Fiske, Brooke Scelza, Daniel Hruschka, Nancy Levine, Yan Yunxiang, Robert Boyd, Clark Barrett, Daniel Fessler, Robert Lemelson, Seinenu Thein, Andrew Grant, Chen Chen, Kuang Jianjing, and Yang Xi. In particular, I am grateful to Nancy Levine and Andrew Grant, who, also working in the Amdo region, generously shared their recent works with me and answered my questions.

When I began to formulate new understandings of the art market and social changes in Rebgong, I participated in events organized by the Yale Himalaya Initiative (YHI)—sadly, it does not function anymore—and the Third Association for Nepal and Himalayan Studies conference, where I met teachers who have guided my way, including Mark Turin, Sara Shneiderman, Andrew Quintman, Tenzin Jinba, Carole McGranahan, and Tami Blumenfield. I thank Alark Saxena, who invited me to give a talk about Rebgong's art market at the YHI in 2016, where I received valuable feedback that helped me shape the writing of chapter 2. With Timothy Gregoire as the go-between, I screened my documentary film *A Woman Who Paints Thangkas* (2019) and celebrated Tibetan Losar with the Yale Himalaya Students Association in 2020, just before the pandemic put a halt on everything. I feel blessed to have been able to do that and cherish the stimulating conversations we had about art and gender at the event.

I am not the first anthropologist to study Rebgong thangka or thangka painters. I am indebted to my predecessors, particularly Chen Naihua, who generously introduced thangka painters to me during my initial visits to Rebgong, and Mark Stevenson, who directed my attention to important works of Rebgong art and culture that I would not have known otherwise. I also thank

Elizabeth Reynolds for sharing her early work on Rebgong's art commodification with me. Over the years, public talks, conferences, film screenings, art exhibits, and publications have brought me to many teachers whose comments on my work have sparked ideas in this book. I am grateful to Aaron Reich, Andrew Kipnis, David Morgan, Gonkar Gyatso, Huatse Gyal, Karma Lekshe Tsomo, Lei Jianjun, Liang Junjian, Russell Leong, Shen Yang, Soumhya Venkatesan, Trine Brox, Tsewang Tashi, Wu Di, Zhang Ziling, and Zhu Jingjiang. Special thanks go to Peng Lijing, Xu Jing, and Tenzin Jinba, who read my book draft and provided detailed comments that very much enhanced the manuscript. Inspiration and guidance from teachers I have not named directly can be found in the citations.

Thanks to Lorri Hagman, Stevan Harrell, and Caitlin Tyler-Richards for their faith in this book. I am particularly grateful to Stevan, who saw the value of this work despite the too many signposts of "I argue." Thank you, Stevan, for teaching me how to write with clarity and strength. I would also like to thank the two anonymous readers for the University of Washington Press; the book has been greatly improved because of their thoughtful comments. I also want to thank everyone at the press who has contributed to the book's publication. I alone am responsible for any remaining errors and shortcomings.

This book would not be possible without the support of my family. My husband, Huang Yibing, and my mother, Ni Xiaolin, were always there for me when research and travel distracted me from my other responsibilities. They have tremendous faith in my work and taught me the wisdom of listening. My two daughters, BaoBao and TaoTao, have accompanied me to Rebgong for documentary filmmaking and fieldwork and never got tired of art or lamb stew. Needless to say, their fresh minds open new paths for knowing. I am very grateful that they have become part of this beautiful, ongoing journey.

Many thanks to the journals that gave me permission to reuse previously published articles or portions of them, including "Strategic Commodification: The Object Biography of Tibetan Thangka Paintings in Contemporary China," *HAU: Journal of Ethnographic Theory* 11, no. 3 (Winter 2021): 1153–67; "The Travel of a Thangka: Crossing Gender and Cultural Boundaries with Lutso's Stories," *Journal of Material Culture* 29, no. 1 (2024): 102–21; and "The Life of a Painting after the End of (This) Life: Agentive Images as Relationship Participants," *HAU: Journal of Ethnographic Theory* 15, no. 2 (Fall 2025).

CONVENTIONS

Multiple languages are used in this book. I transcribe Tibetan names and terms phonetically using the Tibetan and Himalayan Library (THL) phonetic transcription guidelines, rendered to approximate the Amdo Tibetan dialect spoken in Rebgong. When a Tibetan term appears for the first time, I also give its Wylie transliteration in parentheses after the abbreviation *Tib.* as it reflects the precise spelling of the Tibetan scripts. For Chinese I use the Pinyin romanization in parentheses after the abbreviation *Ch.* For some names of Buddhist deities and Buddhist terms, I give the Sanskrit terms in addition to Tibetan and/or Chinese translations, since the Sanskrit terms (e.g., *samsara*) are commonly known by non-Tibetan audiences. All diacritical marks for Tibetan, Chinese, and Sanskrit terms are dropped to improve readability. Non-English terms such as *lha zo* (Tib. *lha bzo*) and *ge gen* (Tib. *dge rgan*) are not pluralized with an *s*. The only exceptions are *thangka*, *stupa*, and *mantra*, which I use as Anglicized words, with their plural forms as *thangkas*, *stupas*, and *mantras*.

In addition to public figures and published writers, I use real names for some of the artists in the book. When the real name appears for the first time, I give the Wylie transliteration or Pinyin with the birth year of the artist. When I use a pseudonym for a Rebgong interlocutor, it does not come with the Wylie transliteration or birth year of the person. The pseudonyms are common names among Tibetans in the region. When a pseudonym is used for a Chinese interlocutor, only the Pinyin of the last name is given. In addition, some of the interlocutors' major identifying characteristics have been altered in the case of persons with pseudonyms. For some important sites—such as a monastery, mountain, or museum—I provide both Tibetan and Chinese names, if applicable.

PAINTING THANGKAS ON
THE TIBETAN PLATEAU

INTRODUCTION

My journey in Rebgong started in a shop. In 2009, when I first entered a thangka shop in Rongwo town, a painter and owner of the shop was talking to a monk from Rongwo Monastery (Tib. *rong bo dgon chen chos 'khor gling*, Ch. *long wu si*). The monk was commissioning a thangka from the painter. They discussed the arrangements of deities and details of the painting so the finished image would suit the monk's particular practice needs. A few days later, that painter was chatting with a couple of tourists who wandered into his shop and curiously looked at thangka scrolls displayed on the wall. One tourist pointed to a thangka and asked, "How much is this painting?" The painter gave him a number. "That's expensive!" exclaimed the tourist. The painter explained that the painting was made of natural mineral pigments and that it took a few months to complete one painting. The tourist took a closer look. Eventually, he left the shop without purchasing anything.

This scene intrigued me because the different statuses of Tibetan thangka paintings—as functional objects assisting religious practice and as tourist commodities—existed seamlessly in the space of a tiny art shop, a shop run by the artist himself. I was intrigued again two years later, when I learned about another market for Rebgong thangkas. When I visited a monk painter in Upper Wutun Monastery (Tib. *seng ge gshong ya mgo dgon pa*, Ch. *wu tun shang si*), our conversation was interrupted by a phone call.

"It was a client from Zhejiang," the monk explained to me as he hung up the phone.

"An art dealer?" I asked.

"No," said the monk, "this *lao ban* [Ch. boss] and his family have been following Tibetan Buddhism for some years. They order my paintings for *xiu xing* [Ch. practicing Buddhism]."

According to the monk painter, this client trusted him and always commissioned paintings from him because his family had high standards for iconography and they knew the monk would not cheat them of their money.

Like the shop owner, well-known Rebgong thangka painter Namgyal accepts commissions from local monasteries and nearby regions and opens the door of his art school to tourists and visitors who are interested in Tibetan art. Like the monk painter, Namgyal paints thangkas for non-Tibetan devotees of Tibetan Buddhism—mostly affluent entrepreneurs residing in China's urban centers or abroad. Meanwhile, Namgyal's works are also featured in government-organized exhibits as folk art (Ch. *min jian yi shu*). One of his apprentices, Lutsojam (Tib. *klu mtsho byams*, b. 1993), known as Lutso, is the first Tibetan female thangka painter to open a studio and train her own apprentices in Rebgong.

Ready-made Tibetan thangkas with price tags, Buddhist images exhibited in national art museums as crafts, paintings commissioned by Han disciples of Tibetan Buddhism for religious practice, women who have acquired a full set of painting skills as men do and have become professional thangka painters—a little over two decades ago, these would have been inconceivable in Rebgong.

Encountering Rebgong Thangkas

Rebgong (or Repgong, Tib. *reb gong*) is located in Huangnan Tibetan Autonomous Prefecture (TAP) in Qinghai in Northwest China. It has been an important center of Tibetan Buddhist thangka art since at least the eighteenth century (Linrothe 2001, 6). Tibetan thangkas—*thang ka* in Tibetan and *tang ka* in Chinese—are scroll paintings on canvas or silk, usually depicting the Buddha and Buddhist deities, religious figures, historical scenes, or mandalas (plate 1). In Tibet commissioning a Buddhist image is an essential way of merit making (Jackson and Jackson 1988, 9; Lopez 2018, 150). Thangkas thus not only serve as important tools for teaching and meditation in Tibetan Buddhism but also play a vital role in the daily lives of Tibetan people. For instance, a thangka is often made and dedicated to the better rebirth of a recently deceased person (Bue 2017) or commissioned under the guidance of a monk or diviner to dispel illness or misfortune (Bentor 1993, 110). Currently, Rebgong thangka paintings are circulated within Tibetan communities and on China's national art market. The commodification of Tibetan Buddhist art in Rebgong began roughly in the 1990s (cf. Stevenson 2002, 211; Catanese 2019, 114) and was intensified after 2000, when China launched the Great Western Development (Ch. *xi bu da kai fa*) campaign. The status of Rebgong thangka art became even more complex after it was recognized as an "Intangible Cultural Heritage" (ICH) by the state in 2006 and by UNESCO in 2009.

This book examines how Rebgong thangka painters, *lha zo* or *lha zo pa* in Tibetan, situate their artwork and themselves between their own identities as Tibetan Buddhists, a state-fostered tourist market promoting thangka paintings as folk art or ICH, and an emerging market of non-Tibetans who pursue the very religious significance of Tibetan thangka elided in official narratives.[1] Although no Buddhist teaching unequivocally prevents women from painting thangkas (McGuckin 1996, 39), Rebgong did not have any female thangka painters until the late 2000s—the new markets have drawn Tibetan women into art production. Now both Rebgong women and men face new constraints and possibilities in making Buddhist images. How do Rebgong Tibetans interact with thangkas? How do they make them? By this I mean not just the materials they use or the artistic skills they hone but also the "enchanted technologies," in Laurel Kendall's (2021) words—the protocols, rituals, energies, art makers' intentions, and even accidents that make an image *work*. What is the image made for? If a thangka painting sits with a price tag in a commercial art gallery, has it lost its religious value, or "aura" (cf. Benjamin 1969; Brox 2019)? Are women's paintings considered as effective as men's? What happens when certain protocols are not followed or rules are broken? What if participants— monastic and lay, painter and patron, Tibetan and non-Tibetan, women and men, young and old—disagree with each other? Who receives the religious merits, and who gets the punishment? When Rebgong painters present their artwork in a cultural expo organized by the government, do they paint their religious conviction and the sacred seed syllables *om ah hum* on the back of a thangka, or do they omit both?[2]

Today Rebgong art makers produce for both internal audiences (monastic and lay communities in Tibet) and external ones (tourists and art merchants) as well as an intermediate market of non-Tibetans who follow and practice Tibetan Buddhism (Caple 2020; Osburg 2020) and commission Rebgong thangkas for ritual purposes.[3] For these clients, the thangka's intended use is neither purely commercial nor sacred in the most traditional sense. The variety of relationships between thangka painters and their clients (especially non-Tibetan clients) is a missing piece in previous studies of Rebgong thangka art and its commodification (e.g., Reynolds 2011; Catanese 2019). Among all painters, Tibetan female *lha zo* face particular challenges. Rebgong women painters are mastering what was historically a male domain of art making.[4] Female *lha zo* not only enter the same complex regime of sacred art production but also need to compete in a market that has been dominated by men. Furthermore, both female and male *lha zo* constantly contribute innovations and adjust to the process of art making and distribution.

As Rebgong thangkas now circulate beyond the local community and Rebgong thangka painters respond to challenges and opportunities in the new markets, the thangkas they paint, unlike many other Indigenous artworks (e.g., Graburn 1976; Price 1989; Errington 1998; Morphy 2007), do not change significantly in form or content and often not in function either. Commodification does not necessarily reduce the aura of Tibetan thangka paintings. The efficacy of Rebgong thangka is *made* in the process of art production, circulation, consumption, displaying, and veneration. Some Rebgong *lha zo*, including women, paint thangkas and participate in the art market in order to authenticate their religious identity, preserve a cultural tradition, and establish artistic authority within and beyond Tibetan communities. Amid conflicting pressures from the state's overarching goal of cultural development, from the seemingly overwhelming forces of commodification, and from painters' own understandings of art making, different *lha zo* may accomplish these goals via somewhat different pathways—the heterogeneity is an important aspect of art making in today's Rebgong.

Rebgong's ethnographic context enables us to understand Tibetan thangka from multiple perspectives—religious, artistic, economic, political, social, and personal. This provides new insights into how anthropologists understand traditional or functional art. The example of Rebgong thangka shows how people relate to things and how people relate to each other through things, expanding an "anthropological theory of art" (Gell 1998) to an unusual terrain in Tibet.

Art Making in the "Golden Valley"

In many Chinese language travel guides, exhibition catalogs, and TV shows, Rebgong is mistakenly translated as the "Golden Valley" or the "Golden Valley where dreams come true" (see critiques from Kalzang Tseden 2011, 6). One might suspect this is a misinterpretation of Tibetan literature, which praises

Rebgong as the "golden land" or "golden stone" (Tib. *gser mo ljongs*) because of its topography and abundant natural resources (Dhondup 2011, 36). Located in the northeastern part of the Tibetan Plateau and about 112 miles south of Xining, the capital of Qinghai, Rebgong enjoys a relatively mild climate most of the year (map 1).[5] The Guchu River (Tib. *dgu chu*, Ch. *long wu he*) nurtures the valley, which sits at an altitude of about 8,200 feet, and provides for more than 18,500 acres of farmland, divided into small patches cultivated by individual households (plate 2). Although Rebgong has been defined in different ways across time (Stevenson 2002, 198; Kalzang Tseden 2011, 9; Dhondup 2011, 36), today the names Rebgong and Tongren—the administrative center of Huangnan TAP—are often used interchangeably by local residents, non-Tibetan tourists, and visitors, especially after "Regong arts" were recognized as an ICH.[6] According to the 2020 census, Tongren is the home of 101,519 people, the most populous county in Huangnan TAP.[7] While the majority of the residents are Tibetans, as in many parts of the Sino-Tibetan borderlands, different ethnic groups, including Han, Monguor, Mongol, Hui, Salar, and Bao'an, have lived in and around Rebgong for centuries (Dhondup 2011, 34; Makley 2018, 7).[8]

Rongwo Monastery, an important historical and cultural site in Rebgong, is also one of the largest Geluk monasteries in Amdo—the Tibetan cultural region now covering the majority of Qinghai, part of Gansu, and the north-western part of Sichuan. According to *The Political and Religious History of Amdo*, Rongwo Monastery was founded by Samten Rinchen (Tib. *bsam gtan rin chen*) in 1301 and originally followed the Sakya school of Tibetan Buddhism.[9] From the late sixteenth to the early seventeenth century, Rongwo Monastery gradually changed its spiritual lineage to that of the Geluk, the school established by Amdo-born religious teacher Tsongkhapa (Tib. *tsong kha pa*, 1357–1419). With the rise of the Geluk influence and the emergence of the Shartsang lineage, the demand for religious images grew.[10] Buddhist art making in Rebgong became institutionalized and flourished (Kalzang Tseden 2011, 184; Menchok Dondrub 2016, 55). The work of Rebgong *lha zo* was commissioned not only by Tibetan monasteries near and far but also by monasteries in Beijing and Chengde (the Qing emperors' summer retreat).[11] Despite debates about the origin of Rebgong's art, Tibetologists and art historians generally agree that in the eighteenth century Rebgong was already an important center of Tibetan Buddhist art making (Linrothe 2001, 6; Stevenson 2002, 200–204; and Kalzang Tseden 2011, 187–91).

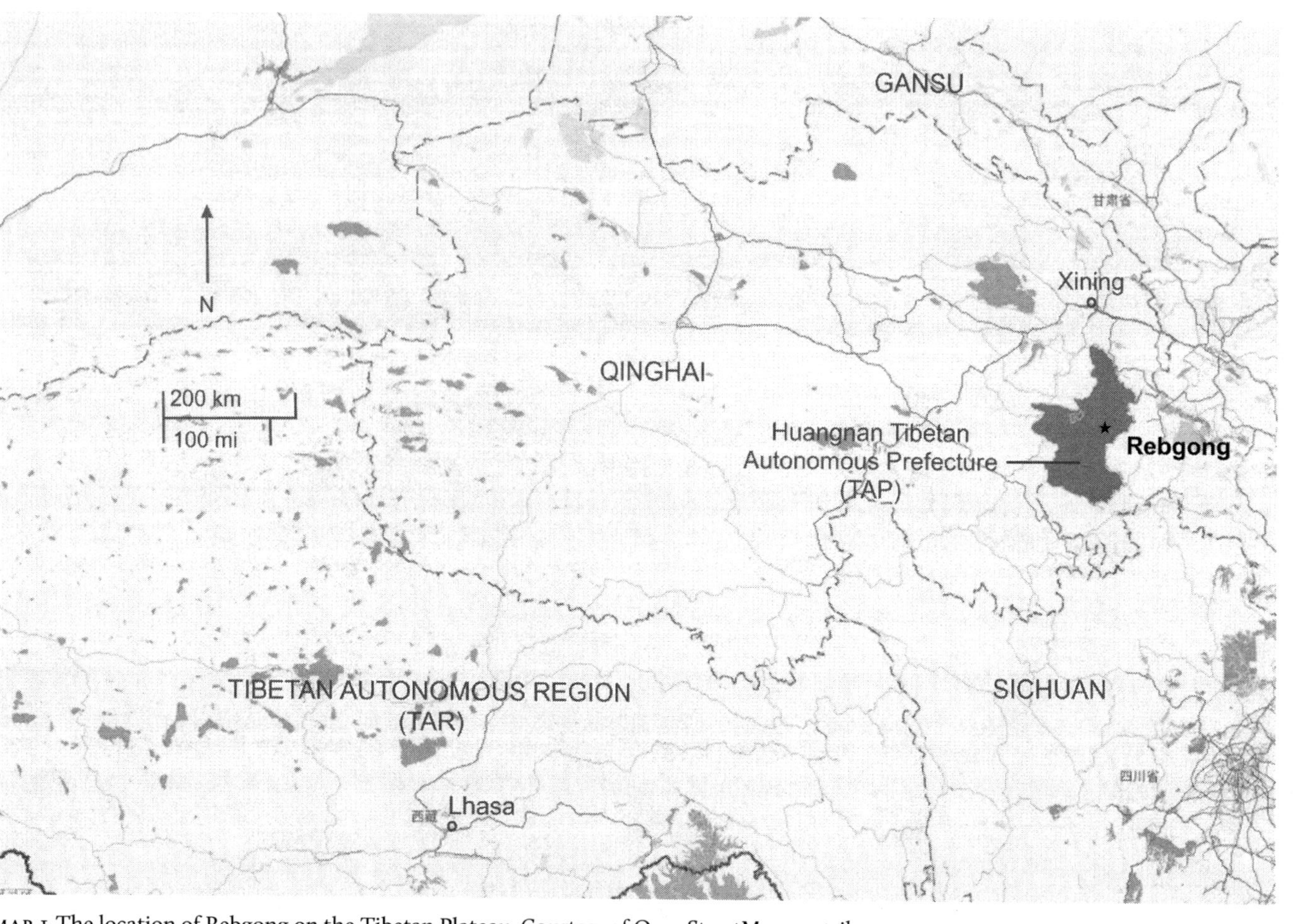

MAP 1 The location of Rebgong on the Tibetan Plateau. Courtesy of OpenStreetMap contributors.

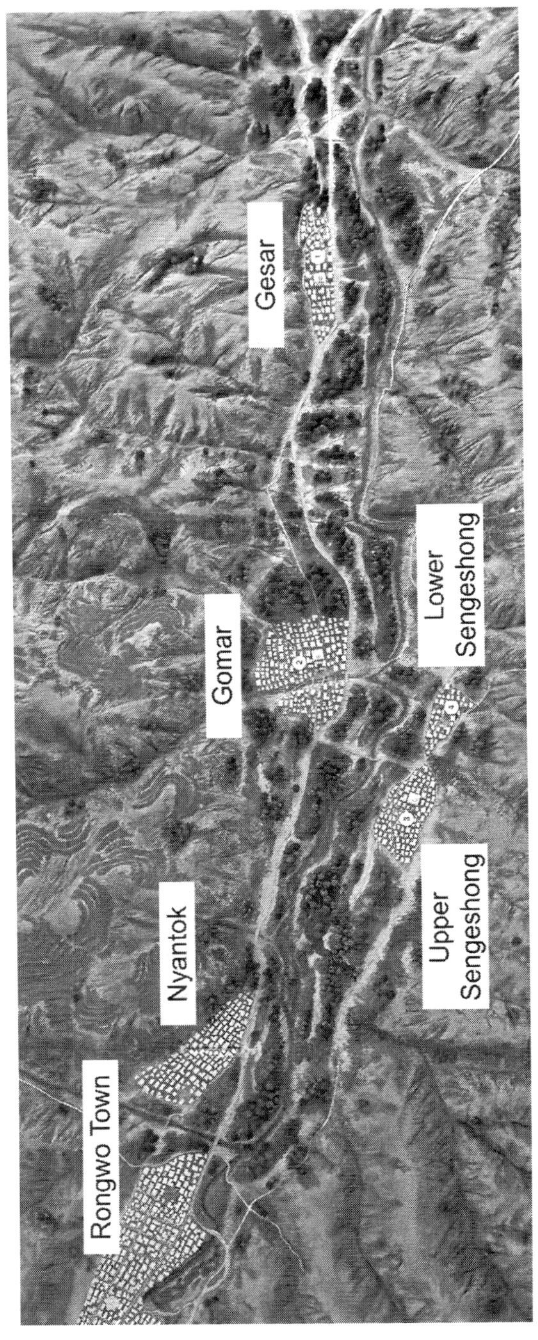

MAP 2 The art making villages in Rebgong.

Although Rongwo Monastery keeps important wall paintings, thangka scrolls, and sculptures, the monastery itself is not the hub of art making. About six miles north of Rongwo Monastery, along the Guchu River valley, monks and lay *lha zo* from several villages have dominated the art production in Rebgong (map 2).[12]

The valley would look just like Tibetan farming communities elsewhere, if one did not see the canvases or wooden stretchers sitting in the courtyard of each household. On my first trip to Rebgong in 2009, the similar scene at different homes familiarized me with the rhythm of life in the village: *ge truk* (apprentices, Tib. *dge phrug*, Ch. *tu di*) and their *ge gen* (teacher or tutor, Tib. *dge rgan*, Ch. *shi fu*)—usually the household head—sit in front of the canvas and paint thangkas during the day. Women in the house prepare food and drink for the painters, attend to farmwork, and take care of household chores. Apprentices are often the *ge gen*'s own children or children of his relatives and friends. When it gets dark, painters gather their paintbrushes and pigments, covering the unfinished thangka with a cloth. Apprentices and their *ge gen*'s family sit together to enjoy dinner, watch TV, and catch up on news and gossip in the village. Some apprentices go back to their own homes for the night. Many others live in their *ge gen*'s home. The *ge gen* never charges tuition or a fee from apprentices. The apprentices pay the *ge gen* back by helping with his art commissions; they also help the teacher's family when extra hands are needed for agriculture work or heavy labor—an arrangement that is part of the *ge gen–ge truk* tradition in Rebgong.

Ge truk learn painting both from written materials and directly from their *ge gen* (Linrothe 2001; Fraser 2011). There is no single manual used in Rebgong today for Buddhist iconography or iconometric theory.[13] According to painters, local scholars, and art historians, possible references that painters consult include, but are not limited to, texts from the Buddhist canon *Tengyur* (Tib. *bstan 'gyur*, Ch. *dan zhu er*); painting manuals assembled by the Potala Palace; *The Wish-Granting Gem* authored by the fifteenth-century artist Menla Dondrub (Tib. *sman bla don grub*); and the eighteenth-century Chinese-language art making treatise *The Buddha's Teaching on the Iconometry in Image Making*.[14] But most Rebgong apprentices do not learn thangka painting by directly reading the scriptures or treatises. Rather, they rely on their *ge gen*'s hand-drawn sketches and verbal instructions to study and practice Buddhist iconometry and iconography (figure 1).

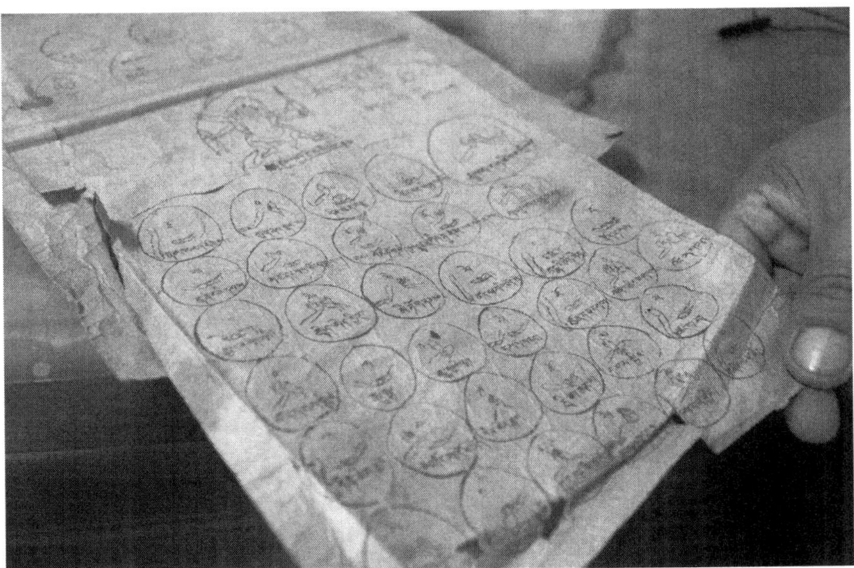

FIGURE 1 A sketch by Namgyal's teacher, possibly produced in the 1980s, for demonstrating the various hand gestures of the Buddha to his apprentices, 2012.

A beginner starts by learning how to construct the proportional grid (Tib. *thig khang*) on paper, using the lines as guidance to portray the image of a deity.[15] By repeatedly copying examples of Buddhas and deities, the student gradually internalizes the rules of measurement and the configuration of each divine figure—this usually takes a few years.[16] Then the apprentice advances to coloring, first learning to grind and mix mineral pigments, next to apply base colors, then how to add various washes of shading (Tib. *mdangs*) to different objects.[17] A more advanced apprentice will practice gold lining and finishing details, including refining facial features and painting or dotting the eyes, called "opening the eyes" (Tib. *spyan 'byed*, Ch. *kai yan*) for the deities.[18] Although many contemporary works produced in Rebgong seem to follow the Menri style (Tib. *sman ris*, Ch. *mian tang pai*), established by Menla Dondrub, given the dynamic cultural exchange between Rebgong *lha zo* and the outside world, their works constantly assimilate elements from other Tibetan painting schools and Chinese, Nepalese, and Indian art (Linrothe 2001, 22). While all painters work under similar iconographic and iconometric rules, each workshop has its own specialty or preferred motif (Linrothe 2001, 25), which apprentices also acquire through "working on commissions in a collaborative environment" (Fraser 2011, 129).

When Tashi Gyatso (Tib. *bkra shis rgya mtsho*, b. 1967) and Chodrak (Tib. *chos grags*, b. 1971), brothers and renowned *lha zo pa* in Rebgong, say that they think about others when they paint thangkas (see the book's epigraph), they are emphasizing the religious function of thangka painting and the essential responsibility of thangka painters. Above all, Tibetan Buddhist paintings and statues are sacred receptacles (Tib. *sku rten*, the "body support") that host the divinities. After an image is made and properly consecrated (Tib. *rab gnas*, Ch. *kai guang*), it is transformed into the Buddha, the deity, or the religious teacher it depicts (Bentor 1996; Lopez 2018; Tythacott and Bellini 2020).[19] To commission a Buddhist image and worship it in one's daily life is to accumulate merits and, in some cases, to overcome obstacles.

Since an artist paints a thangka to fulfill the patron's specific need, art making is considered a meritorious act (Tib. *dge las* or *dge ba*). The *lha zo* relies on her or his artistic skill and selfless virtue to serve as the essential medium between the divinity and the devotee. Citing the early Chinese Buddhist scripture *The Scripture [Spoken by] the Buddha in His Golden Coffin about the Merit of Devotion* (Ch. *fo zai jin guan jing fu jing*), Alex Catanese points out that a painter accumulates merits through depicting the image of the sacred (2019, 25) and that "such moral attributions are alive and well" among contemporary *lha zo* (Catanese 2019, 75). Rebgong painters and scholars also refer to another scripture, *The Buddha on the Merits of Image Making in the Mahayana* (Ch. *fo shuo da cheng zao xiang gong de jing*), to emphasize the meritorious nature of thangka painting. On the other hand, no matter for whom or what a thangka is made, incorrect iconography or inappropriate practice would incur bad karmic consequences for the painter (Bentor 1993, 131), which some *lha zo* understand as a punishment from the sacred being(s) depicted in the thangka (Chen 2013, 218).

A Synergy between the Anthropology of Art and "Material Religion"

Like locally produced tourist or commercial arts (e.g., Graburn 1984; Phillips and Steiner 1999; Kisin and Myers 2019), Tibetan thangka paintings have entered the global marketplace as fine art, artifact, antiquity, and following the Chinese government's designation, folk art or craft. Rebgong thangka painters, like Australian Aboriginal dot painters (Morphy 2007), Ghanaian sculptors (Steiner 1994), or Zapotec weavers (Stephen 2005), need to negotiate the meaning of their work and define themselves in these "intercultural fields" (Myers 2001, 41). Yet Rebgong *lha zo* also face unique opportunities and challenges. Rebgong thangkas, no matter where they are circulated, largely maintain their traditional medium, form, and content.[20] More important, Rebgong thangkas are now commissioned by both Tibetan and non-Tibetan patrons for religious use. These thangkas thus differ from Aboriginal acrylic paintings displayed in museums or on collectors' walls—these are derived from the "traditional designs involved in ritual and body decoration and cave painting" (Myers 2002, 2), but the paintings themselves are not used in any ritual by local communities. Unlike Navajo singers who intentionally alter or omit details of the traditional design so that the sandpaintings they produce can be sold to nonbelievers (Parezo 1983, 75), hardly any *lha zo* dare to change the Buddhist iconography, no matter what the intended destination of the painting. This indicates that Tibetan thangka art today does not divide neatly into the categories of "traditional art" intended for internal consumption and "tourist or commercial art" for external audiences.[21]

In today's market, many Tibetan thangkas are made for religious use and intended to be "ensouled" (Kendall 2021) through self-conscious human acts—in this case, the consecration rituals performed by monks. Historically and into the present, thangka paintings and other ritual images, understood by devotees as social actants (Gell 1998; Keane 2003), establish special relationships with viewers beyond aesthetic appreciation (Kendall 2021, 12). Scholars of material religion have helpfully oriented our gaze toward the material fabrication and ritual masters' practices that equip the image's agency as well as people's response to its potency.[22] While this approach encourages a fluid understanding of ritual objects, it focuses too exclusively on people's direct interaction with the object, leaving out the important relationships between the makers of the art and its audiences. Art makers' intentions and expectations are too often shadowed under terms such as *out of piety* or *to accumulate merit*. Both are meritorious acts (Tib. *dge las*), but for a *lha zo*, is painting a thangka commissioned by an outside client the same as painting for one's mother? What has been missing is a sophisticated look at how personal relationships and social conditions intertwine with the making and use of functional or ritual objects.

Anthropologists of art, by contrast, have offered insights into the complex web of social interactions in which the art and the artist are embedded.[23]

By bridging the anthropology of art and the study of material religion, this book forges a novel intersection between the material, ontological, and social discourses in anthropology. Ethnographic encounters in Rebgong reveal how personal relationships and social conditions mediate the making of a thangka that *works* (or not) as well as the plurality of engagements people have with thangka paintings. These various kinds of engagements, in turn, depend on the context—where, when, and for whom is a Rebgong thangka defined as "sacred object," "art," or "craft," and how have thangka painters internalized or challenged these categories?[24] This approach not only highlights Rebgong *lha zo*'s agency and their ownership of the cultural heritage but also illuminates how we can better view, understand, and contextualize religious and ritual images in intercultural settings.

The Diverse Meanings of Thangka

Rebgong art has changed and developed in many directions since 1982, when it made its debut in China's national museums. Exhibitions in that era not only recognized the artistic significance of Rebgong thangkas and energized their revival after over twenty years of suppression but also facilitated their commodification—broadening Rebgong art from the religious realm to tourist or folk art and promoting it on China's national art market.[25] The Great Western Development campaign and the Intangible Cultural Heritage recognition have intensified this process, with both national and local governments viewing Tibetan thangka as a "cultural resource" and painting as a useful skill that contributes to the alleviation of poverty (Ch. *tuo pin*).[26] One significant change is that ready-made thangkas (i.e., thangkas made without a commission) and mass-produced religious objects have become prevalent on the market (Catanese 2019). The emergence of art schools and government-sponsored training programs has also made a substantial impact on the *ge gen–ge truk* relationship and the mode of cultural transmission in Rebgong. In that sense *Golden Valley* is perhaps not a careless translation appearing on travel brochures or TV shows but precisely the goal of cultural development—the wealth of Rebgong is also embedded in the canvases sitting in thangka painters' courtyards.[27]

The revived story of Rebgong artist Shawo Tsering (Tib. *sha bo tshe ring*, 1922–2004) and his 1940 encounter with Chinese artist Zhang Daqian (1899–1983) in Dunhuang inspired local artists, scholars, and some government officials to recognize the uniqueness of Rebgong art—the knowledge and skills of Rebgong *lha zo pa* not only enabled them to repair peeled murals in monasteries but also connected them to an earlier tradition that few contemporary artists could decipher.[28] In the Reform era, leading artists and local officials managed to choose a different pathway for Rebgong thangka than for other types of local art available on the national market (e.g., Garze New Tibetan Painting and Yangliuqing New Year Prints).[29] In addition, *The Great Thangka* (Tib. *kun 'dus zhal thang chen mo*, Ch. *cai hui da guan*), the 618-meter (2,028-foot) thangka scroll designed by a Rebgong *lha zo* and created in 1999 through the collaboration of over three hundred artists, not only "put Reb gong on the world map" (Stevenson 2002, 216); it also transformed the mode of art production and distribution in Rebgong. While the artistic "renaissance" (Linrothe 2001) that Shawo Tsering and his fellow painters experienced in the 1980s was largely nurtured by monastic commissions, *The Great Thangka* was an overture to Rebgong art in the twenty-first century—the preservation of cultural traditions and experiments of artistic innovation require the support of new patrons and painters' carefully crafted narratives that negotiate space for Buddhist art making between the state's overarching agenda of cultural development and the increasing intensity of commodification.

At the turn of the century, Tibetan thangka paintings were no newcomers to the global art market. When, however, Tibetan thangkas are appreciated as canonical art in the mainstream art world—in fine art museums, galleries, and auction houses—they usually enter these places as differently contextualized objects intended to represent a certain geographic region, artistic genre, or aesthetic excellence. For instance, for the Metropolitan Museum of Art's first exhibition about Tibetan paintings in 1998, its director, Philippe de Montebello, wrote in the catalog's foreword, "The paintings were chosen primarily for their aesthetic quality and condition; their iconography was considered only secondarily."[30] His words resonate with the dominant narrative of Tibetan art in China, which appreciates thangka paintings for the artistic skill or the natural pigments involved in the work but often downplays or outright neglects their religious meaning. Without being properly introduced to the religious meaning and function of Tibetan thangkas, many audiences who encounter the image of a thousand-armed Avalokiteshvara or wrathful deities in China's national art museum would likely be impressed by the exquisite craftsmanship—the major selling point in the narrative—but be perplexed by what the image is for or mistake it as a mysterious invention arising from the psychology of the art maker.[31]

At another extreme, some audiences, including some who have commissioned or purchased Rebgong thangkas, would likely consider Tibetan art as transcending any aesthetic value and pointing to a hidden truth of the cosmos—viewing a Tibetan thangka is like performing psychological therapy on the viewer.[32] Those prevalent but biased views of Tibetan art are very distant from how Tibetan people, Rebgong residents included, view and use their images. In Rebgong, thangkas, murals, and statues are commissioned for "reasons more quotidian than mystical" (Lopez 2018, 150), including the *kye go* (Tib. *skyes sgo*) thangka—a genre of Tibetan thangka paintings made for the recently deceased to help them find a better rebirth. The *kye go* image in Rebgong is not only used in funeral rites but is also kept and venerated by family members in their domestic shrine (Tib. *mchod khang*) long after the funeral and mourning have ended. The personal, familial, and local memories are preserved in the *kye go* images commissioned on behalf of the deceased family member, art teachers, and religious leaders. This aspect of Tibetan art, unfortunately, is ignored even in the immersive display of Tibetan shrine room exhibits intended to encourage visitors to appreciate the religious art and objects from a more "authentic" perspective.[33]

With the expanded reception for Tibetan thangkas, the question of who should determine the meaning of Tibetan art has no straightforward answer. Donald Lopez leaves the space open for discussion, raising questions such as "Is perspective of the Tibetan, in the end, the determinative perspective? And, if so, which Tibetan, the artist in exile or the artist in Tibet? And which artist, the one producing *thangkas* for the Dalai Lama, the one producing *thangkas* for tourists, or the one producing modernist paintings?" (2018, 154). Many diaspora Tibetans consider that "the 'real' Tibet ceased to exist after 1959" (C. Harris 2012, 10). Their material cultures, many of which have flowed from the Tibetan Plateau to New York, London, and other global metropolitan centers since then, are preserved and displayed as cultural relics that "paint a portrait of a Tibet unlocated in history" (Lopez 2018, 136–37). The Western representation of Tibetan art has fostered a timeless or static view of Tibetan art, which boosts the economic and political value of Tibetan objects possessed by Western museums and private collectors but denies the agency and innovation of contemporary Tibetan people who continue making art.

For instance, the thangka painting *Three Kings*, commissioned by the fourteenth Dalai Lama for the newly built Namgyal Temple in Dharamsala and painted by the Amdo-born Tibetan artist Amdo Jampa (Tib. *a mdo byams pa,*

1916–2002) in the 1980s, was strongly rejected by the exile community because the artist's innovation, depicting the kings' portraits as well as objects around them three-dimensionally, reminded Tibetan exiles of Socialist Realism, a predominant art style in Maoist China, even though it was certainly not the artist's intention to sinicize Tibetan religious figures (Harris 1999, 49–52; Tsewang Tashi 2018, 54–55).[34] In addition, the Lhasa-born Tibetan contemporary artist Gonkar Gyatso (Tib. *gong dkar rgya mtsho*, b. 1961) decided to leave for London in 1996 after four years in Dharamsala because he felt "the only acceptable form of art in Dharamsala was traditional thangka"; his works, then (e.g., an abstract form of the Buddha's silhouette), were considered inauthentic, inappropriate, or even profane (personal communication, July 28, 2016).

The Perspectives of Rebgong *Lha Zo*

It is thus clear that no one constituency and no one interpretation governs how Rebgong *lha zo* should make their arts—not national or local governments, not art historians or museum curators, not Tibetans in exile, not devout Buddhists who commission thangkas on the intermediate market. This provides Rebgong *lha zo* with more varied ways to exercise their agency and contribute to the evolving Tibetan art tradition. Rebgong thangka painters' agency and originality work in diverse arenas, including the Buddhist/monastic tradition, the state's ICH agenda, and wealthy patrons' "money-mediated spirituality" (Osburg 2020), directing our attention to how painters define themselves as artists and how they present themselves and their artwork to various audiences. When some Rebgong painters bring their artworks to private galleries in China's urban centers, they seek to challenge the view that reduces Tibetan thangka to a craft while making and exhibiting their work in response to the "pure gaze" (Bourdieu 1984, 3) of non-Tibetan audiences who simultaneously look for spirituality and creativity in thangka art.[35]

At the same time, most Rebgong painters understand "art" very differently from how it was defined by the Western hegemonic system that undergirds the art world. These *lha zo* rely on their artistic skills, knowledge of Buddhism, and thoughtful use of visual language to create scenes that exist in Buddhist scriptures only as text. This is illustrated in the works produced by Tashi Gyatso and Chodrak, particularly in their recent paintings commissioned by a monastery in Mount Wutai (Shanxi) for a Chinese Buddhist ritual. Their practices resonate with what Shawo Tsering and his fellow *lha zo* accomplished in Dunhuang eighty years ago—it seems that only artists with sophisticated art skills and profound knowledge of Buddhism can decipher the messages embedded in religious scriptures and visual images and translate them back and forth in skillful ways. From their point of view, this level of creativity has always been part of Buddhist art making practice and defines the meaning of the "true artist" (Tib. *lha bzo dngos ma zhig*).[36]

This creativity within a tradition is, however, different from that of the Tibetan contemporary artists Clare Harris introduces in *The Museum on the Roof of the World*.[37] Influenced by Tibetan, Chinese, and/or Western art styles, these artists produce modern art as a way to reconstruct their identities. By analyzing their artwork and practice, Harris seeks to answer the question of creativity and agency in Tibetan art, suggesting that Tibetan art may have a life "in the rarefied atmosphere of the art world" (2012, 263). Though illuminating, this conclusion unfortunately reinforces Tucci's view that Tibetan artists who produce religious or functional images are not much more than "copyists." In contrast, art historian Rob Linrothe observes, based on his field trips in Rebgong in 1998 and 2001, that Rebgong painters today are "permitting contemporary elements to affect their painting . . . attuned to both the past and the present, but ideological slaves to neither" (2001, 7). Even when Rebgong *lha zo* produce for their "own people," as in the case of the *kye go* thangkas, painters constantly make compromises, changes, and/or artistic innovations—whether or how something works are "practical theories" (Venkatesan 2020, 448) that thangka painters reconcile with physical materials, religious protocols, artistic concerns, and social conditions.

The experiences and relationships of several male *lha zo* with their non-Tibetan patrons show how actual transactions take place, how patronage is established and maintained (or broken) over time, and how different painters explore alternative ways to engage with the various markets. Although some painters exploit the government's agenda in order to gain personal benefits, other *lha zo* strategically participate in the market to proclaim the religious identity of art making challenged by the state. They contextualize their artwork in ways that make thangkas a kind of commission in a reimagining of the tradition, especially with clients from the intermediate market. Some *lha zo* use the "profits" made from their affluent non-Tibetan clients to nourish their monastic commissions or to sustain the operation of their art schools, financially independent from government support, so that they can cultivate their apprentices following the traditional mode of art transmission.

Rebgong female *lha zo* are in a unique position (plate 3). Although Rebgong women's participation in art making may have improved their economic status, enhanced their personal competence, or provided them with a new way to exercise their creativity and agency (Babcock 1993; Niessen 1999; Stephen 2005; Li 2020)—unlike Zapotec weavers, Pueblo potters, or even some Tibetan women weavers in pastoralist communities (Bauer 2006; T. Harris 2012)—most Rebgong women did not engage in art making before their participation in thangka painting.[38] Moreover, since women have started painting thangkas in Rebgong, there has been no gendered division of labor in art making.[39] Rebgong women *lha zo* are mastering what was previously a male domain, a domain requiring an extended period of learning to acquire the full complement of artistic skills as well as religious protocols and knowledge behind art making. Rebgong women painters also accept commissions and produce art used for religious purposes, in contrast to female modern artists who explore various mediums—oil paint, acrylics, and sculpture, for example—to create artworks about their intimate experience as Tibetan women from a feminist point of view.[40]

Instead of seeing Rebgong female *lha zo* as embodiments of women's liberation, as asserted by the state, or viewing structural arrangements as absolute constraints, I join other feminist scholars, Lila Abu-Lughod (2008) and Karma Lekshe Tsomo (2019), in seeing women as subjects of their own lives and situate their aspirations, struggles, and choices in the dynamic context of art making. Experiences of female apprentices in local art schools and married women who paint with their husbands at home embody a paradox. Although women are acquiring art making skills, hardly any family expects women painters to operate their own art studios or participate in the market as men do. The stationary work of a painter reinforces ongoing gender and cultural expectations for Tibetan women in the village. Women's responsibilities to their family and the community regularly interrupt their art making—many women have to cease painting after getting married or having children. This is rendered even more acute by the heightened mobility of Tibetan men who engage with the new markets. However, in a society where religious identities are highly esteemed but deeply gendered (Gyatso and Havnevik 2005; Makley 2007; and Gayley 2016), Tibetan women *lha zo* expect to accumulate Buddhist merit through painting thangkas and to help others with their artistic skills—a virtuous act (Tib. *dge las*) that was not available to women in the past. Many female *lha zo* see art making and their continuous engagement in familial and communal activities as reinforcing the sense of home (Tib. *khyim*) while many things around them are changing.

While most female painters paint with their husbands at home or stay in art schools as apprentices or assistants, one exceptional Tibetan woman, Lutso, broke this mold and became the first woman in Rebgong to open a thangka studio and train both female and male apprentices on her own. In particular, Lutso's life experiences are intertwined with the meaning of her thangka *Avalokiteshvara with Mind at Rest*, which I followed from its birth in Rebgong to its visit to an art gallery in Beijing and, finally, to its entrance into the collection of an ethnographic museum in New York. Through painting thangkas and training her apprentices (especially female *ge truk*), Lutso is able to support her family financially, empower other Tibetan women, and authenticate a religious identity that has been denied in the official narrative of Tibetan thangka art. The practices of Rebgong women *lha zo*, including Lutso and other female painters, suggest an alternative narrative to the official rhetoric that purposefully mutes the religious significance of thangka and emphasizes the economic incentives in art making. They also add a new layer of complexity to the discourse of Tibetan women's empowerment, which often emphasizes individual competence or achievement.[41]

Not all art makers in Rebgong are ethnic Tibetans (Ch. *zang zu*); some of them are recognized by the government as Monguor (Ch. *tu zu*) or Mongolians (Ch. *meng gu zu*), for instance. However, many of the "non-Tibetan" art makers, since they make Tibetan thangka art and practice Tibetan Buddhism in their daily lives, strongly identify themselves as Tibetan or Tibetan Buddhist.[42] Some ambitious ones have even successfully changed their ethnic identity formally to Tibetan (also see Roche 2019, 118). Tenzin Jinba points out that "ethnicity is just one of the multiple identities of the locals" and that it does not play a decisive role in defining people's practices (2014, xiv). What Rebgong art is and who are Rebgong *lha zo* reveal the complex problem of identity (Stevenson 2002, 199). While open conflict and resistance to change have occurred across Tibet (Barnett 2006; Yeh 2013; and Makley 2015), especially with the 2008 unrest and its repercussions, the daily reality of Rebgong *lha zo* is complex and belies the simple dichotomy of oppressed Tibetans and authoritarian Chinese overlords. While recognizing the reality of ethnic conflict, here I focus on the subtle and day-to-day decisions Rebgong *lha zo* make in order to paint thangkas and to cope with change. By looking at the different art markets, the context of the actual exchanges, and the specific relationships forged between thangka painters and their clients (especially non-Tibetan clients), this ethnography unravels the ongoing and intricate "social life" (Appadurai 1986) of Tibetan thangka paintings in contemporary China as well as the agency and creativity of Rebgong thangka painters.

The Lost Smells and the Unlearned Painting Skill

I thought I had all the things I need for writing. Field notes, voice recordings, photos, videos, scanned documents, sketches, Buddhist paraphernalia, and actual thangka paintings, large and small, which I commissioned or was given during various trips to Rebgong. When I started writing, the first thing that jumped into my mind was what I could not preserve: the smells.

Jampa's breath reeks of Tsingtao beer when he gets off the motorcycle, after "just borrowing some pigments from Wande" turns into a three-hour drinking party in the summer heat. Lutso's thangka studio mixes the smells of mineral pigments, animal glue, and nail polish she and her female apprentices have tried on during the break. The overwhelming odor of Hunan-manufactured Fu Rong Wang tobacco traps us in a shared car ride from Rebgong to Xining, while a helpless monk keeps his window open the entire 112 miles through snow-covered mountains. In Tsering Gyal's family shrine, the brocade frame of a thangka painting is soaked with the smoke of butter lamps. The embracing fragrance of baked *go re* (Tib.), the unleavened wheat flour bread, escapes from Drolma's pink wrapping scarf. As slowly waking households greet each other with dogs' barking, white smoke rising, toddlers' crying, and elders' chanting, the scent of burning juniper branches (Tib. *shug pa*) disperses into the chilly morning air.

The smells stopped registering in my brain, often after the first few days of my field trips, but they became salient, almost a craving, as I was writing this book, sitting over seven thousand miles away from Rebgong. Being a participant observer, an "oxymoron" that still largely defines the methodology of anthropology, have I lost more "smells" as I jot down what painters said to me, clumsily sketching the arrangement of family shrine rooms, snapping photos of women's circumambulation, or trying to catch up with others in the wheat field while carrying my camera and tripod?[43]

After my initial trip to Rebgong in 2009, I spent thirteen months between 2011 and 2012 in Rebgong for my doctoral research and returned for fieldwork in 2013, 2016, 2018, and 2019. Being Chinese, it may have been easier for me to stay in the village and conduct my research in rural Tibet.[44] I spent most of the time living in the village, staying with painters and their families in Sengeshong, Gasar, and Thokya, while occasionally paying visits to Nyantok and Gomar. I observed painters' daily lives in their home studios or their studios in town and participated in agricultural work, communal events, and religious ceremonies. I interviewed painters about their experiences of art making and their engagement in the art markets. Usually, these conversations took place in the studio (in Rebgong or elsewhere), over dinner, at karaoke parties, or during holiday breaks, when painters spent time with their families. I also traveled with some Rebgong *lha zo* to museums and galleries in Beijing and Shanghai, where they put up their own exhibitions or met potential clients. When traveling became difficult due to the COVID-19 pandemic and the subsequent travel restrictions, I was able to communicate with many Rebgong painters and keep up with their news and updates via WeChat (known as Weixin in its Chinese-language version), the pervasive messaging and social media app in China.

Rebgong residents speak Amdo Tibetan, Mandarin or Qinghainese (a Mandarin dialect spoken in Qinghai), and various local languages or dialects (e.g., Wutunhua is spoken in Sengeshong, Dor skad is spoken in Gasar)—sometimes the language or dialect used in one village is incomprehensible to residents from another village.[45] I am a native speaker of Mandarin. While I used multiple languages in my research, most of the interviews were conducted in Mandarin, especially when the conversation was about the art market, painters' interactions with their non-Tibetan patrons, or the changing status of Rebgong thangka in contemporary China. I gradually picked up Qinghainese, Amdo Tibetan, and Wutunhua during my fieldwork while relying on two local research assistants to help me interpret the conversation if it was in Tibetan or in one of the local languages or dialects. Some details in Rebgong residents' daily conversation were out of my grasp as a result of this methodology—a kind of lost smell— which I acknowledge is a limitation of my research. For the same reason, I do not simply present my illustrations in the book as "evidence" secondary to the text. I use the visuals to capture the complexity and sensibility—another type of smell—that might have been lost in the written words.

In 2018 I received a fellowship from the American Association of University Women (AAUW) for my research with female thangka painters in Rebgong. Between 2018 and 2019 I visited female apprentices in art schools and married women who paint with their husbands at home. Together with women painters I had encountered in previous years, I was able to interview twenty-eight female painters from Sengeshong, Gasar, Thokya, and Nyantok. Although all Rebgong residents recognize me as a woman, my positionality—a Han, an American-trained anthropologist, an urbanite, and a scholar—granted me access to the sacred hall in a monastery where Tibetan women do not dare enter except for on special occasions (also see Makley 2007, 160–61), but I was confined to the kitchen to eat lunch with *a ce* (Tib. sisters) and *a ma* (Tib. mothers) while monks and male family members enjoyed their meal in the living room or courtyard. In that regard, my presence at every social event was a negotiation of the gender and cultural boundary drawn between women and men, outsider and insider. Although it has influenced what I could observe or hear—another partiality in my research—I also take it as an opportunity to understand how gender and cultural norms actually function in a society where change and resistance to change are both important repertoires in people's daily lives.

At the early stage of my fieldwork, I might have taken participant observation too literally. I thought I would not be qualified as a competent anthropologist studying Rebgong thangka without actually learning how to paint a thangka. When I stayed with Jampa and his family in Gasar, I brought up this inquiry a couple of times, hoping Jampa could teach me thangka painting. Jampa replied with a grin but never put it into action. When I again raised this topic, after a trip to a neighboring village, where I had tried drawing the proportional grid and a few hand gestures of Manjushri (Tib. *'jam dpal dbyangs*, Ch. *wen shu*) on sketch paper, Jampa seemed displeased. Looking at the sketch paper, he said, almost a rebuke: "You should focus on your research. Don't spend time on drawing!"

Why? Was that drawing so bad? Though I had never learned Tibetan thangka or chosen art as a major, I had received years of training in Chinese ink painting and had experimented with different mediums in college and graduate school in my spare time. My drawings on that sketch paper were unprofessional, of course, but I did not think them poor either. In fact, I showed my drawings to Jampa because I wanted to prove that I was not completely ignorant of art—the way new apprentices show their drawings to the *ge gen* to prove they are worthy *ge truk*. Was it because I am a woman, a Han, an outsider? Was I too old to learn thangka painting from scratch?

These questions hovered in my mind, but I did not say anything. I wondered how to explain to Jampa that I considered learning thangka painting as participant observation, the core methodology of my research. Jampa might have guessed some of my thoughts. He put down his paintbrush and said:

> I began to learn thangka painting when I was a kid. My life is destined to be a *lha zo*. I spend days, months, and years sitting in front of the canvas and painting thangkas, in order to make merits, to help others with my skills. You are a scholar. You spend days, months, and years sitting in a classroom, reading books, acquiring knowledge. You have the privilege I do not have. Your skill can help more people. But if you really want to be a *lha zo*, you should put away your notes and books. You should sit in front of the canvas, like me, spending years to practice your painting skills until you can make the image of the Buddha that brings merits to others.

I put down the piece of sketch paper and never again asked Jampa to teach me painting.

But in a way, Jampa has become my *ge gen*. He and his wife, Drolma, taught me not how to paint thangkas but how *they* paint thangkas. They baked me *go re* and provided me shelter; I lent a helping hand whenever they needed. "Apprenticing" with them and with many other Rebgong painters like them, I navigated the valley and reached the corners of life otherwise inaccessible to me.

In writing this book, I hope my skill—the one I had chosen over thangka painting—can make merit that goes to Jampa and other painters who have taught me the value of work and also to readers who would like to know about Rebgong thangka and the lives of *lha zo* in this so-called Golden Valley that shines with different reasons energizing my journey.

CHAPTER 1

Painting a Regional Art Tradition

Twice in recent history, Guinness World Records recognized Rebgong thangka art: first, *The Great Thangka* in 1999; and twenty years later, "the most people drawing thangkas simultaneously."[1] Both records seem to celebrate the magnificent scale of art making ("the biggest" and "the most"). While these two notable events may look similar, during those two decades the art making in Rebgong changed significantly in terms of production and distribution. One reason for this is the commodification or secularization of Tibetan thangka art, especially after the recognition of Rebgong art (thangka painting included) as an Intangible Cultural Heritage (ICH) by the state in 2006 and by UNESCO in 2009. Both the state-fostered secular market for Tibetan thangkas and the local government's participation in the ICH campaign intend to reconfigure the meaning and function of thangka painting, expanding it from the religious realm to tourist or folk art.

Although the art historical and anthropological discussion on "non-Western art" now rejects the "one culture–one style" paradigm and encourages us to understand cultural authenticity in more flexible and malleable ways (Price 2007, 607; also see Steiner 1994; Morphy 2007; Phillips 2015), the trajectory of the regional art development in Rebgong since the 1980s offers something new to consider. The commodification of Rebgong thangka expands its audiences, but the form and content (and in many cases function) of Rebgong thangkas have largely remained the same as pre-1950 paintings. Therefore, Rebgong art has not been reduced completely to a craft or transformed into a hybridity, like the New Tibetan Painting developed in Garze

(Sichuan) in the 1980s that combines styles of Tibetan thangka and Chinese Socialist Realism. This chapter focuses on how Rebgong *lha zo* have nurtured a proud regional tradition of Tibetan Buddhist art, by examining several art projects initiated by Rebgong thangka painters in the 1980s and 1990s and painters' participation in the ICH campaign since the 2000s.

Shawo Tsering (Tib. *sha bo tshe ring*, 1922–2004) is one example. He traveled with Chinese artist Zhang Daqian to Dunhuang to copy Buddhist mural paintings in the early 1940s, and his practice made a considerable impact on contemporary Rebgong *lha zo* (Linrothe 2001; Fraser 2011). In addition, the work of *The Great Thangka* not only "put Reb gong on the world map" (Stevenson 2002, 216), but it has also shaped the direction of Rebgong's art development, despite the various motives in carrying *The Great Thangka* project to fruition (Linrothe 2001, 40; Kalzang Tseden 2011, 31–33). Since the post-1978 Reform era, local artists, scholars, and government officials have advocated for a regional art tradition on the national level. Their narratives, though not always homogeneous, have encouraged the transmission of art making skills and the use of traditional materials and, to various extents, have preserved the religious meaning of Tibetan thangkas. These have negotiated space between the state's overarching agenda of cultural development and the demands of the market for the growth of Rebgong Buddhist art making.

A Different Pathway

After over twenty years of suppression, the religious and artistic revival in Rebgong was made possible by political changes after the Third Plenary Session of the Eleventh Central Committee (Ch. *shi yi jie san zhong quan hui*) in 1978 (Stevenson 2002, 208; Kalzang Tseden 2011, 315). Alongside this, the tenth Panchen Lama, who supported the reconstruction of monasteries in Amdo and held two important teachings in Rebgong in the early 1980s (Chen 2013, 165; Makley 2020), facilitated a revival of Tibetan Buddhism in Rebgong. In 1982, however, when Rebgong art made its debut in Beijing and Shanghai, through the exhibition *Qinghai Wutun Tibetan Folk Painting and Painted-Sculpture Art*, Beijing officials from various art organizations criticized its content.[2] These officials praised the Rebgong artistic techniques but disapproved of the tradition's overly religious themes and subjects, when they had expected to see themes that "celebrate life under the Four Modernizations [Ch. *si ge xian dai hua*]" or scenes showing "the oppressive Lamaist theocracy"

(Stevenson 2002, 211–13). Their criticism should be understood within a context of emerging new art styles in China, such as the updated Yangliuqing New Year prints in Tianjin and, notably, Garze New Tibetan Painting in Sichuan; both illustrated contemporary themes in a modernizing China, like "new wine poured into old bottles," as the Chinese political slogan suggested.

New Tibetan Painting (Ch. *xin zang hua*), also known as the Garze school (Ch. *gan zi hua pai*), emerged in Garze (Tib. *dkar mdzes*) Tibetan Autonomous Prefecture in Sichuan around 1980. This collaboration between Tibetan and Han artists created a series of artworks combining traditional thangka painting techniques with Socialist Realist styles to depict historical figures, legends, and contemporary social and political events (Harris 1999, 151–58; Tsewang Tashi 2018, 196–200).[3] For instance, in 1980 this group of artists produced the painting *The Meeting of General Zhu De and Getag Tulku in 1936*.[4] Partially painting in the style of the Karma Gadri school (Tib. *karma sgar bris*), the artists illustrated how the tulku welcomed and assisted General Zhu and his troops as they arrived at the tulku's monastery during the Long March. The two central figures, sitting together on a platform, were drawn in the manner of Socialist Realist portraiture of the Maoist period but were framed against a bright-yellow halo, a motif that is usually reserved for the sacred in traditional thangka paintings. Another painting, *Thangtong Gyalpo* (Tib. *thang stong rgyal po*), completed by two Tibetan artists in 1984, also depicted the prominent Buddhist siddha and Tibetan architect (also known as "the iron bridge maker") in this realistic style.[5] In the painting the architect Thangtong Gyalpo stood and held an iron bridge model in his hand, instead of sitting as in standard thangka paintings. Tibetan landscapes, architectures, Buddhist statues, stupas, and scenes from Tibetan opera were skillfully arranged around him.

New Tibetan Painting was generally well received within China; it was praised for the artists' courage to explore new directions for Tibetan art in the Reform era.[6] This was certainly what Beijing officials had in mind when they offered their critiques on Rebgong art in 1982—more innovative content would have been welcomed. However, the Garze school has been largely dismissed by art historians, especially by scholars of Tibetan art in the West. Researchers such as Tibetologist Per Kværne and art historian Clare Harris not only criticize the use of Tibetan motifs in Socialist Realist paintings as exploiting "'mythic' resonances to create a parable of political power" but also worry about the disappearing Tibetan Buddhist heritage; among artworks produced by the Garze school, for instance, paintings of King Gesar, a figure essentially from a secular tale, override images of Guru Rinpoche or Milarepa (Harris 1999, 154–55). In the same vein, Mark Stevenson asserts that New Tibetan Painting has not only revolutionized style and subject matter but has also redefined the function of Tibetan art (2002, 214).

Neither the criticism from officials in Beijing nor the promotion of New Tibetan Painting in Reform China drastically changed the scene of art making in Rebgong, however. According to Stevenson (2002) and Linrothe (2001), as well as my own interviews with painters, Rebgong *lha zo* did not produce art celebrating socialist themes on a large scale. Nor did Rebgong thangka painters create other forms of new art, as Sepik carvers (Silverman 1999) and Yolngu painters (Morphy 2007) create tourist or commercial arts derived from traditional designs. Why did Rebgong not choose the same route as Garze? How did contemporary Rebgong artists largely maintain the style, content, and function of thangkas, which were similar to paintings made in the pre-1950 period?

One straightforward answer is that since the 1980s Rebgong *lha zo* had been too busy working on monastic commissions—commissions not only from Rebgong but also from distant Tibetan communities including Garze. In the previous three decades or so, various political movements—including the Anti-Rightist Campaign (1957–59), the Great Leap Forward (1958–62), and the Cultural Revolution (1966–76)—had strongly disrupted Buddhist teaching and religious practices in Tibet (Goldstein 1997; Shakya 1999). In many Tibetan communities, Rebgong included, monasteries and temples suffered neglect or severe destruction (Slobodník 2007; Demick 2020). During the Cultural Revolution, for example, the assembly hall of the Lower Wutun Monastery (Tib. *seng ge gshong ma mgo dgon pa*, Ch. *wun tun xia si*) was turned into a barn to store grain and farming tools (Namgyal, personal communication, May 18, 2012; also see Linrothe 2001, 8). Most Rebgong thangka painters during that period put down their paintbrushes and became carpenters or blacksmiths.[7] When bans on religious expression were somewhat relaxed in the 1980s (Potter 2003; Kalzang Tseden 2011), a large number of remaining monasteries and village shrines were in need of restoration, not to mention additional buildings needed to be built. Hence, art historian Rob Linrothe does not use the word *renaissance* lightly while describing the artistic revival in Rebgong since the 1980s.

A few competent *lha zo pa* in Rebgong were facing an explosion of demand from monasteries within and beyond the region.[8] To meet this demand, young monks and laymen were apprenticed with their *ge gen* (teacher)—sometimes their own father or relative—to work on hundreds of wall paintings and thousands of thangka scrolls as well as Buddhist statues in various sizes and made of diverse materials (Linrothe 2001, 11). The challenging job and heavy workload had provided extensive and solid training to many young artists living through this "renaissance." They not only knew the iconography or brushwork but were also equipped with diverse training (e.g., in architecture, sculpture, carpentry, and silversmithing) as well as the religious and cultural knowledge needed to accept and work on monastic commissions (Fraser 2011, 116). The footprint of the Rebgong painters also stretched beyond Rebgong to Labrang Monastery, Kumbum Monastery, and as far as monasteries in Sichuan and Lhasa (Tang 2009; Kalzang Tseden 2011).

In addition to artists' enthusiasm, donations from eager devotees, and financial support from the government (Linrothe 2001, 15), the artistic revival in Rebgong was also energized by scholars and officials at various levels. From the late 1950s, the Qinghai Art Association (Ch. *qing hai mei xie*) organized scholars and specialists to conduct fieldwork in Rebgong, not only to preserve Tibetan paintings, statues, and architecture but also to research the history of its local art, especially through talking to leading artists in the region (Tang 2009, 18). Some of the local artists, including Kunzang (Tib. *kun bzang*, 1919–96) and Shawo Tsering, later became major forces in establishing the Rebgong Art Research Group (Ch. *re gong yi shu yan jiu chou bei zu*), administrated by Qinghai, in 1979 and promoting Rebgong art on the national level (Stevenson 2002, 206–8; Kalzang Tseden 2011, 218). The 1982 Rebgong art show in Beijing and Shanghai also encouraged the Huangnan Tibetan Autonomous Prefecture to support construction of the Rebgong Art Gallery (Ch. *re gong yi shu guan*), which not only functioned as a museum to exhibit Rebgong art but also oversaw funding and research to preserve the transmission of traditional knowledge and art skills. In 1986 Huangnan took over the Research Group from the province and changed its name to the Rebgong Art Research Institute (Ch. *re gong yi shu yan jiu suo*) (Stevenson 2002, 209; Tang 2009, 18).

An "Apprentice" of Rebgong Painters

Among all the stories of contemporary Rebgong artists, one frequently told by thangka painters and local scholars concerns Shawo Tsering's encounter with Chinese artist Zhang Daqian and their trip to Dunhuang in the 1940s.

Shawo Tsering was born in Sengeshong in 1922 and started to learn thangka painting at eight, when he was a monk in a local monastery. In 1941, at the age of eighteen, Shawo Tsering met Zhang Daqian while working with his *ge gen* and fellow monks at Kumbum Monastery (Tib. *sku 'bum byams pa gling*, Ch. *ta er si*) to repaint murals and make thangka scrolls. Zhang paid a visit to Kumbum Monastery on his way back to Dunhuang from Sichuan. In his initial visit to Dunhuang in 1940, Zhang Daqian was intrigued by the Buddhist wall paintings preserved in the caves but realized he did not have the expertise to copy or study them. Zhang specialized in ink painting (Ch. *shui mo hua*) and meticulous painting (Ch. *gong bi hua*) in the Chinese art tradition. The materials and techniques required for the Buddhist painting in Dunhuang were alien to him. Additionally, Zhang was not equipped with adequate knowledge of Buddhist texts or iconography. When Zhang met Shawo Tsering and other Rebgong *lha zo pa* at Kumbum Monastery and observed their work, he believed they were the people he was looking for, whose "knowledge of Buddhist art and iconography could illuminate and unlock the meaning of medieval paintings in Dunhuang" (Fraser 2011, 121).

In March 1942 Shawo Tsering and four other Rebgong *lha zo* left with Zhang for Gansu and began their fifteen-month project of copying Dunhuang cave paintings. Zhang was trained to paint with ink and water on rice paper (Ch. *xuan zhi*). His initial copies on paper were judged as "unprofessional" by the Rebgong painters (Kalzang Tseden 2011, 97). The Rebgong painters taught Zhang how to treat the fabric—they used cotton canvas—with gesso (Tib. *'dam*) and polish it with a stone (Tib. *dbur rdo*) after mounting the canvas on a wooden stretcher (Tib. *rkyang shing*).[9] Only the hard surface, instead of the soft paper, could support the meticulous and precise brushwork needed for religious images. Zhang also practiced Buddhist iconographies under the guidance of the Rebgong artists and continued to learn the religious meaning behind each image from them. To reproduce the wall painting in its original size, Zhang's team copied sections of the wall on separate stretched canvases (approx. 29 x 29 in. each) and later combined them.[10] Meanwhile, Zhang made sketches and took notes of the painting compositions, colors, styles, and other details. As Zhang became more familiar with the iconography and material, he joined his Rebgong teammates and started to copy murals himself. Despite their humble equipment and the harsh physical environment, Zhang Daqian and Rebgong *lha zo* completed over two hundred copies of Dunhuang cave paintings before they parted in June 1943.[11]

According to Kalzang Tseden, whose father was a relative and close friend of Shawo Tsering, when Shawo talked about his Dunhuang trip, he proudly claimed that Zhang Daqian, the acclaimed Chinese artist, was once "an apprentice of Rebgong painters" (2011, 97). In no way intending to dwarf the accomplishment of Zhang Daqian, Shawo Tsering was inspired to understand the tradition of Rebgong art from the perspective of an "outsider." Zhang was not a random outsider, however, but a seasoned artist with a cultivated eye (Bourdieu 1984) whose interests and expertise spanned various types of art. When Zhang praised Tibetan thangka art for "leading him into an entirely novel artistic space" (Kalzang Tseden 2011, 98), his affirmation encouraged Rebgong *lha zo pa*, Shawo Tsering included, to reposition themselves on the artistic map in China. The tradition of Buddhist art had spread across East Asia by the eleventh century, but "the technical expertise required to execute complex paintings with the necessary fineness" seemed lost in the Chinese art lineage over the following two hundred years, while such sophistication in art making was "primarily in the hands of painters of the Tibetan-Mongolian lineage of Buddhist art" (Fraser 2011, 131). Though it is difficult to chart a clear genealogy between Rebgong art and the various art styles exemplified in the Dunhuang caves (Fraser 2011; Kalzang Tseden 2011; Wu 2022), the encounter between Shawo Tsering and Zhang Daqian in Dunhuang helped Rebgong *lha zo* recognize the importance of their practices—their knowledge and skill enabled them not only to repair the peeled wall paintings in local monasteries but also to connect an older artistic tradition that very few artists in contemporary China could decipher.

Because of his experience with Zhang Daqian in Dunhuang, Shawo Tsering was given a leading role in the Rebgong Art Research Group. In 1988 he was awarded the title "National Art and Craft Master" (Ch. *quan guo gong yi mei shu da shi*), the first artist in Qinghai to enjoy such an honor (Stevenson 2002, 208). While Zhang had learned and benefited artistically from his Rebgong teammates much more than the other way around, when Zhang published the 276 copies of Dunhuang cave paintings in his book *Caves of Mogao Mountain* (Ch. *mo gao shan shi ku ji*), the contribution of the Rebgong *lha zo* was not clearly acknowledged (Kalzang Tseden 2011, 98).[12] Perhaps Zhang considered himself a patron to Shawo Tsering and his fellow *lha zo pa*. In Buddhist art it is usually the patron, instead of the art maker, who may leave his name on the artwork (Linrothe 2001, 30; Kieschnick 2003, 162).[13] But when Zhang exhibited and promoted his Dunhuang paintings to various audiences as the artist, it was unfortunate that Zhang had failed to give credit to his *lha zo* teachers from Rebgong.[14]

Notably, there is a fundamental difference between Shawo Tsering and Zhang Daqian in art making. Zhang emerged from an artistic tradition "based on the literati ideal of the expressive artist," whose personality or identity is "the defining factor in a painting" (Fraser 2011, 131). Shawo Tsering and the other four Rebgong painters, on the other hand, came from a system of collaborative workshops (Linrothe 2001, 27), in which the painter's identity was much less important than the correct iconography. Copying the cave paintings did not drastically change the practice of Shawo Tsering and his fellow painters in Rebgong, whereas a significant change in style and subject matter can be observed in Zhang's artwork after his Dunhuang trip. In Linrothe's words, Rebgong *lha zo* were "not intent on fundamentally reinventing Tibetan painting afresh based on exposure to modernist aesthetic values and a model of personal expressionism" (7). To some extent, the encounter with Zhang Daqian in Dunhuang highlighted the importance of traditional art transmission in Rebgong, which became one major goal guiding the work of Shawo Tsering and other members in the Rebgong Art Research Institute.

When Shawo Tsering and many leading *lha zo pa* in Rebgong once again picked up their paintbrushes after the Cultural Revolution, they not only produced a large amount of work for monasteries but also trained numerous young painters, many of whom became prominent artists and leading teachers in today's Rebgong.[15] Their wall paintings and thangka scrolls kept in monasteries also became important references and templates for both monastic and lay successors in Rebgong. Zhang Daqian, by commissioning Rebgong artists to work with him in Dunhuang, might have accumulated enough merits to advance his career as an individual artist. Shawo Tsering and his fellow *lha zo pa* had nurtured a generation.

The Great Thangka

Shawo Tsering and other painters of his generation might not have expected to see a six hundred–meter thangka painting emerge in Rebgong at the end of the twentieth century. *The Great Thangka of Tibetan Art and Culture in China* (Tib. *krung go bod kyi rig gnas sgyu rtsal kun 'dus zhal thang chen mo*, Ch. *zhong guo zang zu wen hua yi shu cai hui da guan*), otherwise known as *The Great Thangka*, was completed and shown to the public in 1999 (plate 4).[16] According to official records, *The Great Thangka* is 618 meters long and 2.5 meters high, including more than seven hundred thangka paintings mounted on embroidery brocade with numerous decorative panels. Over three hundred artists, from Rebgong and other regions all over China, participated in the making of this gargantuan painting. The seven hundred constituent paintings, claimed to have been painted with traditional pigments, narrate the entire span of Tibetan culture and history, including Tibet's origin, Tibetan Buddhism, important historical and religious figures, Tibetan art, medicine, literature, philosophy, linguistics, mathematics, opera, folklore, as well as monasteries and natural sites in Tibet.[17] Upon its completion, Guinness World Records certified it as the biggest thangka in the world. It was later exhibited in Xining, Beijing, and even South Korea.

Anthropologist Mark Stevenson concludes that although the title of this painting situates the artwork within China, "the logic of enlargement that defines the project, or its monumentalism, is an innovation that says as much about [Tibetan] national consciousness as it does about cultural revival" (2002, 216). However, this does not seem to be the most plausible motivation for Rebgong artists and officials to take part in this project. If *The Great Thangka* were made to deliver the message of the Tibetan "national consciousness" or the "idea of the Tibetan nation" (Stevenson 2002), how could Western scholars (or Western audiences) decipher its implication while local and state officials, Tibetan cadres included, overlooked its Tibetan nationalist overtones and even exhibited the work at the Museum of the Chinese Revolution in Beijing as part of the celebration of the People's Republic of China's fiftieth anniversary? Instead of assigning *The Great Thangka* a single symbolic value, we need to understand the particular local context—artistic, cultural, economic, and political—for this project to come into being. What *The Great Thangka* contributed to Rebgong art making at the turn of the century is much more than a Guinness World Record.

The Great Thangka was not a project commanded from above but was originally conceived by Tsondru Rapgye (Tib. *brtson 'grus rab rgyas*, b. 1951), a thangka painter and member of the Rebgong Art Research Institute. Tsondru Rapgye grew up in a village in Xunhua County and later learned thangka painting from the prominent artist Kunzang (1919–96) in Rebgong. Tsondru Rapgye began to plan and prepare for this project in 1980 (Kalzang Tseden 2011, 91). As a sophisticated painter and former monk, Tsondru Rapgye visited and consulted with a long list of lamas (Tib. *bla ma*), *khenpos* (Tib. *mkhan po*), scholars, and artists in Lhasa, Qinghai, Gansu, Sichuan, Yunnan, and Beijing for this project over the following years. During his travels (or in a sense, his fieldwork), he also took photos and made sketches of monastery paintings, sculptures, architecture, folk customs, and the natural environment. Since this was not a government initiative or a project of the Research Institute, in the preparation phase, Tsondru Rapgye largely used his own money to cover the expenses of travel and painting supplies. It is not hard to understand why some Rebgong monks and painters considered that he "had sacrificed for the sake of a greater goal" (Linrothe 2001, 40). In his original design, *The Great Thangka* was to be approximately five hundred meters long.

After a series of discussions, Huangnan TAP and Tongren County decided to support the project by giving Tsondru Rapgye a loan from the prefecture's Agricultural Bank as start-up capital.[18] In 1996 Tsondru Rapgye set this project in motion and extended its length from 500 to 618 meters. He organized over three hundred artists from various places; most of them were from Rebgong, but they came together with Tibetan, Mongolian, and Han artists from other regions who specialized in Tibetan art. They rented the third floor of a commercial building in town as their workshop. In addition to covering rent, utility bills, painting materials, and artist compensations, the money Tsondru Rapgye sought from various sources was also used to produce an encyclopedic text in Tibetan called *The Bright Mirror Illuminating the Meaning of the Great Thangka of Tibetan Art and Culture in China*.[19] This 700,000-word book includes materials Tsondru Rapgye collected from his earlier fieldwork as well as interviews and documentation made possible with the support of local and state officials (e.g., Ngapoi Ngawang Jigme and Zhao Puchu), especially Tibetan officials at various levels (Tsondru Rapgye 2002, 531–32; Kalzang Tseden 2011, 91).

Unlike many other promotional materials of Rebgong art published by the government at that time, the emphasis of *The Great Thangka* and its accompanying text is on religion (Stevenson 2002, 215). Painted in a mural style, *The Great Thangka* largely follows traditional iconography and iconometrics. While certain parts of the thangka differed slightly from Rebgong's regional style—parts by artists from Lhasa or Kham, for example—the organizer and artists made efforts to ensure the composition, use of color, and refinements were consistent across the scroll, most importantly to avoid the type of "hybridity" observed in New Tibetan Painting. Besides painting styles, both official promotions and academic publications about *The Great Thangka* highlighted the use of natural pigments, which, they claimed, added much authenticity to the work (Stevenson 2002; Kalzang Tseden 2011).

What previous scholarship has failed to notice or emphasize, however, is the fact that *The Great Thangka* was consecrated and was viewed as sacred by Buddhist audiences. Upon its completion in August 1999, *The Great Thangka* was taken to Jokhang Temple in Lhasa, where monks and religious leaders from different sects of Tibetan Buddhism attended its consecration ceremony (Tsondru Rapgye 2002, 532). About a month later, *The Great Thangka* was shown to the public in Rongwo town, where the eighth Shartshang lama and local monks performed another consecration ritual for the painting.[20] In that sense, the Buddha, deities, or reincarnated lamas depicted in the painting are not simply symbols. Their very presence in *The Great Thangka* bestows blessing and protection to those who venerate and worship them. For villagers and visitors who poured into Rongwo town to see *The Great Thangka* in 1999, it was not merely an art show but a merit-making event even understood by some as analogous to the display of giant appliqué thangkas in monasteries.[21]

Monk Rinchen from Sengeshong was nineteen years old when he first participated in the making of *The Great Thangka*. He also led a team of three apprentices, aged fourteen, thirty-three, and fifty-four years old. Rinchen and his apprentices worked full-time between 1997 and 1999 on *The Great Thangka*. They arrived at the commercial building every morning and went back home after sunset; sometimes they worked into the night. Their days were spent sitting in front of a fifteen-meter metal frame, upon which the long scroll was mounted, painting with other artists who were working on the same section of *The Great Thangka*. Rinchen regretted not asking a journalist for the photo of him working on the painting. "That'd be nice to show to my clients," Rinchen said later and laughed. Rinchen's favorite memory was when he showed two Kham painters from Sichuan how he drew Yamantaka (Tib. *rdo rje 'jigs byed*, Ch. *da wei de jin gang*), one of the most complex iconographies in Tibetan art, on a palm-sized piece of paper. They were awed by Rinchen's skill and later learned many techniques from him. As a young painter who had not yet set foot outside Amdo Tibet, Rinchen also found much to learn by talking to artists from other places and observing their work.

In contrast, Rinchen was less excited about the payment he received for participating in this project. Tsondru Rapgye had commissioned Rinchen to make ten paintings and paid him RMB 30,000 (about USD 3,600), an amount largely conforming to Rinchen's "market price" at that time (about RMB 3,000 per painting). However, this payment also had to cover the compensation for Rinchen's apprentices, so Rinchen earned considerably less by working on *The Great Thangka* than he normally would by painting alone. Perhaps some other established artists in Rebgong were "faintly disparaging about the project" for this reason; one painter considered that "he was not offered enough money to make it worth his while" (Linrothe 2001, 58). Unlike the painters who considered Tsondru Rapgye to be profiting from cheap labor, Rinchen believed Tsondru Rapgye was in a real financial deficit from time to time. According to Rinchen, in the beginning, Tsondru Rapgye brought flour and oil from his home to cook for the painters. When his food pantry could not feed all the mouths, Tsondru Rapgye brought prefecture officials and businessmen to observe the painting in progress and tried to secure their investment or more loans from the government. Before *The Great Thangka* found its permanent home in the Tibetan Culture Museum (Tib. *mtsho sngon bod kyi rig gnas rten mdzod gling*, Ch. *qing hai zang wen hua bo wu yuan*) in Xining, Tsondru Rapgye had to return the twenty-two hundred–pound giant to the local bank after each exhibition, since he had not paid off his loans.[22]

The Great Thangka no doubt made a significant imprint on Rebgong's art history. Tsondru Rapgye's ambition to produce an innovative work was achieved by the painting's unparalleled size and the scale of collaboration among Tibetan artists, scholars, monastics, and officials across many years. More important, with *The Great Thangka* in hand, Rebgong made a gesture to reject the type of innovation observed in the New Tibetan Painting. The prefecture's support of Tsondru Rapgye's project could be understood as a strategic response to the type of requests made in the early 1980s by Beijing officials, who wanted to see Rebgong art adapting to the spirit of the new political era. *The Great Thangka* emerged at a time when economic growth was steady and ethnic groups in China were involved in a market economy encouraging the "revival of ethnic cultural forms and customs" (Harrell 2001, 53) and the display of their religions (Oakes and Sutton 2010). With the painting's majestic scale and the artists' meticulous skill, *The Great Thangka* positioned Rebgong as a self-sustaining center of Tibetan art and suggested a unique path for Rebgong's cultural development. Following Tenzin Jinba's analysis on the permeable identity of Gyarong Tibetans on the Sino-Tibetan border, who "activate and invigorate an intertwined network of sociopolitical restructurings" (2014, 9), *The Great Thangka* can also be seen as reinforcing three layers of identity for Rebgong painters: as "worthy" Chinese citizens, "authentic" Tibetans, and "distinctive" Rebgong artists.

On the other hand, *The Great Thangka* did change the equilibrium of art making in Rebgong. Some painters criticized the "entrepreneurship" of this project (Linrothe 2001, 58), while some others disliked the "insider" and "outsider" distinctions that the project created (Stevenson 2002, 216). Like their Native American or Australian Aboriginal counterparts, Rebgong *lha zo* face new questions that have challenged the traditional system of patronage and art production: who should lead or "own" such a project, who should be invited to work on such a painting, where should the money come from, how much should each participant be paid, and whose name should be recorded and remembered, among other details. Moreover, although the central government was receptive to *The Great Thangka*, to this day local officials and artists still struggle to preserve the religious meaning associated with art making as Rebgong thangkas are commodified on China's national art market. We should notice that *The Great Thangka* was not commissioned in a traditional sense. Tsondru Rapgye's motive aside, he sought money and support from various sources to realize this project, including his own family, local government, monasteries, the market, and the state. While the artistic "renaissance" Shawo Tsering and his fellow painters experienced in the 1980s was largely nurtured by monastic commissions, *The Great Thangka* is an overture to Rebgong art in this century. The preservation of cultural traditions and experiments of artistic innovation need to look for new patrons, usually relying on carefully crafted narratives that negotiate space for Buddhist art making between the state's agenda of cultural development and the increasing intensity of commodification.

The Ambiguity of Intangible Cultural Heritage

Not long after Tsondru Rapgye exhibited *The Great Thangka* in Rebgong and Beijing, the Chinese Kunqu Opera was included in UNESCO's 2001 Intangible Cultural Heritage Representative List; the recognition is often regarded as the beginning of China's full-speed national ICH campaign (Su 2020).[23] However, the cultural display and the heritage discourse are "powerful tools of modernization and development" in the "field of governance and social regulation" (Oakes 2012, 380). What has driven the enthusiasm of cultural elites in China to take part in the ICH discourse involves not only national and ethnic pride or the worries about cultural traditions threatened in a rapidly modernizing China but also the political authority—the power of "telling stories about the past and present" (Silverman and Blumenfield 2013, 4)—and the incentives of economic development (Chio 2014; Su 2020).[24]

For the local government, taking part in the ICH boom was not simply a way to boost ethnic pride or the "external visibility" of Rebgong art, as indicated in UNESCO's purpose for establishing its ICH Representative List (UNESCO 2009). Under China's Great Western Development campaign, Rebgong's participation in the ICH discourse supported a new cultural industry and tourism centered on art production, opening Rebgong to broader economic opportunities. Stories like Shawo Tsering's Dunhuang encounter and the making of *The Great Thangka* became stepping stones for Rebgong to generate persuasive and appealing narratives to demonstrate local residents' tradition, authenticity, and living practices—essential characteristics to qualify Rebgong art as an ICH. After all, heritage is not a preexisting or fixed quality but arises "in the process of making" (Maags and Svensson 2018, 13). From the beginning of the twenty-first century, prefectural and county officials rolled up their sleeves and worked on gaining this new identity for Rebgong art (Kalzang Tseden 2011, 92). In 2006 Rebgong art was successfully included in the national ICH list. In 2008 Qinghai established the Rebgong Cultural and Ecological Protection Zone (Ch. *re gong wen hua sheng tai bao hu qu*; hereafter Protection Zone). A year later UNESCO added Rebgong art to its Representative List of ICH of Humanity.

Although Rebgong painters and officials I've talked to do not necessarily agree on how the concept of ICH is translated in the context of Rebgong art—what part of the heritage is intangible, what needs to be preserved, or what falls within the Protection Zone—most of my interlocutors agree that labeling Rebgong art as an ICH (Ch. *fei yi*) is preferable to calling it folk art (Ch. *min jian yi shu*). After Rebgong art was recognized as one of the first national Intangible Cultural Heritages, the local art market boomed as well. An important incentive for the government to set up the Protection Zone was to vitalize and regulate the art market, through identifying ICH inheritors, organizing the transmission of art making skills, supporting art schools, and finding new clients for Rebgong thangka beyond local audiences.[25] Many young residents in Rebgong stopped migrating elsewhere for work. Instead, they stayed in Rebgong to learn thangka painting—participating in the making of an ICH was economically and reputationally more appealing. In that sense, the local

ICH campaign has motivated younger generations and encouraged the transmission of the Rebgong art tradition (Menchok Dondrub 2016, 72). Meanwhile, Rebgong painters face new challenges over how to understand the meaning of their practice, or more specifically, how to situate themselves between cultural preservation and economic development—a dilemma essentially shared by all ICH practitioners (Smith 2006; Harrell 2013; Maags and Svensson 2018).

There is always a wobbly line between protection and commodification. Although the state issued the Law on Intangible Cultural Heritage (Ch. *fei wu zhi wen hua yi chan fa*) in 2011, which aims at protecting its ICH for political and cultural purposes, the same national law explicitly regards ICHs as "important resources for cultural industries and tourism" (Su 2020, 165). Su interviewed officials at various levels (including national, provincial, and local) regarding heritage management in Lijiang, Yunnan, and reveals that the implementation of ICH policies on the local level is a dynamic and contested process that usually encourages sympathy for the development of tourism and commodification (Su 2020, 182). In Rebgong's case, ICH is also used as a convenient label that, on one hand, mitigates the weight of the religious component in thangka art and, on the other hand, avoids the resentment elicited by reducing Tibetan thangka to decorative or folk art. Therefore, the ICH discourse becomes a preferable strategy for the local government to elicit support from the province and the central government and manage local cultural resources.

Not surprisingly, the ICH discourse elicits mixed feelings and responses from local participants. A monk painter in a local monastery questioned the definition of *intangible*. To him, almost all measures of heritage preservation in Rebgong were directed to protect, or in a sense to produce, the "tangible" forms of cultural practice, such as a painting or sculpture, and transform them into commodities. The religious knowledge, the patronage system (especially the monastic patronage), or the use of Buddhist images in both monastic and secular lives—essential parts of intangible culture, in the monk's opinion—were missing. His view, and that of some other painters, resonates with Christina Maags and Marina Svensson's criticism, which considers the ICH as "a new form of governance and a way to control religious and ethnic communities" in China (2018, 20). On the other hand, some local officials and painters—"stakeholders," in Maags's words (2018, 122)—do find room to enhance their agency and contest the top-down polices in the heritage-making process (Robertson 2012; Ashworth 2014). Today Rebgong *lha zo* simultaneously experience increasing competition, uncertainty, and distrust, intertwined with ethnic pride, cultural agency, and economic incentives catalyzed by the ICH discourse.

Who Becomes Inheritor or Master?

When Lutso, the first Tibetan female *lha zo* to open a thangka studio in Rebgong, clicked on the website of the online art shop featuring her thangka paintings, she found that the shopkeeper had introduced her as both an "ICH Inheritor" (Ch. *fei yi chuan cheng ren*) and an "Arts and Crafts Master in Qinghai" (Ch. *qing hai gong yi mei shu da shi*). She was confused since she had never applied for any title like this and, certainly, had never obtained one. She called the shopkeeper, who told her that because Lutso came from Rebgong and painted thangkas, "naturally" she was an inheritor of an ICH. Besides, in the shopkeeper's opinion, Lutso, along with some other contracted artists, were excellent thangka painters with the level of skill equivalent to those "masters" recognized by the government. For that reason, the shopkeeper did not consider it off the mark to label Lutso in such a way. Obviously, it was a marketing tool. The shopkeeper was reluctant to delete or change the titles, but Lutso felt unsure. She turned to *ge gen* Namgyal and asked for his advice. Namgyal thought it would be better to eliminate the titles or at least remove the label "Arts and Crafts Master"; otherwise, Lutso "might run into trouble."

If it had been several years earlier, Lutso or Namgyal would not have been so concerned. Before the prefecture established regulations and local legislation on the recognition of various types of craftsmen (Ch. *gong yi shi*), masters (Ch. *da shi*), and inheritors (Ch. *chuan cheng ren*) as part of national and provincial ICH policies, painters and merchants had a certain leeway to use these labels in their promotional materials. Besides, in the early 2000s, before any regulations came into effect, social ties, or *guan xi*, with local officials and specialists were essential in the selection of masters and in winning art competitions.[26] The local legislation "Criteria for Accreditation and Rules of Implementation for the Selection of Huangnan Prefecture Folk Craftsmen and Prefectural Representative ICH Inheritors" (hereafter "Criteria and Rules") was established in 2014.[27] With the legislation and regulations in effect, Namgyal worried that if a client found out that Lutso was not an officially accredited inheritor or master (i.e., by asking for an official certificate), the shopkeeper or Lutso could be prosecuted for fraud. Or if another painter in Rebgong noticed that Lutso was falsely featured as a master on a commercial site, they could use this case against her in peer competition.

As we can see from its name, the "Criteria and Rules" oversees two systems of accreditation: the Folk Craftsmen and the ICH Inheritors. While the Folk Craftsman status emphasizes painters' artistic achievements, the title of ICH Inheritor takes other factors into consideration, particularly the transmission of cultural practice. According to a manager of a local art school, a painter needs to be first recognized as a "County-Level ICH Inheritor," by filling out the forms and submitting evidence of training apprentices. The prefecture will then select from the pool of county-level ICH Inheritors to promote some to "Prefectural ICH Inheritors" based on their artistic skills, teaching effectiveness, and contribution to the local community (e.g., donating to the poor). While the selection of ICH Inheritors is a relatively straightforward process, the accreditation of a Representative ICH Inheritor (Ch. *fei yi dai biao xing chuan cheng ren*) is much more complicated. Representative ICH Inheritors belong to the highest level of recognition among all ICH Inheritors. Until 2019 Rebgong had only had seven national, twelve provincial, and twelve prefectural Representative ICH Inheritors, who are acclaimed artists and concurrently directors of art schools or transmission centers (Ch. *chuan xi zhong xin*).[28] The art shop might get away with using the title ICH Inheritor without any specification—a common practice among many art merchants—but labeling Lutso as an "Arts and Crafts Master" might be a greater sin.

In 2021 I sent my congratulations to Tsering Gyal, a painter from Sengeshong village, for being accredited as a Provincial Folk Craftsman (Ch. *sheng ji min jian gong yi shi*). Tsering Gyal's accreditation journey started as early as 2013, when he began to submit application forms and draft the thangka that he planned to submit to a major art competition organized by the prefecture. In 2014 over nine hundred local painters, Tsering Gyal included, took part in the competition aimed at selecting the first prefectural-level Folk Craftsmen and Arts and Crafts Masters in observance of the newly established "Criteria and Rules." All thangka entries were exhibited to the public in town. At the end of that year, a committee consisting of prefectural officials, specialists, and prestigious local artists (e.g., National Arts and Crafts Masters) judged the artwork. Tsering Gyal won third place in the competition and was immediately accredited as a Prefectural Arts and Crafts Master (Ch. *zhou ji gong yi mei shu da shi*), the highest rank for thangka painters at the prefectural level and a prerequisite for his future application for any provincial titles.

On the provincial level, the Folk Craftsman (Tsering Gyal's accreditation) is the lowest rank of accreditation, with Folk Crafts Masters (Ch. *min jian gong yi da shi*) as the next rank, and Arts and Crafts Masters (Ch. *gong yi mei shu da shi*) the most prestigious of the three. Within each rank, there are also different levels. For instance, Tsering Gyal was accredited as a Level 2 Folk Craftsman (Ch. *er ji min jian gong yi shi*), the lower level of the lowest rank. There is no skipping a step in the accreditation process; Tsering Gyal has to advance to a Level 1 Folk Craftsman (Ch. *yi ji min jian gong yi shi*) before he can apply for Level 2 Folk Crafts Master (Ch. *er ji min jian gong yi da shi*). The province holds the review every three years, but it can take longer to prepare for the application of provincial accreditations than for prefectural ones because the competition is more intense. Applicants come from all over the province and are not only thangka painters but also artists and craftsmen of all sorts, of which Qinghai has plenty.

Tsering Gyal thinks it is worth pursuing accreditation. With the "Criteria and Rules," Tsering Gyal considers the selection process fairer and more transparent than how painters won their titles or were promoted by the government in the early 2000s. He likes the idea of exhibiting all applicants' artwork in public so everyone can judge if an accredited artist lives up to his or her title (though Tsering Gyal admitted if someone appropriated another's painting for the competition, things would be more complicated). The accreditation track gives Tsering Gyal, self-characterized as "born without money or status," hope to "move up" in society with his own hands. Moreover, since the Folk Craftsmen system emphasizes artistic achievement, the art market adapts well to this accreditation system. Many art galleries and shops prefer to attach a copy of the accreditation certificate to the painter's biography for promotion. The price of Tsering Gyal's thangkas also increased after he received provincial recognition. Upon hearing me explaining the academic tenure track, Tsering Gyal laughed and said the painter's track might be more exhausting. He was in his early thirties when he was recognized as a Provincial Folk Craftsman. "My realistic goal is to become a 'Provincial Arts and Crafts Master' in my fifties," said Tsering Gyal, "That'd be my tenure." Given the efforts and time invested in a painter's "tenure," it is not hard to understand why Namgyal considered the art shop's (careless) use of the term *Arts and Crafts Master* as doing more harm than good to Lutso.

Unlike Tsering Gyal, some other painters, including Tsering Gyal's friend and neighbor Norbu, distance themselves from this accreditation system, even after the "Criteria and Rules" and other local regulations came into effect. Besides distrusting the system, Norbu thinks it takes too much time to prepare for the application and to participate in all the social events associated with the process, including exhibitions, heritage festivals, trainings, meetings, and banquets with officials and other artists. Norbu is satisfied with his current patron from Shanghai, a Han art dealer specializing in Buddhist art. "As long as I can feed myself and my family, I don't need any title," said Norbu. "I don't want to get involved in those complexities—village fellows sometimes fight with each other because of those art competitions." This is also why Lutso was reluctant to apply for any official titles. Namgyal has encouraged Lutso to start on the accreditation track as early as possible. On one hand, he considers the current accreditation system "healthier" and thus a possible means to improve women painters' status. On the other hand, since Namgyal sits on several review committees, he knows the level of competition and the time it takes to obtain a desirable result. Like Norbu, Lutso does not like complexities, nor does she like to deal with officials at any level. Being a woman, she thinks her participation in the accreditation process is also likely to trigger jealousy and resentment from male painters who are already anxious about the competition.

Because Lutso has not yet applied for any accreditation, she urged the shopkeeper to delete those titles from her profile. The art shop finally took them off. However, I am not sure if the shopkeeper was sympathetic to Lutso and Namgyal's concern or if the shopkeeper simply figured out something better. The shop now highlights the fact that Lutso's artwork has been collected by a world-class museum in New York.

A Thousand Painters and Ten Thousand Thangkas

Twenty years after *The Great Thangka* was recognized by the Guinness World Records as the biggest thangka in the world, Rebgong set two other world records. On a hot day in July 2019, over a thousand Rebgong thangka painters gathered in Sengeshong village. Each painter brought a canvas mounted on stretcher, a few paintbrushes, and pigments. They sat in the open square in front of the Rebgong Thangka Art Museum (Ch. *re gong tang ka yi shu guan*) in Sengeshong and started to paint the head portrait of Buddha Shakyamuni (figure 2). Meanwhile, Guinness World Records officials were counting the number of thangka paintings displayed inside the museum—thangkas submitted by

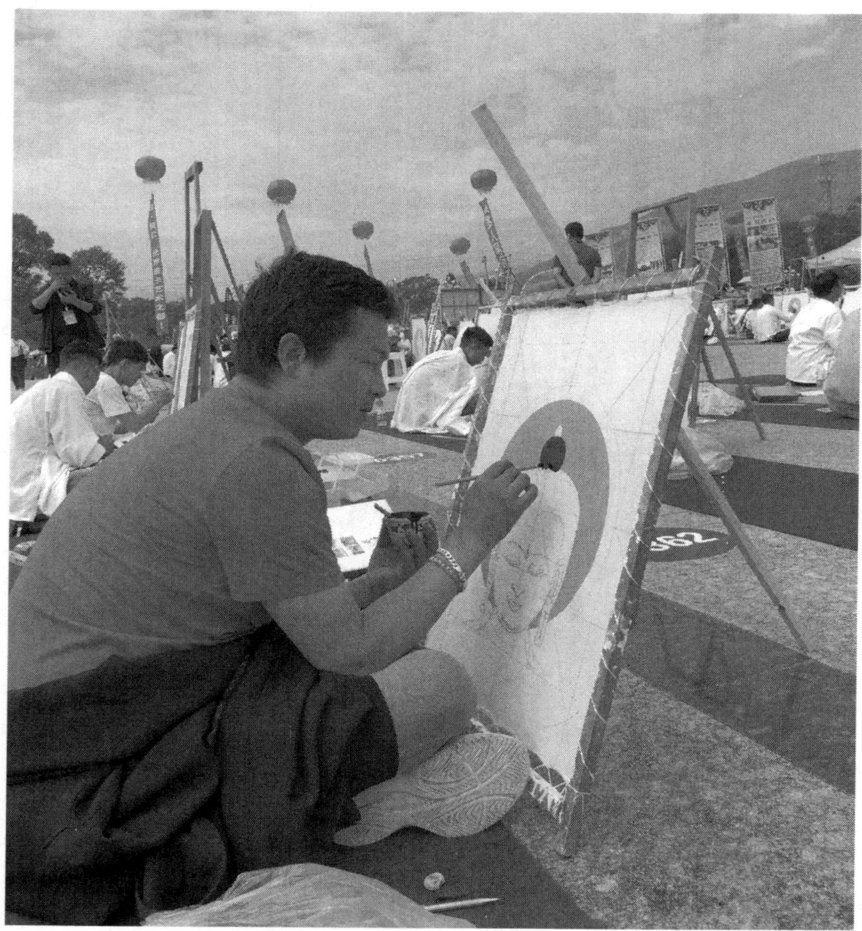

FIGURE 2 Rebgong *lha zo* painting the Buddha's head portrait for the Guinness World Records event, 2019.

painters from various villages in Rebgong. The counting took about five hours. As a thousand Buddha's heads emerged outside the exhibition hall, the World Records officials announced that Tongren County People's Government had successfully achieved "the largest display of thangka paintings," which consisted of 10,031 paintings, and "the most people drawing thangkas simultaneously," which included 1,005 people. Before participants went back home, they were invited to take a photo with the Guinness World Record certificate.

Both Tsering Gyal and Lutso participated in this event. Tsering Gyal told me that the choice of painting subject was made by the county officials. They chose Buddha Shakyamuni because his iconography is a basic skill of all thangka painters, whether they were trained in family workshops, art schools, or government-sponsored training programs. Painting his head portrait instead of the whole body was largely a logistical consideration—no painter would wish to sit under the summer sun for the entire day. Because it was just the head of the Buddha (though fully colored), painters did not write the sacred syllables *om ah hum* behind the image. And because it was not a whole image of the Buddha, no one took these paintings for consecration. Tsering Gyal kept his painting at home and never took it out again. Lutso brought the painting back to her studio. When a non-Tibetan client visited Lutso and saw the Buddha's head portrait, she quite liked it and asked about the price. Lutso told her this was a painting made for a cultural event, not a thangka for sale. The client still liked it, so Lutso gave the painting to the client without any charge.

To painters like Tsering Gyal and Lutso, the Buddha's head portrait was not a sacred or functional image but a piece of decorative art using the Buddhist motif, like what one might find in the backyard of a California house (Catanese 2019, 4; Tythacott and Bellini 2020, 4). A reader might detect an irony here: since these paintings only depicted part of the Buddha and they were not consecrated (nor intended for religious use), they are not thangka in the strict sense, despite how the Guinness World Records characterized them ("the most people drawing thangkas simultaneously"). Using a religious image for secular purposes is not something new to Rebgong painters, as many of them have traveled to other places and encountered a sculpture of Buddha's head on a bar counter or in a garden fountain. Yet some local painters indeed felt uncomfortable toward the "iconography" chosen by the officials. One painter told me that even on mini-thangkas, paintings smaller than the size of a palm, the body of the Buddha or deities had to be kept intact.[29] When painters practice their techniques, they draw parts of the Buddha on sketch papers—a hand, an arm, a pair of eyes, or a head. However, they do not call such a drawing a thangka. Another painter considered this Guinness World Records event a "gimmick" played by the county officials to attract tourists and money. After all, painters who sent their thangkas for exhibition or participated in depicting the Buddha's head did not receive any compensation, except a copy of the Guinness certificate that arrived a few months later.

Although the Guinness event is not part of the prefecture's Cultural Heritage Festival (Ch. *wen hua yi chan ri*) held every summer, it is not entirely irrelevant to Rebgong's ICH discourse. Most painters who had sent their works to the Rebgong Thangka Art Museum for the Guinness exhibition were recognized as County-Level ICH Inheritors, a prerequisite for the accreditation of Prefectural ICH Inheritors. Though participation in the Guinness event was voluntary, for painters who wanted to pursue the ICH Inheritor accreditation, their participation seemed necessary because it not only gave them an entry-level title but also counted as a "social contribution" or "public engagement," which would be valuable on their résumés.[30] This is why Norbu thinks it is time-consuming to pursue any accreditation—the Guinness case is only one of many such events an applicant for ICH Inheritor or Arts and Crafts Master would not want to miss.

Local implementation of national ICH policies often varies and suits local stakeholders' particular economic, political, and cultural needs (Shepherd and Yu 2013; Su 2020). Because of the ambiguity of ICH, cultural practitioners have some room to exercise their agency between the government agenda and the changing demands of the markets (Maags 2018). The village, county, or prefecture may each provide its own footnote to the provincial or national ICH agenda. The 2019 Guinness event, for instance, was an initiative of Tongren County instead of the prefecture or Qinghai. As a consequence, it was held in Sengeshong village instead of in Rongwo town. Painters living in this complex social system find various ways to negotiate a niche for art making and identity shaping. Some are like Tsering Gyal, who has chosen to march the accreditation track (and attend the Guinness event). Some are like Norbu, who distances himself from the ICH discourse and seeks audiences in other contexts. And others are like Lutso, who has not yet decided which way to go and explores various opportunities.

In 2019 the Guinness World Record might not have created the level of enthusiasm it had in Rebgong two decades earlier, partly because Rebgong painters now know that this record was initially established by an Irish brewing company and is largely commercial. Yet we cannot say that painters in Rebgong necessarily condemn commodification. Between *The Great Thangka* and "the thousand Buddhas," Rebgong painters' involvement in the art market, especially the secular market, has hit a new level. Yet Rebgong thangka is hardly transformed into a pure commodity or a hybrid art, a characterization many local painters feel sensitive about. During the artistic revival, Rebgong apprentices spent years acquiring a complete set of painting skills as well as sufficient knowledge to accept and work on monastic commissions. As in the story of Shawo Tsering and Zhang Daqian, Buddhist art making is not immediately accessible to "outsiders," not even to sophisticated artists like Zhang. Stories like this have motivated the local government to preserve its distinct art tradition and, later, to participate in the national ICH discourse. Rebgong's success in the ICH campaign, on both national and international levels, has encouraged the transmission of thangka painting skills and largely maintained the form and content of Rebgong thangkas—setting Rebgong on a unique trajectory of art development that is different from many other local arts going on global markets (e.g., Graburn 1969; Steiner 1994; Myers 2002). However, even as the government intended to preserve the traditional way of art making, what belongs to the tradition is a question of much debate.

The story of *The Great Thangka* indicates that in today's Rebgong the preservation of religious value and cultural tradition may need to find new patrons beyond audiences within Tibetan communities. But what will happen as more and more Rebgong thangkas are acquired by non-Tibetan clients? If a thangka painting is featured in a commercial art gallery, is it still sacred? Can it be used for religious purposes? Whether a thangka is a sacred object or a piece of decorative art depends on the context of art production and distribution and can be gleaned by looking at how Rebgong *lha zo* make meaning in their work. Notably, painters may accomplish this via somewhat different paths—the 2019 Guinness event is a reflection of this heterogeneity. Because of painters' involvement in today's markets, it may no longer be possible to gather hundreds of painters to work *together* on one piece of thangka painting, as they did with *The Great Thangka* twenty years ago. Instead, the 2019 Guinness World Record documented the display of ten thousand different thangkas and a thousand Buddha's heads that ended up at separate homes.

CHAPTER 2

"Aura" in the Art Market

In February 2020 Namgyal received a phone call from a Han gallery owner based in Beijing. The gallery owner wanted to order a hundred thangka paintings depicting a healing deity in Tibetan Buddhism, Loma Gyonma (Tib. *lo ma gyon ma*, Ch. *ye yi fo mu*), who lives in the forest and is known to be able to pacify all illnesses, especially contagious diseases such as SARS and AIDS.[1] From the beginning of the COVID-19 outbreak, Namgyal had been tracking the news and felt deeply sad about people who were suffering from the illness. At first, however, he held off on painting Loma Gyonma, uncertain if he would receive enough orders to cover the painting costs. Enshrining one thangka of Loma Gyonma in the local monastery could give the entire region sufficient blessing, while non-Tibetan people, in Namgyal's opinion, had very likely never heard of this deity. The order from the gallery owner gave Namgyal a sense of assurance. He completed the commission and made extra thangkas of Loma Gyonma to send to his close non-Tibetan friends residing in China and overseas as a blessing. In the following months, Namgyal received continuous orders from these places for thangka paintings of Loma Gyonma.

Do painters producing for the contemporary market continue viewing thangka paintings as sacred objects that possess blessings, wisdom, and healing powers? How do painters respond to an emerging art market that largely consists of non-Tibetan clients? In the story recounted here, why did Namgyal first keep the idea of painting Loma Gyonma on hold, and what made him paint extra copies of Loma Gyonma to send to his non-Tibetan friends later on? Furthermore, how do Rebgong *lha zo* operate within a state-fostered tourist market that has reduced the religious meaning of thangka art, and how do they position themselves in relation to an increasing number of Han clients who follow and practice Tibetan Buddhism and pursue the religious significance and efficacy of thangka paintings elided by the state?

When things once considered too sacred for sale become commodities on the market, it usually triggers discomfort or a sense of profanity on the part of people who still practice religious rituals with these objects. This happens in Rebgong (Catanese 2019, 202), as in some other places (e.g., New Mexico: Kalb 1994; Korea: Kendall, Yang, and Yoon 2015; Vietnam and Indonesia: Kendall 2021). Some Rebgong residents, seeing mass-produced religious paraphernalia piled in shops in town might give a nod to Walter Benjamin (1969), who laments that the endless reproduction of copies has destroyed the authenticity, mystery, and originality of art—or as he calls it, the "aura" of art. Does it mean when the painter announces the price of a ready-made thangka hung in his shop, like the one I encountered on my very first day in Rebgong, that the painting could not be used for hosting a divine spirit and later for worship and veneration?

Economic practices do not preclude the possibility of creating sacred objects and their aura through processes that mingle ritual with material production (Gernet 1995; Kieschnick 2003). The Buddhist statue sold in a shop in Chengdu is handled with care and respect: the shopkeeper puts the statue in a wooden box and wraps ceremonial scarves (Tib. *kha btags*) around its neck to ensure its safe journey to the client (Brox 2019, 115). Commercially produced ritual goods and commoditized religious services are prevalent in urban Japan, Korea, and Vietnam, but they are first made for sacred purposes (Reader and Tanabe 1998; Kendall 2015). Even Balinese masks made in an unconsecrated assembly line and targeted to the tourist market have been known to become enlivened or possessed by spirit entities, demanding to be treated as "sacred" (Slattum and Schraub 2003, 13; Kendall and Ariati 2020). The "life" of Rebgong thangka paintings can embody all these aspects.

While the growing body of material religion studies rejects any simple dichotomy of sacred object and commodity, anthropologists of art direct our gaze toward how various actors in the markets negotiate and reconfigure the values—in Rebgong's case, the religious, economic, artistic, and cultural values of Tibetan thangka paintings in contemporary China.[2] The synergy between these two fields suggests that commodification should be understood as a dynamic process in which some Rebgong *lha zo* tactically participate in different markets in order to authenticate their religious identity, preserve a cultural tradition, or establish artistic authority within and beyond the local community. Contextualizing the biography of Tibetan thangka paintings in different social spheres (Kopytoff 1986), by looking at the different motives behind Rebgong *lha zo* and the various values of thangka paintings they make, helps us solve the seeming contradiction inherent in the commodification of sacred objects.[3]

The Three Markets for Rebgong Thangka Art

To understand the art making scene in Rebgong, we have distinguished three kinds of markets for Rebgong thangka. In the *internal market*, Rebgong thangka paintings are circulated among monastic and laypeople within Tibetan communities (plate 5). This market was revitalized during Rebgong's artistic revival, beginning in the Reform era. In the internal market, the religious and social practices associated with Tibetan art making have not changed very much, even after thangka paintings came to be promoted on the national level as an Intangible Cultural Heritage (Reynolds 2011; Catanese 2019). In this market, thangka paintings are usually acquired by commission, for occasions such as meditations, Buddhist teachings, funerals, or to dispel illness and misfortune.

Since Buddhist art making is "almost always a social rather than individual activity" (Kieschnick 2003, 54), the *lha zo* and the patron (Tib. *yon bdag*) are bound in the internal market by the sacredness, or "inalienability," of the painting, as they are in exchanges of sacred objects in other places (see Weiner 1992; Mauss 2002). Many Tibetan textual sources, including the fifteenth-century art treatise *The Wish-Granting Gem*, provide abundant descriptions of the proper relationship between the patron and the artist.[4] The *lha zo* works hard because making a sacred image is a meritorious act (Tib. *dge las*), and the artwork is venerated and worshipped by the patron and his family in their everyday lives. For this reason, artists usually do not leave their names on the Buddhist image, while the patron's name might be inscribed on the back of the painting (Linrothe 2001; Quintman 2013). The patron should provide generous compensation—conceived as voluntary offerings (Tib. *yon*), including food, lodging, or cash—to the painter, who serves as a medium between the sacred spirits and secular people (Jackson and Jackson 1988, 12; McGuckin 1996, 33).[5] The Tibetan word *lu* (Tib. *blu* or *glud*), used for this type of commission, is applied in an honorific sense to the acquisition of a sacred image (e.g., thangka *lu* means to commission a thangka painting). In contrast, the word *tsong* (Tib. *tshong*), which describes commercial transactions for profit, was rarely paired with Buddhist art before Tibetan thangka paintings entered into China's national art market.

Although there is little record documenting how the exchange between the patron and the painter actually happened in Rebgong prior to the Cultural Revolution (Catanese 2019, 74), contemporary thangka painters generally agree upon certain conventions for accepting and working on a commission, following the ideal relationship between the patron and the *lha zo* that has been described in various textual sources (Catanese 2019). A painter told me that to refuse a commission because of the size of the compensation was not only impolite but could also incur bad karmic consequences for the art maker. Besides money, many forms of material compensation are acceptable, such as meals, butter, livestock, tea, and clothing. A local monk painter told me he had once painted a thangka commissioned by a poor woman for her deceased husband, for which only a brass bowl was offered as the payment. Also, a painter needs to be honest in producing the religious image. For instance, if a patron has paid for the materials, including valuable mineral or plant pigments and gold leaves, the artist should use up all the materials for the patron's painting. Nor should a painter use synthetic pigments, such as acrylic colors, as a substitute for natural mineral pigments without the patron's approval. On the other hand, the painter may adjust details, such as the amount of gold details and embellishment, according to the patron's budget.[6] However, monastic commissions are somewhat different from commissions made by laypeople. Many Rebgong *lha zo* today, including both painters and sculptors, make Buddhist images for the monastery for minimum or even no charge, since making an image that is kept and venerated in a monastery brings tremendous merits to the art maker.

After China launched the Great Western Development campaign in 2000, which aims at directing domestic and foreign investments to China's marginalized western regions (Goodman and Edmonds 2004; Fischer 2013), the secularization of Rebgong's art intensified. With new resources, Huangnan Tibetan Autonomous Prefecture and Tongren County have invested a considerable amount of money to develop Rebgong's cultural industry and tourism, including staging art competitions, heritage festivals, and cultural expos, and initiating low-interest loans for local art makers to open family-owned thangka shops or galleries (figure 3). In this way the state has fostered an

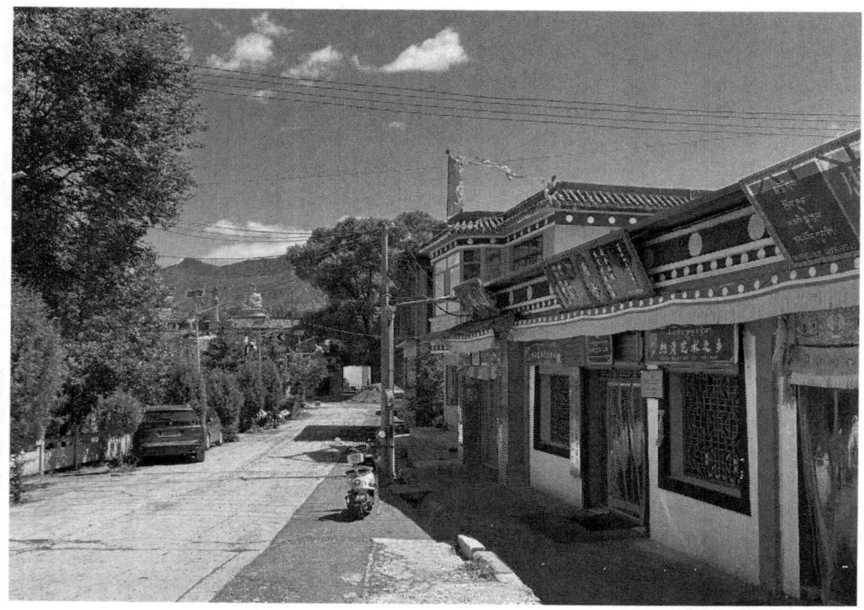

FIGURE 3 Thangka shops built onto residents' own houses along the village road in Sengeshong, 2024. Their proximity to the Lower Wutun Monastery (*far left*), today also a tourist attraction, makes them popular places for visitors.

external market in which Tibetan thangka art is tailored to the taste of secular consumers, including tourists, art merchants, and non-Tibetan entrepreneurs who are looking for exotic and expensive gifts for their business partners.[7] With the development of ethnic tourism and the promotion of Rebgong thangka art in China's urban centers under the ICH banner, painting has become a lucrative profession for Rebgong residents (Catanese 2019, 217). Precisely for this reason, the state and the prefecture treat thangka art as a valuable "cultural resource" (Makley 2018, 237), with painting as a pragmatic skill that contributes to the alleviation of poverty. In the external market, the official narrative of Tibetan art emphasizes artistic techniques and materials, such as the rarity of natural mineral pigments or the exquisite craftsmanship, instead of the religious content of the paintings.[8] This state-led commodification, with such tangible forms as "an art institute, sinecures for lay artists, publications with glossy color photographs, tourist promotions, and national-level exhibitions," has downplayed, if not completely muted, the religious value of Tibetan art and expanded thangka paintings beyond the Buddhist sphere (Linrothe 2001, 34).

Today many Tibetan Buddhist objects, thangkas included—premade objects with a fixed price—have come to be sold in an emerging market dominated by non-Tibetan clients. Although there is "a long-held and deeply embedded" religious prohibition on selling religious objects in Tibet (Catanese 2019, 111), Rebgong art makers, monks, and merchants seek to project and preserve their ethnic identity through selling Buddhist objects (156–57). Some Rebgong *lha zo* also operate their art shops and sell thangka paintings to non-Tibetan clients in distant places, such as Shangri-la in Yunnan (Reynolds 2011, 100–103). One major motive driving Tibetan merchants and painters to engage with the external market seems to be the worry that if Tibetans did not sell religious objects, other ethnic groups (most likely Han and Muslim) would sell them anyway or, worse, sell them in culturally inappropriate ways (Catanese 2019, 118, 158). If we only focus on the act of selling, however, we would unequivocally accept a dichotomy between sacred object and commodity and sigh with Walter Benjamin for the loss of its aura.[9] In fact, within the complex structure of the art market, Rebgong thangka painters constantly translate their own changing values and aspirations into the production and circulation of Buddhist images.

The gallery owner from Beijing, as well as Namgyal's non-Tibetan friends who ordered thangkas of Loma Gyonma from him, belong to a third market. These non-Tibetan clients follow the guidance of their monastic teachers, commission religious images and venerate them at home, and practice Tibetan Buddhism in their daily lives. These clients are very different from tourists and art dealers who treat thangka paintings simply as folk art or ethnic commodities. The *intermediate market*, a term I adapt from Yael Bentor's (1993) research on the thangka market in Nepal, consists of non-Tibetans (mostly Han) who practice Tibetan Buddhism and value the religious meaning, correct iconography, and social practices associated with art making in serious ways. To them, Buddhist ethics are not polluted by the market economy; instead, the economic activities associated with Buddhism could be a "reaffirmation of the significant religious influence that Buddhism has amidst global market forces" (Brox and Williams-Oerberg 2017, 510). With the rising popularity of Tibetan Buddhism among Han people (Yü 2012; Zhang 2012; Osburg 2020), the intermediate market plays an important role in shaping the biography of Rebgong thangka art, which neither conforms to the official narrative imposed on Tibetan thangka for external audiences nor strictly follows the norms governing the internal market.

Most Han involved in Tibetan Buddhism since the 1990s are well-educated and well-off people whose engagement in Tibetan Buddhism could be driven by an emerging spiritual or religious market in China after the economic reform and by the pursuit of "truth and spirituality" in a rapidly changing society (Caple 2020, 69). There are various intentions behind these "belief consumers": for some, thangka paintings, religious practices, or Tibetan Buddhism in general serve as "an extension of worldly projects of social distinction and wealth accumulation," while others imagine Tibetan Buddhism as "an isolated spiritual retreat from those same concerns" (Osburg 2020, 69). Yet little is known about the other end of this chain—that is, how art producers respond to consumers' desires and needs associated with the spread of Tibetan Buddhism in China. In today's market, a single *lha zo* may engage in different kinds of transactions with various types of clients, including the local community, non-Tibetan patrons who practice Tibetan Buddhism, and tourists or art dealers from the venues fostered by the state. Even in the intermediate market, clients possess diverse motives, aesthetic preferences, and understandings of Tibetan Buddhism, which complicate the nature of their commissions and their relationships with individual thangka painters.

Navigating the Intermediate Market

MONK RINCHEN

On my first visit to monk Rinchen in a local monastery in 2011, he half-joked, "Han collected artworks by their ears, not by their eyes." He meant that many Han clients indiscriminately preferred thangka paintings from famous painters who have been designated "National ICH Inheritors" or "National Arts and Crafts Masters," promoted through national exhibitions, or featured in news reports and TV shows.[10] Rebgong painters often used the Mandarin term *thangka masters* (Ch. *tang ka da shi*) to describe them; it is not a term for artists in the Tibetan tradition.[11] Rinchen, who had participated in the making of *The Great Thangka*, felt that some of these star painters, or so-called masters, do not live up to their titles because of their ordinary or even poor painting skills. Unfortunately, many non-Tibetan clients do not possess a connoisseur's eye to distinguish the quality (or the author) of a thangka painting. While Rinchen was not perfectly happy with the fact that some thangka paintings were now sold as decorative art or souvenirs in the market, he was even more annoyed when poor-quality paintings were sold at skyrocketing prices because of someone's fame and felt that such cheating not only incurred very bad karma but also damaged the future of Rebgong thangka art.

Not long after my first interview with Rinchen, he joined my conversation with one of his friends, a Tibetan official who worked for the Cultural Bureau of the Prefecture. Rinchen's friend and I were talking about the village's plan to build its own art museum. Rinchen listened for a couple of minutes and broke in, "How do you know this isn't going to be another showroom for those 'thangka masters'?" Giving a nod to Rinchen, his friend put an ambivalent smile on his face, indicating that it was not the first time he had heard such a complaint, or perhaps not even the first time from Rinchen. Diplomatically (in front of an anthropologist) or out of sincerity, Rinchen's friend said he was willing to file a report to prefectural officials to discuss the issue of the disqualified "thangka masters." Rinchen laughed. In a sarcastic tone, the monk joked to his friend that he would have to wait after all his teeth had fallen out for this problem to be solved. The topic was dropped.

Being a sophisticated painter himself, Rinchen turned to the market to look for patrons who would treat Tibetan Buddhism and thangka art in respectful and serious ways. One of Rinchen's recent patrons was a Chinese entrepreneur from Shanxi. The entrepreneur and his family had been practicing Tibetan Buddhism for many years before they got to know Rinchen, who gave the family a tour of his monastery in 2011. Impressed by his knowledge and charisma, the patron invited Rinchen to his mansion in Shanxi. For several months each year, Rinchen lived with the patron and his family in Shanxi and taught them Tibetan Buddhism and how to paint thangkas. With the help of this patron, Rinchen was able to hold a solo exhibition of his thangka paintings in a private art gallery in Shanxi in 2013. The show brought Rinchen a good sale and subsequent commissions. Rinchen was pleased with this patronage. He also felt that through this work, he had helped to spread Tibetan Buddhism and the tradition of thangka art among non-Tibetans.

LESHE

When I googled "Re gong tang ka" in 2011, Leshe's blog showed up as I scrolled down the search list. Leshe addressed himself as a "Rebgong thangka artist" (Ch. *re gong tang ka yi shu jia*) on the home page. I opened his blogs: a photo of his pencil sketch of the White Tara, with a brief explanation of iconometric theory in Tibetan thangka art; an enlarged view of a deity's apparel, accompanied by a description of the gold lining technique he applied to paint the exquisite patterns on that dress; and his recent thangka painting of Manjushri, followed by the story of this bodhisattva. Although some information was too general or brief to be accurate, I was intrigued by this well-organized and educational blog in both Tibetan and Chinese, under the name of a Rebgong thangka painter.[12] In the contact information, I not only saw his phone number but also noticed that Leshe had a thangka shop in one of the most expensive districts in Beijing.

A few months later, I met Leshe in Rebgong as he returned from Beijing to celebrate the New Year with his family. Leshe was in his late twenties when I first met him. Talking to me in Mandarin with a Beijing accent, Leshe told me it was the fourth year that he had lived and painted thangkas in Beijing. In 2008 Leshe had a chance to attend an event in the city's Olympic Village. During that time Leshe began to realize there was a market for Tibetan thangka paintings in the capital. After the Olympics, Leshe did not go back to Rebgong. He borrowed RMB 400,000 (about USD 57,553, at the exchange rate in 2008) from a client, who came from Hong Kong and lived in Beijing, to open his thangka shop in the center of the city.

According to Leshe, his business was quite difficult in the beginning. Tourists were not interested in buying the expensive thangka paintings he had on display, let alone commissioning any new work. Leshe did not have an extensive network with Tibetan Buddhist practitioners or art collectors in the city either. Yet he needed to pay rent, which was over RMB 80,000 (about USD 11,510) per year, as well as considerable living expenses. Leshe told me the Hong Kong patron who had lent him money helped him again, on the condition that the patron shared half of the profits from selling Leshe's thangka paintings, in addition to the interest on his loan. The patron introduced Leshe to businessmen who were interested in Tibetan Buddhism or Buddhist art. Being a Tibetan Buddhist practitioner, the patron also set up the online promotion for Leshe's thangka paintings—the patron had written the blogs I read, and Leshe had done the Tibetan translations.

In a practice that Trine Brox would characterize as "packaging"—operating the thangka shop under Leshe's name, publishing personal blogs of Leshe with the image of his artwork in progress, accompanied by "flashcards" of Tibetan Buddhism or Buddhist art in two languages—Leshe and his Hong Kong patron have proclaimed the sacrality and authenticity of his thangka paintings, so "they become unlike any other mundane commodity" (Brox 2019, 114). I once praised Leshe for his beautifully presented blogs. He smiled and said: "That's my patron's idea. I don't know how to take photos or publish a blog. But my patron said it's important to let people know what Tibetan thangkas are and how beneficial it is to have a thangka painting. So, we keep doing that." As Leshe's social network expanded, his business started to grow. By the time I met him, he had been quite successful. In 2014 Leshe was able to open a second thangka shop in Beijing. He also employed several apprentices from his own village to work at both shops in the capital.

NORBU

Another thangka painter, Norbu, in his early twenties in 2007, was introduced through a Tibetan friend to "the boss," Mr. Liu, a Han who claimed that he worked for the Religious Bureau in Beijing. Liu was recruiting thangka painters from Rebgong and Lhasa to work on his commissions. He provided Norbu and other painters with a shared apartment in Beijing as well as a monthly salary of RMB 4,000 (USD 575). Norbu never asked Liu where his commissions came from. Through Liu's phone calls and conversations with others, Norbu speculated that Liu was trying to open his own shop in Beijing featuring Tibetan arts and religious objects. Therefore, Liu not only needed thangka paintings for sale in his shop but also sent some of the paintings as luxury gifts to government officials and business partners for networking. Liu did not paint, but to Norbu he appeared very knowledgeable about Tibetan Buddhism. For every commission, Liu took out a piece of paper and sketched the arrangement of deities for his painters. Norbu and other painters admired Liu's charisma and enjoyed eating out and touring with him around Beijing. What Norbu enjoyed most was looking at illustrated catalogs of Tibetan art Liu brought to them and listening to Liu telling stories from Tibetan Buddhist scriptures, albeit in Mandarin.

Unable to adjust to food and climate in Beijing, Norbu decided to go back to Rebgong after spending three years in the capital. Yet he continued painting for Liu and brought thangka paintings to Beijing once or twice a year. Norbu did not consecrate these paintings in Rebgong. Liu insisted on bringing these paintings to a reincarnate lama residing in the Yonghe Temple (Tib. *dga' ldan byin chags gling*) for consecration.[13] Norbu knew by that time that Liu was operating a shop in an antique market in Beijing, where he sold Norbu's paintings—signed by a "Rebgong thangka painter" instead of Norbu's name—for a price about two or three times what he paid Norbu. Norbu never visited Liu's shop, knowing Liu would be annoyed if he did. On the other hand, Norbu was quite pleased with the money Liu offered for his paintings: though it could not match the price tag in Liu's thangka shop, it was still better than the price of most thangka paintings sold in Rebgong.

Their collaboration broke down after a couple of years. For two consecutive commissions, Liu failed to pay Norbu, insisting that he would pay Norbu back with interest once he sealed an important business deal. Norbu knew from another friend in Beijing that Liu was experiencing financial hardship and had probably also lost his job. After reminding Liu several times and getting no money back, Norbu gave up. Norbu lost about RMB 40,000 (USD 5,714) on these two commissions, yet he refused to consider Liu greedy or malicious. Instead, he thought Liu was an old man with good intentions but bad luck. Norbu ceased painting for Liu but said they occasionally exchanged text messages. Neither of them ever mentioned the unpaid thangkas. Currently, Norbu works on commissions for a gallery owner from Shanghai.

When the Thangka Master Becomes a Middleman

In Rebgong, Liu was not Norbu's only client. One day in 2012, when I visited Norbu in his home studio, another painter from the same village, Sangyal, dropped in and asked if Norbu had thangka paintings of Yamantaka. Sangyal was an apprentice of a Tibetan thangka master, who was designated as one of the first "Inheritors of the National ICH" in Rebgong. This was before the establishment of local laws and regulations on the recognition of inheritors or masters. According to some other painters and local officials, this master had not earned his title through exceptional painting skills but through skillful networking with government officials.[14] With this title, the thangka master received financial and other support from the government to purchase land and build an art institution (Ch. *hua yuan*, Tib. *sgyu rtsal gling*) of his own.[15] In a time when Rebgong art was being promoted on the national level, media looked for distinctive but safe subjects like this master to feed their news stories. Because of his fame and connections, the thangka master was overwhelmed with orders from non-Tibetan clients. Unable to complete the orders by himself and his apprentices alone, the thangka master purchased paintings from local painters and resold them to clients under his name. Norbu told me that the master once acquired a thangka painting from him for RMB 7,000.

Norbu somehow found out that his painting was eventually sold (of course, under the master's name) for over RMB 100,000. On the day of my visit to his home studio, Norbu did not have the painting Sangyal was looking for, nor did he want to sell any painting to the thangka master.

Ready-made thangka paintings are common in Rebgong nowadays (Reynolds 2011; Catanese 2019). Reselling is not unusual for Rebgong thangka painters either, although none of the Tibetans I know has ever resold a thangka she or he made or commissioned for religious use. Ready-made thangkas are not only sold to tourists or dealers but also exchanged in the social network of local painters. From time to time, clients order paintings a painter does not have or is unable to complete within the desired time frame. Being more comfortable with sharing paintings than sharing clients, a painter would turn to other painters to "borrow" their artworks and resell them to his clients.[16] Though technically one cannot commission a ready-made thangka, some painters still use *lu* (commission) in this context. For instance, several painters used a similar expression to make such a request: "Can I take your thangka to show to my client? If the client likes it, I will commission it from you."[17] Every painter is aware of the fact that his painting will be resold at a higher price than what he is paid for it, often under the name of the other painter who has borrowed it. Many painters told me the exchange between trustworthy relatives or friends could ensure the actual author of the painting gets a fair share.

However, borrowing and reselling do not necessarily result in a win-win situation for thangka painters. Resourceful and well-connected painters, like the thangka master, could accumulate more economic and social capital by reselling paintings from less resourceful painters. Even close friends or relatives sometimes argue over the payment or authorship of a resold thangka. When Tibetan thangka paintings enter the secular or capitalist market, where the pursuit of financial profits overrides the religious protocols of art production and distribution, the Buddhist convention of not leaving the artist's name on the painting results in much ambiguity in the authorship and the originality of an artwork and becomes a convenient tool for the thangka master and middlemen to appropriate works from others. The selling of Tibetan religious objects, in fact, does not create a "high degree of social cooperation and unity" (Catanese 2019, 220). With increasing competition, there are more conflicts in the local community (plate 6).

Both Norbu and monk Rinchen (as well as many other painters) deliberately reject the official recognition of the title thangka master. At first glance, monk Rinchen seemed to complain about Han clients, who in his opinion lack expertise in distinguishing the quality of thangka paintings. However, the real targets of his criticism were the officials who have chosen particular "thangka masters" to be the public face of Rebgong art and have little interest in educating external audiences about what Tibetan thangka really is—a criticism that had embarrassed Rinchen's friend on the village road. Painters like Rinchen, Norbu, and Leshe were able to negotiate with the official narrative by looking for or even cultivating patrons in the intermediate market. However, many less resourceful painters felt they were being exploited but did not have better options other than selling their paintings to the thangka masters.

Making Meaning across Different Markets

Not all thangka painters chase after wealth and fame. Namgyal was highly respected and admired by local painters long before he received any title from the prefecture or the central government. Namgyal used to be a monk in a local monastery. With his *ge gen* or through the teacher's introduction, Namgyal had traveled to several important religious institutions since the 1980s, including Kumbum Monastery, Labrang Monastery, and Jokhang Temple, to work on their commissions. After Namgyal returned to secular life and operated an art school of his own, he still had strong connections with these monasteries and continued painting for them. In 2019 more than half of Namgyal's commissions came from monasteries.

Commissions from monasteries require more time to complete than commissions from elsewhere because monasteries set the highest standard for the iconography and content of paintings. Painters need to do extensive research on Buddhist scriptures and revise their sketches multiple times until they receive approval from the commissioning monks or religious teachers. However, monasteries usually run on a tight budget. What monasteries can pay Namgyal often barely covers the material cost of a painting. In order to continue painting for monasteries and sustain his school as an art institution, Namgyal accepts commissions from Han clients who practice Tibetan Buddhism, art collectors, and gallery owners residing in Beijing, Hong Kong, and overseas.[18] These clients are willing to offer generous payments for Namgyal's thangka paintings because of their exceptional quality, in both an artistic and religious sense. Namgyal's history of being a monk becomes particularly appealing to clients in the intermediate market, who take it as assurance of the proper religious content and efficacy of the painting. Moreover, now that his artworks have been bid at seven-digit prices (in RMB) at auctions held in Beijing and Hong Kong, many non-Tibetan clients consider Namgyal's thangka paintings "collectible."

Namgyal does not like advertising his thangka paintings to clients and strongly objects to selling thangkas on social media platforms. This explains why he kept on hold the idea of painting Loma Gyonma for his Han friends—besides the painting cost, Namgyal did not want his friends to mistake this virtuous gesture as a marketing strategy. Namgyal met most of his non-Tibetan clients (and friends) at exhibitions, expos, or auctions held in China's urban centers. In these places, Namgyal got to know a few well-off patrons (who also practice Tibetan Buddhism) and maintained good friendships with them. These patrons are not only wealthy; they are also well connected (Osburg 2013; Bian 2018). After a patron of Namgyal, Mr. Chang, received the thangka of Loma Gyonma and displayed it in his private art collection in Taiwan, his relatives, friends, and business partners asked for identical paintings. Intentionally or not, patrons like Chang helped Namgyal "advertise" his artwork in a market that otherwise would have been inaccessible to him. According to Namgyal, the financial support from the government (in the form of loans, grants, or awards) covered less than 10 percent of the annual operating cost of his art school. The income made from his non-Tibetan clients helped to subsidize his monastic commissions as well as keep the art school running.

Being a student of Namgyal, however, is not an easy task. Beginners must learn to draw grids and proportions with him for about three years before they can advance to coloring. All students need to acquire basic knowledge of Tibetan Buddhism along with painting skills. Most of his students spend at least eight years in the art school to master all the painting techniques. His curriculum follows the mode of thangka transmission practiced before the 1950s, which is in stark contrast with the trajectories of many young painters today, especially those who have attended accelerated training programs (Ch. *su cheng ban*) sponsored by the local government under the name of poverty allevi-ation.[19] Namgyal understands that for their livelihood, young painters want to enter the market and make money as soon as possible. However, Namgyal thinks this rapid learning sacrifices the artistic creativity one could achieve in a painting career. From his point of view, the artistic creativity of thangka painting takes root from skillful techniques and a thorough understanding of

Tibetan Buddhist scriptures. Without proper training, "the best thing a painter could wish to become is a Xerox machine," Namgyal said.

In painting thangkas of commonly portrayed figures, most painters simply follow—or in Namgyal's word, "Xerox"—the content of previous paintings. But artists do have a certain amount of freedom. Instead of being constrained by rules of iconography and composition, a painter could, for instance, illustrate scenes from Buddhist text that have not been depicted before or examine the life story of a religious or historical figure and visualize such research through the paintbrush.[20] The sixteen arhats (Tib. *gnas brtan bcu drug*), a painting (or a set of paintings) frequently commissioned by monasteries in contemporary Tibet, is a particular subject that allows an artist to exercise creativity because, unlike tantric texts, arhat scriptures do not provide definitive visual characteristics for individual arhat (Linrothe 2004, 7). When Namgyal worked on the arhat paintings in the Kumbum Monastery in the 1990s, he found that previous paintings kept in the monastery and images circulated on the market contained mistakes and flaws, such as misplaced dharma instruments (e.g., drum, conch shell, and Vajra) or incorrect postures for a particular scene. Namgyal and his apprentices spent months reading scriptures with monks in Kumbum Monastery and then worked on the sketch. After completing the Kumbum commission, Namgyal kept doing research on the arhat images from various sources. Recently, he has updated the content of the thangka depicting Buddha Shakyamuni and sixteen arhats, an image also popular among audiences from the intermediate market. Rebgong *lha zo* such as Namgyal see this artistic freedom—the ability to create images from texts—as an important component of thangka art.

The Thangka Painters' Motives

In contrast to Pintupi acrylic paintings or Oaxacan wood carvings (Myers 2002; Chibnik 2003), Rebgong thangka paintings are not specifically designed for the external or the intermediate market. The external market of Rebgong thangka art is largely fostered by the state with the intention of commoditizing this religious art, while audiences in the intermediate market emphasize the religious value of thangka paintings to various extents. Painters caught between the two markets avoid, exploit, or contest the different "intercultural fields" to serve their own purposes (Myers 2001, 41), which also include the continued production of thangkas for internal sacred use. Many Rebgong *lha zo* believe that their thought, will, or intention matters to the aura of thangkas they paint, just like people who believe images of deities bestow blessings in response to worship but punish disrespect or neglect (Kendall 2021, 12). Thus, the relationship between *lha zo* and the artwork they produce should be understood in the same way anthropologists understand other types of human relationships: as defined by rights, obligations, and mutual expectations (Gell 1998, 16–18). Although in today's market some transactions associated with thangka paintings are purely commercial, some Rebgong painters carry their religious, cultural, and artistic intentions in art making and have thus reshaped the biography of Tibetan thangkas in contemporary China.

In an era of promoting "socialist culture under the market economy" (Makley 2018, 237), the official narrative has largely replaced the religious value of thangka paintings with their economic value and made them more accessible to consumers who might be unfamiliar with Tibetan Buddhism or Buddhist art. Some painters, like the thangka master, exploit this agenda in order to gain personal benefits—for example, acquiring land to build their own art institutions, receiving financial support from the government, or being promoted in state-sponsored exhibits, all of which further secularize and commoditize Rebgong thangka art. Although the government intended to foster a cultural industry and an ethnic tourism centered around Tibetan thangka to boost the local economy, especially for rural residents who often find themselves less competitive in regular job markets than other ethnic groups (particularly Han) (Fischer 2013; Demick 2020), it has failed to deliver the economic benefits promised to many locals. Painters like the thangka master take advantage of less resourceful painters by appropriating their artworks. Many painters are trained in home studios, private art schools, and government-sponsored programs for an increasingly competitive market. As a consequence of heightened competition, Rebgong painters have had to spend more time on painting, explore various marketing strategies, or travel farther away from home to seek their fortune.

Although Buddhists' engagement in economic activities has long been recognized as a way to project or reaffirm religious identities (Brox and Williams-Oerberg 2017; Catanese 2019), Rebgong *lha zo*'s participation in the art market goes beyond this. The crux of the problem for Rebgong painters is how the religious value of thangka art is perceived and treated by different actors in the market. One major motive for painters like Rinchen, Leshe, and Norbu is their "politics of presence"—Tibetans' materialization (through things like thangka art) of "the links people claimed between types of persons, authorities, exchange, and jurisdictions that legitimated forms of control over resources and livelihoods" (Makley 2018, 16). These painters subtly contest the substance of state-led developments that reduce the ethnic minority culture to "a set of exotic and photogenic beliefs, things, places, and performances" (15).[21] By strategically participating in the new markets, these *lha zo* exploit the social spheres (especially the intermediate market) in which the values of the painters and the clients can be in accord and the religious significance of thangka paintings are affirmed for new audiences.

Norbu refused to sell his paintings to the thangka master and avoided participating in government-organized exhibits or competitions altogether. Interestingly, Norbu was upset when the thangka master resold his painting for profit but did not blame Liu, who did virtually the same thing. Besides the fact that Norbu received better payment from Liu than from the thangka master, the relationship between Norbu and Liu had been strengthened by Liu's devotion to Tibetan Buddhism and their shared interests in Buddhist art throughout the years they worked together. The concept of fairness Norbu negotiated with respect to Liu and the thangka master (who Norbu described as "losing his beliefs") reveals that religious identities, independent from ethnic identities, play an important role in the specific relationship forged between the painter and the client. Negotiating these interactions, in turn, shapes moral arguments associated with the exchange of thangka paintings in remarkable ways. Similarly, monk Rinchen and Leshe chose to look for, or even cultivate, patrons who would respect and follow the teachings of Tibetan Buddhism. Leshe entrusted the Hong Kong patron to put up a personal blog under his name because the patron had shown engagement in Tibetan Buddhism and Buddhist art, even if it was partially incentivized by economic concerns. Although Rinchen's solo exhibition in a private gallery in Shanxi or Leshe's well-maintained blog did not compare with the scale or influence of state-sponsored exhibits, both of them were content that the religious aspects of thangka art could be preserved through their engagement with audiences from the intermediate market.

For Namgyal, to project and preserve a religious identity goes beyond the choice of clients or where to exhibit his artworks. His history of being a monk and extensive painting experience have led him to place a heavy focus on the religious content of thangka paintings and how painting techniques and knowledge of Buddhism are transmitted. Namgyal sets very high standards for himself and his students, hoping that the "traditional" mode of thangka transmission can be preserved even amid the seemingly overwhelming process of commodification. Unlike Rinchen or Norbu, he has never openly criticized any individual painter or opposed art events organized by the government. His "criticism" takes the form of gathering resources and negotiating conditions to, in his words, "get important things done," that is, to preserve the religious knowledge and cultural practices associated with Tibetan thangkas for generations to come. Although sending thangkas of Loma Gyonma to his non-Tibetan friends was an effective way of disseminating knowledge of Tibetan Buddhism, his engagement with the new markets has had other practical and important purposes: he has been able to subsidize his commissions from monasteries and keep the art school running, financially independent from government support, so that he can cultivate *ge truk* in his own ways.

Monastic commissions also enable painters like Namgyal to establish their credentials and artistic authority within and beyond Tibetan communities. Rebgong *lha zo*, though they follow rules of iconography and composition, display their understanding of religious texts and knowledge of historical accounts by visualizing them in paintings (Jackson and Jackson 1988, 144–45). In monasteries, artworks by Namgyal, as Lothar Ledderose would put it (2000, 7), "naturally" grow up from his study and conversation with monks about Buddhist scripture.[22] The finished thangkas, as well as this dialogical process of art making, have in turn enhanced monastic disciples' learning of religious texts. Moreover, the images displayed in monasteries are not only objects of veneration for visitors from near and far but also references or templates for other artists and scholars. Places like Kumbum Monastery are important sites for tourists and scholars as well as for Tibetans, Mongolians, Han, and other ethnic groups who follow Tibetan Buddhism. In Kumbum Monastery, Namgyal's artworks exemplify the artistic tradition of Rebgong, which contests the government narrative that portrays the officially selected thangka master as "the representative" of Rebgong art. Therefore, "the politics of presence" in Rebgong extends to the intercultural space occupied by monasteries, where *lha zo* reaffirm the religious, cultural, and artistic values of thangka art.

The Biography of Tibetan Thangka Paintings in China

Rebgong *lha zo* today do not view the marketplace as a distinct secular sphere (Weber 1981) that fails to accommodate sacred objects and their aura, nor for that matter do Chinese artisans, who have mass-produced sacred goods—

Buddhist images and votive objects, among others—to accommodate market demand for more than a thousand years (see, Cave 1998; Swergold et al. 2008). The painters in this chapter "sell" Tibetan thangkas beyond the internal market, yet there is no clear distinction between thangkas made for functional or religious use and those for secular consumption. Although selling religious objects is a traditionally prohibited practice in Tibet and goes beyond the comfort zone of some residents in Rebgong, we should look at how transactions actually take place and assume a permeability of categories. Practices of Rebgong *lha zo* inform us that the biography of Tibetan thangka is contingent on the sites of thangka painting within the complex structure of the art market, the context of the actual exchanges, and the specific relationships forged between thangka painters and their clients. Compromises and moral arguments associated with the circulation of Tibetan thangkas do occur, but many of them still take place inside the frame of religious practices.

The thangkas of Loma Gyonma painted by Namgyal for his non-Tibetan clients are no less efficacious than his arhat paintings commissioned by Kumbum Monastery—for both, he follows the Buddhist iconography, carefully arranges the composition, and takes the thangkas for consecration upon completion. While Namgyal's arhat paintings kept in the monastery preserve the tradition of religious image production and showcase the artistic achievement of Rebgong *lha zo*, his thangkas of Loma Gyonma, as well as his other commissions from patrons in the intermediate market, embody the same values and additional ones.

In today's Rebgong, thangka painters are involved in three markets, although the boundaries between them are not so clearly defined or policed. Since there is always a "moral economy" behind the visible economic exchange (Kopytoff 1986, 64; Saxer 2012), the aura of Tibetan thangkas is not an ascribed status but something Rebgong *lha zo* make as they strategically participate in the new markets. Painters like monk Rinchen, Norbu, and Leshe contextualize their artworks in ways that make thangka paintings a kind of commission in a reimagining of the tradition; others, like Namgyal, negotiate conditions to preserve the transmission of artistic skills, religious knowledge, and cultural practices. As a consequence, the biography of thangka painting does not only switch between sacred object and commodity; it also serves as a medium on which *lha zo* hope to connect the past with the future while making sense about the present with narratives of their own creation.

CHAPTER 3

Women Who Paint Thangkas

In 2019 television viewers tuned into a live broadcasting show in which different towns in the People's Republic of China competed with each other to be the most charming place in China. One episode of the show featured several prefectures in Qinghai. Huangnan Tibetan Autonomous Prefecture opened its presentation with an introduction to Rebgong, extolling its exquisite and mysterious Tibetan art and proclaiming Rebgong as the "homeland of Tibetan thangka art." The presentation was followed by a skit telling the story of a Tibetan girl in Rebgong who tried to become the first female thangka painter, allegedly in defiance of Tibetan tradition. In the end, performers invited the real people who had inspired the characters in the skit onto the stage, including Namgyal, the teacher who had opened the door of his art school to women to learn thangka painting, and Tsomo, one of Namgyal's female students. When the TV host asked Tsomo what she wished to do in the future, she responded in Mandarin, "After I graduate, I would like to have female students and teach them how to paint thangkas." Her words received warm applause from the judges and audience, who then gave Huangnan enough votes to advance to the next phase of the tournament.

I first met Tsomo and other female painters in 2013. In real life Tsomo was not Namgyal's first female *ge truk* nor one of his first female graduates. Her interest in painting aside, Tsomo was admitted to the art school in 2012 largely because she came from a poor, single-parent family. After a few years in the art school, Tsomo paused her painting because she constantly felt ill. During her convalescence, Tsomo thought of giving up painting and becoming a migrant worker. In 2019, when the TV crew came to Namgyal's art school to look for a female student who would go with Namgyal to the live broadcasting show, Tsomo was nominated by her *ge gen* because of her proficiency in Mandarin, which she had picked up by watching Mandarin TV shows and movies. After the broadcast, Namgyal successfully persuaded Tsomo to go back to school and resume thangka painting.

The emergence of female thangka painters is a new phenomenon. Rebgong did not have any female *lha zo* until the late 2000s. New markets have made thangka painting a lucrative profession in Rebgong and opened the door for Tibetan women to participate in art making. In the skit, the thangka master accepted the Tibetan girl as his apprentice because of her love for art. However, it took more than a passionate heart for women in Rebgong to be able to paint thangkas. Rebgong female painters are now mastering what was historically a male domain of art making. This is different from female artisans who transform locally produced textiles, ceramics, embroideries, and the like—the female domain of art making—to "crafts" for global consumption (e.g., Babcock 1993; Stephen 2005; Niessen 2009). Rebgong women *lha zo* not only enter the same complex regime of religious art production but also need to compete in a market dominated by men. This directs our attention to the particular challenges Rebgong women painters face and prompts us to ask, why do Tibetan women pursue a profession as thangka painters? Can women establish themselves as professional *lha zo* as men do? Or does painting impose an extra burden on women, who are already busy fulfilling the village ideal of Tibetan women as daughters, wives, mothers, and neighbors? Furthermore, what does painting thangka mean to Rebgong women? Is it just an additional source of income or a new way of life? Is women's participation in art production a "tokenistic gesture," as two male painters from Sengeshong put it, supporting the government's claim to have brought the region, and its women, into the process of national modernization?

If thangka painting is understood from purely economic notions of development and self-improvement (cf. Rajan 2015), as asserted by the state and accepted by many local families in Rebgong, women's participation in art making is destined to be disrupted. Although many families prefer the paid apprenticeship from art schools to other economic opportunities available to women, such as being a migrant worker, few families who send their daughters to learn thangka painting expect them to eventually open their own studios or become professional *lha zo* in their own right. Market biases (e.g., that women's painting is not efficacious or authentic) and gendered stereo-typing (e.g., that women entrepreneurs are promiscuous) make it very chal-lenging for Tibetan women to establish themselves as professional painters following the path available to their male counterparts. Moreover, as male painters like Leshe and Norbu are traveling farther away from home to seek economic fortune in China's urban places, for women painting reinforces a cultural expectation of immobility. Tibetan women's presence in household, childcare, agricultural, and communal events, serving as the "feminine hinge" (Schein 2000; Makley 2007), is expected and essential to holding the rural community together.[1]

Yet we should not see women's response as entirely passive or constrained by structural arrangements. Many women *lha zo* make efforts to balance their multiple roles—as daughters, wives, mothers, neighbors, and painters—to defend the diminishing sense of "Tibetanness" that is being threatened by social, economic, and political changes happening around them. Moreover, unlike Mexican weavers, Pueblo potters, or Tibetan modern artists whose audiences mostly come from the global market, Rebgong female *lha zo* rarely see thangka painting as an artistic outlet for self-expression or transform the Buddhist iconography to meet the modern aesthetics of external audiences. Within the complex structure of the art market, Rebgong women painters, like male painters, not only produce thangkas for tourists, merchants, or art collectors, but they also make paintings commissioned for their religious effi-cacy by devotees within and beyond Tibet. Because thangka painting brings merits to both the patron and the painter, art making enables female *lha zo* to accumulate religious merit—for this life and the next—and reimagine them-selves as social actors, an opportunity that was not available to women in the past. Therefore, women's understanding of art making offers an alternative narrative to the state's project of packaging art production in Rebgong as a palatable story of "good minorities" and the alleviation of poverty.

The Art Market: An Open Door for Women

Monks, painters, and local scholars in Rebgong generally agree that there is no explicit rule in Tibetan Buddhism that prevents women from painting thangkas. In his interview with thangka painters in Dharamsala, Eric McGu-ckin found a similar response that "the Buddha never said one word against it (women painting thangkas)" (1996, 39). In theory, uninitiated women, like uninitiated men, are forbidden from practicing certain tantric teachings and are not allowed to paint or view images of deities associated with such teachings (Makley 1994; Lopez 2018). In practice, several interlocutors in Rebgong have mentioned that Yamantaka Vajrabhairava (Tib. *rdo rje 'jigs byed*) and Palden Lhamo (Tib. *dpal ldan lha mo*) should be forbidden subjects for women painters, although such statements are not without debate.[2] According to Rebgong residents and my own observation, another reason that had prevented women from painting thangkas was the gendered division of labor in the village. In art making villages, men contributed to the household economy by making Buddhist art (sometimes working at distant places) and only occasionally participated in agricultural and household work. Women's time and labor were constantly needed for farming, housework, childcare, and other social responsibilities in the village.

Although in today's Rebgong, as in other Amdo communities, lifeways are too dynamic and complex to be summarized by a single type of family arrangement, most married women in the village live with their husbands' families (a patrilocal residence).[3] Women help their in-laws with farmwork and participate in communal events on behalf of their husbands' families.[4] Rural residents in Rebgong have long had reciprocal and obligatory support networks for farming, house construction, and other heavy labor. The norm of reciprocity has vital importance in the everyday life of the villagers (Chen 2013; Xue 2013), who are attentive to exchanges of material goods—flour, tea, *go re*, and cash gifts, for example—and labor assistance, keeping careful records of these favors in gift registers (Tib. *skyes tho*) (Xue 2017).[5] In a village where everyone knows everyone else, social monitoring prevails. Rebgong village residents care about their own reputations and the reputations of others, and transgressions are subjected to social sanction, such as verbal contempt or the loss of social support. While male painters spend most of their time painting, either at home or traveling to distant places on commissions, women are major players in these occasions of social exchange.

With the rising demand for thangka paintings from the new markets as well as the climbing price of thangka art, an increasing number of Tibetan women began to participate in art production in the late 2000s. One incentive is that the profit women make from thangka painting is much greater than the expense of paying substitute labor for agricultural work.[6] In addition, the recent de-agriculturalization in Rebgong reduces villagers' time spent on the farm (Makley 2018).[7] Like some wood carving families in Oaxaca in Mexico, who reduce their time invested in subsistence agriculture or have considerable flexibility in allocating their labor among farming, craft production, and migration (Chibnik 2003, 83), Rebgong *lha zo* are able to prioritize their income source according to the reliability of the food supply and the profit from making thangka paintings.

Drolma lives in Gasar village and only started painting thangkas in 2010, when her husband, Jampa, returned from a trip to Shandong, a coastal province in China, and brought back orders for thangka paintings from an art gallery there. Back at his home studio in Rebgong, Jampa needed extra hands in order to complete a hundred thangkas in ten months, including paintings of Green Tara, Yellow Jambhala, and various manifestations of Avalokiteshvara. In addition to his two male apprentices, Jampa asked Drolma for help. Though Drolma had been helping her husband prepare canvas cloths and grind mineral pigments, beginning with this order, she picked up a paintbrush and applied the first layer of color to the background of a thangka. Because of her art making, Drolma occasionally skips farmwork or a communal event, such as helping a neighbor with house construction. In these cases, Ama, Jampa's mother, or Jampa's younger sister has to fill Drolma's role.

With her skills improving, Drolma gradually began coloring flowers and animals, clothing, decorative elements, and finally the body of the Buddha and deities. But Drolma rarely initiates designs or sketches on canvas. Jampa is in charge of the painting design and occasionally assigns his apprentices to sketch the deities. After Drolma applies base colors, Jampa or his apprentices take over and work on details, including shading, gold lining, and embellishment. Usually Jampa paints the eyes for the Buddha and deities, the last step of the painting known as "opening the eyes" (Tib. *spyan 'byed*). Drolma has only learned a small number of Buddhist iconographies. She is not even confident that she holds the paintbrush in the right way. "Look at her fingers, squeezing like chicken feet," Jampa gently ribs his wife, to which Drolma replies with a laugh. Drolma knows that Jampa is grateful for her contribution. "With the help from the chicken feet," as Drolma herself puts it, going along with Jampa's joke, Jampa is able to produce more than fifty thangkas of various sizes each year, more than what he and his apprentices could do in previous years and at a cheaper cost than employing additional apprentices.

Like Drolma in the early days of the new market production, many Rebgong women helped their husbands or fathers prepare canvas or grind pigments. There was a rare case of a thangka painter who had a store near

Rongwo Monastery and taught his two daughters painting; the elder one even had her painting exhibited in Rebgong in 2010 (Reynolds 2011, 94). Yet most Tibetan women did not have the opportunity to receive systematic training in thangka painting until a handful of Tibetan-owned thangka art schools began to appear in Sengeshong village in the late 2000s. After one school took the initiative to accept female students, the local government encouraged all art schools and training centers to open their doors to women, handicapped students, and students from impoverished rural and pastoralist families, as a way of achieving the county and prefecture's goal of alleviating poverty. The establishment of these art schools made it possible for women to acquire thangka painting skills from start to finish and make some money through paid apprenticeships. Although financial support from the government was limited, schools with female students were able to obtain preferential policies and opportunities, such as applying for low-interest loans from local banks, being featured in government-owned media, or participating in government-organized exhibitions.

Namgyal is one of the first art teachers who openly accepted female students in his art school, yet his intention in doing so is not to compete for government support but to improve the economic and social status of Tibetan women. Having spent over twenty years as a monk in a local monastery, Namgyal does not think there is any Buddhist teaching that unequivocally prevents women from learning thangka painting. The unequal social status between women and men in Rebgong was highlighted for Namgyal when he traveled to China's urban places. He was first shocked to see female artists and then impressed by their artwork. He raised the question: "Why are Tibetan women not allowed to paint thangkas? Tibetans always say *a ma* [mother] is the most valuable treasure one can have. But when we think carefully about the social status of women in Tibet, it does not go with what we believe." When Namgyal began to accept female students, many villagers objected. They expressed worries such as "How can women paint the Buddha? It's pollution [Tib. *grib*]!" or "Men want wives to farm, not paint."[8] Namgyal had anticipated these objections. In order not to invoke hostility toward himself and his female apprentices, he first invited some of his female relatives to his art school as an experimental step.

Lhamo, a relative of Namgyal, was his first female student. She began to learn thangka painting in the late 2000s and is one of the most experienced students in the art school. Because students acquire thangka techniques through apprenticeships, teachers usually give instructions to senior apprentices, who then supervise less-advanced students. In the art school, each apprentice is assigned to work on part of a commission—the sketch, coloring, shading, or gold lining, for example—depending on her or his painting skills. When Namgyal is not in the studio, Lhamo acts almost like an advisor, demonstrating, correcting, and explaining to the less-experienced students. With her level of skill and her contribution to teaching, Lhamo received more than RMB 60,000 (about USD 9,200) in 2019 as a paid apprentice, an income that was much higher than the average annual income of Huangnan residents.[9] As of 2019, Namgyal had ninety-eight apprentices, thirteen of them women.

Trapped by the Canvas

Given the economically marginalized status of Tibetans in China (Costello 2002; Fischer 2013), Tibetan women are more or less expected to be economically productive, especially before they get married or have children. With the improvement of education in Rebgong, most Tibetan girls in the villages attend school.[10] Yet only a few women are able to pursue professional or college degrees that may lead them to stable and well-paying jobs, such as medical professionals, engineers, and government employees; many drop out without completing middle school. There are several economic opportunities available to women (especially unmarried women) besides painting thangkas. Women from various lowland villages in Rebgong make seasonal trips to mountains near and far to pick caterpillar fungus, also known as *yartsa gunbu* (Tib. *dbyar rtswa dgun 'bu*, Ch. *dong chong xia cao*), a highly commoditized natural product pursued by consumers within and beyond China (Yeh and Lama 2013; Stewart 2014).[11] Some Rebgong women have left for urban centers as migrant workers, following in the footsteps of rural and minority women from elsewhere in China (Gaetano and Jacka 2004; Ngai 2005; Zhang 2013). With the rising tourism in Rebgong, many unmarried women have also found new roles as restaurant or hotel attendants, tour guides, or performers in local entertainment companies. Some women may engage in multiple economic activities at various times or to different degrees.

Nancy Levine (2021) and Heidi Fjeld (2021) suggest not viewing kin obligations, family relationships, or social networks as fixed structural arrangements but to see them in light of families' pragmatic concerns. In the community of Tibetan pastoralists, the decisions of "where to live, how best to manage resources and household-contracted grazing lands to meet economic needs, as well as how to maximize kin support to facilitate adaptations to a rapidly changing world" are practical concerns that affect the organization of family life (Levine 2021, 89). The family's calculus is shaped, to various degrees, by the government's implementation of fixed land contracts and the resettlement of pastoralists.[12] For instance, pastoralist children may reside with their parents after they get married (forming a "conglomerate household," in Levine's term) because of the "indivisibility of contracted grazing lands"; a daughter and her husband may move back and forth between her parents' tent and the couple's own place to avoid the problem of inadequate grazing land (Levine 2021, 91–93). Elsewhere in the world, for example in Oaxacan wood carving families, the decision about how one contributes to the household economy (e.g., through art making, migration, wage work, or farming) or how each family makes the best use of available resource is a dynamic conversation based on the family's economic needs at a particular time (Chibnik 2011, 68–70).

In Rebgong, however, such conversation often assumes men's undisrupted painting, while women's choices are much constrained and tailored to the household's specific needs—women are expected to be flexible enough to bandage the family's economic "wound," including when to start, pause, resume, or terminate their art making.

After local art schools have publicly accepted female apprentices, many families begin to seize this new economic opportunity. When the question "What is this daughter going to do?" is brought up over family dinner, painting is usually the preferred choice.[13] This is drastically different from family reactions to the idea of women painting thangkas in the early 2000s. For one thing, the paid apprenticeship through art making is usually more stable and lucrative than working as a migrant worker or tour guide. Besides, several families told me they sent their daughters to learn thangka painting because the daughter could stay in the village and the parents would know where to find her when they needed her. In fact, few families sending their daughters to art schools expect them to eventually open thangka studios of their own or become professional artists in their own right. Instead, many see the work of a stationary painter "fixing" most Tibetan women to the village or at home, where their presence is expected and important to keep the family running. In addition, thangka painting skills can also be a valuable asset for a woman to negotiate a better marriage, boost her bride price, or enhance her bargaining power in the household, especially with her in-laws (Agarwal 1997; Chen

2013, 65; Rajan 2014, 140).[14] The modern-day good wife not only bakes *go re* and feeds babies but can also assist her husband's painting, like Drolma who saved Jampa the cost of employing additional apprentices.

If women painting thangkas is understood from purely economic notions of development and self-improvement, as is asserted by the government and accepted by many local families in Rebgong, women's participation in art production is destined to be disrupted. When the profit from art making is greater than the cost of finding substitute labor for farming, women sit in front the canvas instead of working in agriculture. If the caterpillar fungus is highly lucrative in a given year, women are likely to drop their paintbrushes and spend several months on the contracted land of the *tso wa*, or clan, harvesting the valuable *yartsa gunbu*.[15] If the family is urgently in need of money, daughters in an art school may pause or quit their learning to seek better-paying jobs (as we will see in Lutso's case in the next chapter). As long as men's painting is undisrupted, the tradition of Tibetan thangka art seems to be assured in the next generation of *lha zo*—male painters. Women's time and labor are mobilized around particular familial needs because many families do not view thangka painting as something fundamentally different from other economic opportunities afforded to female family members.

Almost a decade after he began to accept female students, Namgyal told me that a great number of his female students did not complete their study. According to Namgyal, the major reason preventing women apprentices from graduating was marriage. After female apprentices got married, either to partners of their own choice or through marriages arranged by parents, these apprentices seldom went back to art school. Most women who graduated from art schools painted with their husbands at home and found that their painting was compromised by familial and social obligations. At home married women painters are expected to set their artwork aside, whether it be for household chores, weeding the agricultural field, or answering a call to assist a neighbor—such as in the case when Ama or Jampa's sister was not able to help, Drolma had to put down her paintbrush and resume her regular responsibilities in the village. Moreover, women are also expected to meet the demands for an idealized Tibetan mother, to have many children and to maintain a home to which her grown sons may someday return from their trans-local wandering (Makley 2007, 147; Chen 2013).

While male painters reported that they spent about ten hours per day painting, married women painters were never able to paint for such long stretches of time.[16] Some married women managed to paint for five hours daily; a few could only paint for an hour or two. Two married women painters who used to be Namgyal's apprentices insisted on painting for just an hour a day. Like American women writers of another generation—such as Tillie Olsen, who stole a few hours each week to write in her local library—these two Tibetan women worried that once they stopped, they would never paint again.[17] Namgyal had a talented female *ge truk* who had graduated from the art school after six years of study but gave up painting completely after she got married and had two children. When this female apprentice brought him gifts during the New Year celebration, Namgyal found it difficult to accept her gifts because he was so heartbroken.

Convincing Tsomo, the young woman who made her debut on the live broadcasting show, to come back to the art school was a singular achievement for Namgyal. However, Namgyal thought Tsomo would not have given up the idea of being a migrant worker if it were not for her single-parent mother. After a few years of apprenticeship, Tsomo, a teenage girl, began to feel bored sitting in the same studio room in front of the canvas all day long. The boredom worsened her other health issues, which finally prevented her from attending the art school. When she was home for convalescence, she got to know that some of her childhood friends had migrated for work in other cities. Tsomo wanted to join them, hoping it would lead her to the metropolitan life she had long admired, as illuminated in Mandarin TV episodes she watched.

However, her mother opposed this idea. She insisted that Tsomo stay in the village to help her with household chores and farmwork when she needed extra hands, while Tsomo's brother, also a painter, could travel to other places to work on commissions—"like other male painters," in her mother's words. In addition to the sentiments of Tsomo's mother, the wage of a migrant worker (usually less than RMB 2,000 per month) was not as appealing as what Tsomo could earn from the paid apprenticeship, which was about RMB 40,000 per year by the time she paused her painting. The live broadcasting show led Tsomo to a U-turn. Namgyal encouraged her to continue being the public face of female painters in the art school. It meant that Tsomo would have opportunities to travel with her *ge gen* and fellow apprentices to exhibitions or events held in other places in China. Maybe Tsomo was happy with this type of mobility, which she could enjoy while staying in the village and the art school. Maybe Tsomo understood that her mother wanted her daughter—the bandage of the family—to live close by. Maybe Tsomo knew how challenging

it had been for Namgyal to keep female apprentices at school until they finished their training. Tsomo returned to the art school in 2020.

Troubling Presences in the Art Market

When a married woman painter works with her husband and apprentices on
thangka paintings, their collaborative works are usually sold under her husband's name or under the name of the household head, be it her father or father-
in-law. Men are often in charge of buying mineral pigments and other painting
supplies as well as finding clients. Most female painters do not participate in selling thangkas and hardly socialize with clients, especially those from the external
and intermediate markets. Nevertheless, some Rebgong women painters have
explored alternative pathways to pursue the role of professional painters or to
engage with the market, although their choices are still constrained by gender
norms and usually trigger controversies in the community.

Pema Tso is a married woman from Sengeshong. Like Drolma, she picked
up thangka painting to assist with her husband's art commissions, but unlike
Drolma, she also participates in selling thangka paintings. In summer, domestic and foreign tourists pour into Rebgong, especially during the Lurol festival
(Tib. *klu rol*), a ceremony held in the sixth lunar month to worship mountain
deities and pray for a good harvest. With her proficiency in Mandarin—like
Tsomo, Pema Tso picked up Mandarin by watching TV—Pema Tso looks for
visitors and invites them to her home "for tea and to take a look at their
thangka paintings." Pema Tso does more than just brew tea for guests: she
takes turns with her husband in introducing their artwork to guests who are
not familiar with Tibetan Buddhism or thangka art. Pema Tso explained to
me that visitors were less likely to be intimidated by women than by men, so
they were more likely to visit their home studio if Pema Tso, not her husband,
invited them. With Pema Tso's help, her husband did well in selling thangka
paintings to visitors over the three summers before the COVID-19 pandemic.
Nevertheless, her husband admitted that he did not feel comfortable with
Pema Tso chatting with tourists, especially in public. Pema Tso is aware of his
concern and also aware that other villagers gossiped about her. She told me
that many people in the village thought she was flirting with tourists, but she
considered what she did worthwhile. "Doing business takes time," she said.
"Many people in the village cannot see it because they are too conservative or
shortsighted."

Lhamo, the first female student of Namgyal, could have had many opportunities to exhibit her artwork in public or to participate in art competitions as an independent painter, but she never did. For one thing, Lhamo does not keep any artwork of her own. She works on parts of different thangka paintings, which are later sold or exhibited under the name of the art school. More important, in contrast with Tsomo and Pema Tso, Lhamo is shy. Although she gets along well with people in the art school and speaks Mandarin in addition to Tibetan and her native tongue (the Wutun language), she rarely speaks in front of visitors. When important guests such as government officials, TV crews, or Chinese collectors come to visit the art school, Lhamo dresses up in her elegant Tibetan robe and sits in front of a thangka painting, concentrating on her work. She refuses to answer questions, saying that she does not speak Mandarin.

Lhamo realizes that the "weakness" of her personality prevents her from operating a thangka studio of her own. Yet she does not think marrying a painter husband would be the solution. Lhamo is still single in her thirties, which is unusual for a village woman in Rebgong. After years of persuasion, as well as several unsuccessful matchmakings, Lhamo's parents have given up on finding their daughter a husband. Though not quite happy with Lhamo's choice, her parents at least are assured that their daughter can feed herself with the salary she receives from the art school. Nevertheless, village gossip hums around Lhamo's ears, rumors about why she is not married. Surely it is annoying to her, but she is saddened more by how little time her fellow students, now married women, have left for painting. She takes advantage of being Namgyal's relative and uses the art school as a shelter where she does not have to worry about speaking in public, negotiating with clients, or walking into marriage.

In an era when ethnic culture is promoted under the market economy, the live broadcasting show can be seen literally as, to adopt Makley's (2018) phrase, a "battle for fortune": various Tibetan towns in China participated in the tournament and competed with each other for "charm"—the frontrunners not only gaining prestige but also securing real investments for their development projects (Ch. *xiang mu*) from entrepreneurs in the audience from *nei di* (inner China). Female painters in Rebgong find that when they are portrayed in the political propaganda as embodiments of women's liberation or modernity— like Tsomo, whose (edited) story was used as a selling point for the Huangnan TAP—this characterization puts women in a complicated position. Women's participation in art making is perceived by some male painters as a "tokenistic gesture" for the local government to gather resources from the state and other patrons. Some villagers, including some female apprentices' parents, voiced to me their opinion that many art schools accept female students because they are after government funding. Women's thangka paintings or their participation in art making, therefore, are viewed by some as "inauthentic."

Female painters from Rebgong, along with other minority women who engage in ethnic tourism or other opportunities in the new economy, easily become scapegoats for anxious locals, who lament the negative effect that development projects or markets have on "traditional" society. For instance, Danba County, in Garze TAP in Sichuan, holds an annual "Beauty Pageant" that attracts thousands of tourists from all over China and has gained a soaring reputation as the "Valley of Beauties" through news reports and internet posts, objectifying women and making them subject to tourists' gazes.[18] When an unmarried female tour guide was appointed as a receptionist at the county's Reception Office, some villagers, who were annoyed by the tourism and changes in the village, labeled this woman a "Tibetan whore" (Jinba 2014, 58–60, 61–62). The aspirations and mobilities brought by new economic opportunities in China's rural areas, including numerous Tibetan towns and villages, have "hypersexualized young women's bodies and motives if they appeared in commercial spaces" (Makley 2007, 167; see also Schein 2000; Chao 2012). The sexuality of female entrepreneurs is also subjected to moral questions, which devalue these women's professional achievements (Zheng 2006; Osburg 2013).[19]

Behind the backs of Tibetan female thangka painters, many eyes scrutinize not only their artwork but also their activities in the art market. Often these eyes are not readily pleased. Pema Tso receives contempt from fellow villagers for her "openness," while Lhamo is blamed for being single. Such criticism may also carry a measure of jealousy from men: some village women painters, like Lhamo and Pema Tso, have done well economically through art making, even better than some of their male counterparts. Women painters thus have to shoulder men's anxieties, who embrace translocalities and new opportunities but often feel disadvantaged. They are challenged not only by the burgeoning markets, in which their education, language, ethnicity, or religious beliefs are discriminated against by other ethnic groups (Saxer 2012; Fischer 2013; Catanese 2019), but also by the sense of losing their home—a physical and emotional locus in this rapidly changing community (Kang and Li 2021).

Yet neither jealousy nor scapegoating stops at the gender line. Most women painters in Rebgong believe that when male painters socialize with clients from outside, including female clients, they are not accused of bad behavior. This is far from true. When monk Rinchen went to Shanxi to teach Tibetan Buddhism and thangka painting, many villagers, including some of his fellow monks in the monastery, showed their contempt for Rinchen because they thought he had been corrupted by money. When I visited a young painter at his family workshop, where he was working with his two brothers and three apprentices, his girlfriend, a migrant worker in Xining, got to know about my visit and insisted that an anthropologist was the same as those "rich ladies who looked for romantic relationships with Tibetan men." She therefore forbade her painter boyfriend from meeting me again because she thought "[I] had tried to steal [her] boyfriend." Behind the gossip of "corrupted" monks or "promiscuous" painters are broken families or a broken village—the insecurity and distrust grown out of anxiety in the community. Villagers in Rebgong, both men and women who endure the recent economic, social, and political changes, struggle to find the feminine hinge that would signify the unchanged and gendered boundaries in their everyday experiences back home.

"Who Said You Could Decide?"

One spring afternoon in 2012, Jampa went to town to fill out forms and apply for the government allowance for low-income rural families. Drolma stayed at home and worked on a thangka painting in the living room. Generous sunlight streamed through four windows, two on each wall. She chatted with me as I was typing field notes on my laptop. Both of us bathed in the warmth of the sun, relaxed and sleepy, until we heard a car honking outside. We looked out from the window and saw an SUV stopped on the village road. A man got out of the car and waved at us. Drolma went outside.

"Is this Jampa's house?" the man asked.

"Yes," Drolma replied in Mandarin.

"I'm from a gallery in Xiamen. Do you know Wande [Jampa's cousin]? He sent me to look at Jampa's thangka paintings." The man introduced himself as he crossed the street.

"*O le*, Jampa is not home now," Drolma said.[20]

"When will he come back?"

"I don't know. He is in town. Did you call him?"

"He did not answer my call. It's fine. Can I see his paintings? I can't stay long. I need to go to other places."

The man entered the living room and stood in front of the thangka Drolma was coloring. Before bringing Jampa's thangkas, Drolma hurried to make tea, a bag of green tea mixed with Goji berries, longans, dates, and crystal sugar—a special treat reserved for guests.

"Please don't trouble yourself," the man said politely, accepting the tea from Drolma. "I won't stay long." He turned around and put the tea on the dining table.

"Ja tung, ja tung," Drolma said, making a gesture of drinking with two hands.[21] She then cleaned her hands with a towel and brought a poster tube from another room. Drolma pulled a roll of thangka paintings out from the tube and unfolded them on the carpet.

The man looked at the paintings. "How much is this Green Tara?" he asked Drolma.

"You will have to ask Jampa," Drolma said, and the man nodded.

Drolma did not go back to painting. She stood behind the man, rubbing her hands with the towel. After about ten minutes, the man thanked Drolma and left.

An hour later Drolma and I heard Jampa's motorcycle coming down the village road. Jampa came into the house.

"Has the art dealer come already?" Jampa asked.

Drolma nodded.

"Rongwo Gonpa, why didn't you make him stay?" Jampa raised his voice. Sweat beads rolled down his cheeks.[22]

"He said he had other places to go," Drolma replied.

"Did he see the thangkas?"

"Yes, I showed him those in the black poster tube."

"What did he say?"

"Nothing."

"Did you show him the paintings I put in Ama's room?"

"No, I thought those are for the other gallery—"

"Who said you could decide?" Jampa yelled at Drolma.

That night the air in the room was intense and cold. No one talked at the dinner table. Ama and three kids finished their noodles quickly and moved to their shared bedroom. Jampa kept smoking. He had had bad luck in town: the government allowance he applied for required photocopies of his household register, which he had forgotten to bring with him, and a letter from the village head, which he did not yet have. He was turned down by the government clerk before he noticed several missing calls from his cousin and the art dealer. "Not my day," Jampa said as he threw his jacket on. "I will have a drink and get that damn letter tomorrow."

After Jampa left, Drolma hurried to remove dirty dishes from the dinner table together with the cup of untouched tea.

Drolma Performs *Cho Kor* in Spring

One morning in May, a few weeks after the art dealer's visit, Drolma asked me if I would like to go on *cho kor* (Tib. *chos skor*) with her. *Cho kor* literally means "circumambulation with dharma texts." A group of village leaders, *chu dak* (Tib. *chu bdag*), had decided this was the day to ask for blessings from their protector deities (Tib. *lha pa*).[23] I followed Drolma and Ama to the village monastery, where I also saw many other women from the village. Everyone brought a large piece of brocade or embroidered cloth as well as a long scarf. A monk from the monastery and two *chu dak* were distributing Buddhist scriptures—each person got five or six volumes. Women wrapped the scriptures with the fabric and tied them up with the scarf. Ama asked me to help her lift the package up on her back. I felt the weight: the five volumes on Ama's back were over twenty pounds.

After the scriptures were handed out, one *chu dak* asked all the participants to form a line. Following the thangka of a protector deity hung from a pole stick, we made our way out onto the village road.[24] The leading *chu dak* raised his hands. Women in the front began to chant in Tibetan, "om ma ni pad me hung." Women in the middle followed suit. Those at the end of the line joined in last. The chanting continued rising one after another, like breathing, like a heartbeat. The rhythm paved our way as we passed numerous village houses. Dogs barked. Cows mooed. Agricultural fields were touched by green. Pear blossoms greeted us from orchards surrounded by mud walls or iron railings. White petals fell on the women's braided hair and the scriptures on their backs.

As we paused at the courtyard of the largest village temple, I looked around.[25] There were only a few men among us: the three *chu dak* who had been leading the troop, two monks from the village monastery who were responsible for the scriptures, two old men following us after we passed their houses, and a couple of boys coming with their female relatives.

I asked Drolma: "Why don't men come to *cho kor*? Are they not allowed to participate?"

"Of course men can participate. Everyone can participate," said Drolma, "because *cho kor* is a meritorious thing."

"But why are there so few men?" I asked.

"Maybe because men are busy, painting, sculpting, carving, and doing their business. Some men are not in the village. They work as migrant workers outside," Drolma tried to explain.

In my later conversation with one *chu dak*, I was told that every resident in the village was welcome to take part in *cho kor*. To circumambulate the whole village with Buddhist texts helps to protect the village from harmful spirits or energies. It also ensures a good harvest in a few months (Tshe ring skyid 2015, 261). The *chu dak* explained to me that every household could benefit from *cho kor* by having at least one family member participate. Everyone seemed to agree that it is important to attend *cho kor* for the sake of the family and the community. Everyone also seemed to agree that men were busy with painting and other work, so the merits of each household and the blessings of the entire village needed to be accumulated through women's footsteps.

"You know what?" Drolma suddenly said to me in the village temple's courtyard. "Going on *cho kor* is also good for women."

"Yeah?" I was curious.

"They say that carrying the scripture on your back helps you eliminate all illnesses and bad luck."

Seconds later, Drolma said, "I guess it works for men too."

Both of us laughed.

A little past noon, we had walked and chanted along the edge of those large farming fields close to the Guchu River. Taking a few shortcuts, we made our way back to the village road. I thought we were done. Two *chu dak* and a monk asked women to make two lines, standing on each side of the village road.

"What are they doing?" I asked Drolma.

Drolma smiled and answered with some excitement in her voice. "It's time to ask for auspicious money!"

The two *chu dak* stepped forward and stood in the middle of the road. Women followed them from both sides, virtually blocking the entire pathway. A truck was approaching us from the north. The *chu dak* gestured the driver to stop. The vehicle slowed down, the brakes squeaking in front of the human wall. The driver rolled down his window. One *chu dak*, holding a

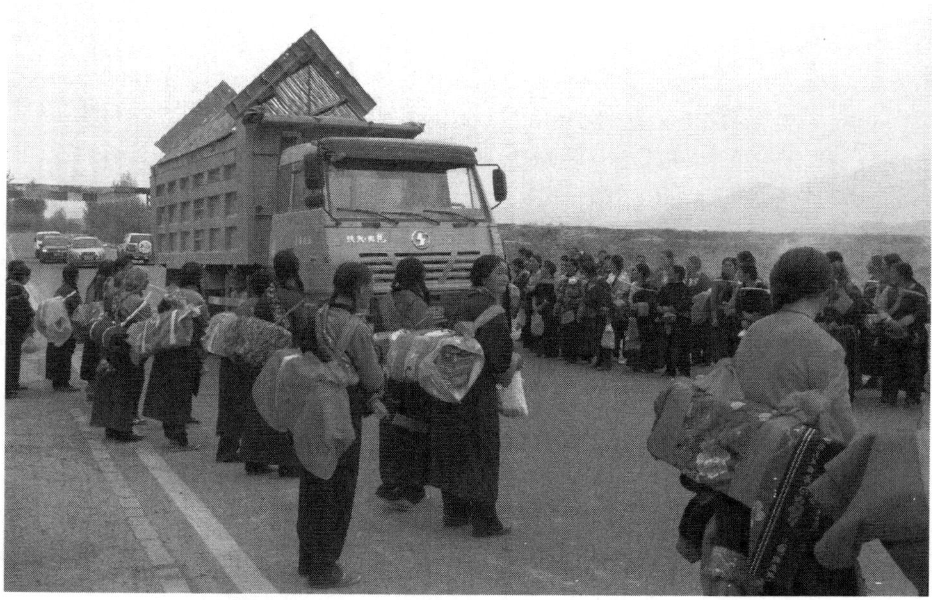

FIGURE 4 Women in Gasar blocking traffic and asking for auspicious money on the village road during their annual *cho kor*, 2012.

scripture with two hands, said to the truck driver in Mandarin: "Today is an auspicious day. Our women are circumambulating the village carrying Buddhist scriptures. Do you mind giving the women and kids some petty cash for candies and snacks? We give you and your family blessings and wish you a safe journey!"[26] The truck driver took out ten yuan from his pocket and handed it to the *chu dak*. The *chu dak* thanked him and waved the cash to the women behind him. Women stepped aside, giving the truck an exit. The truck driver rolled up his window and left (figure 4).

Asking for auspicious money on the village road during circumambulation is not something peculiar to Gasar nor anything new for Rebgong residents.[27] At a time when only a few people ventured out of the village—most of those who did went on pilgrimages to Lhasa and other sacred places or worked on commissions in other Tibetan communities—travelers brought back gifts and food to share with relatives and friends in the village.[28] Children waited on the village road, eager to get a share of the exotic snack.

Today the village road, on which the Gasar women were standing, is part of the provincial highway, one of two roads connecting the town of Tongren in the south to other places, including Xining in the north.[29] In 2002 the village road in Gasar was expanded and partially paved by the local government, which energized the prefecture's plan of attracting tourists to Rebgong and investments to Huangnan's development projects (Costello 2002; Catanese 2019, 115). The much-improved road, along with economic prosperity, also encouraged the mobility of local residents—mostly men. Motorcycles zoomed on the village road day and night. A few minivans owned by Gasar residents transported villagers back and forth between the village and the town. More and more villagers abandoned the government-run "snail" bus that runs between Tongren and Xining. Instead, they squeezed into a shared Volkswagen Jetta or Santana, taking off from town and reaching Xining in as few as two and half hours; this was before the opening of a third highway in 2018 and before many households in Gasar owned private cars.

With the prefecture's development plan, an increasing number of vehicles from outside appeared on the village road too. Those drivers had no idea about *cho kor*. After an explanation was offered, most drivers were happy to donate not food or drink but cash. It inspired the local residents too: with cash, women and children could buy whatever food they liked, and the money left over could be used to renovate the village monastery. On a road where cars pass by at thirty miles per hour, where no kids play anymore because worried mothers have heard too many sad stories of car accidents, the taste of the outside world brought back by travelers from their spiritual journeys has evolved into something else.

It was almost 1:00 p.m. No one had eaten lunch. No one seemed to care about it. The success with the first truck was encouraging. The *chu dak* asked women to stand back and hold the "wall." Over the next two hours, they stopped numerous vehicles from both directions—passenger cars from Gasar and beyond, tour buses, taxis, construction trucks, cargo trucks, tractors, motorcycles, police cars, commercial vans, and even a group of shimmering black Audi A4s carrying high-level government officials from another province (recognizable from their special license plates). Sometimes the road got too busy. Vehicles had to wait in line to get past; some honked impatiently. In those cases villagers did not have time to hold up a Buddhist scripture or offer the driver any blessing. Once the driver handed out money, a green light was granted—like a toll station. A few cars tried to move on without giving anything, and the women yelled to each other, "Stop that car!"

Those were intense hours. It seemed to me a true blessing (or miracle?) that nobody got hurt or had any trouble that day. Several residents from Sengeshong and Thokya made comments like "Gasar villagers are too greedy!" One villager from Sengeshong said, "We also ask for auspicious money but never to the extent like what Gasar has done." But how could Gasar residents not become "greedy"? With an overly economic-oriented notion of development in Rebgong, intervillage competitions are important repertoires in the battle for village fortunes. In Makley's observation, two villages in the north part of the valley compete with each other not only for government recognition and financial support but also for patronage from foreign "gift masters," including Makley herself and her English teacher friend, who helps mobilize money donations from the Dutch Embassy to Rebgong (Makley 2018, 154–57).[30]

Although Gasar is the home base for some prominent artists such as Kunzang (1919–96) and Chogyal (1940–2007), *lha zo* from Gasar always feel overshadowed by their counterparts from Sengeshong. Because artists in Sengeshong outnumber those in other art making villages in Rebgong and because their village is closer to town, Sengeshong is obviously the first choice to establish a Protection Zone.[31] Recent government-sponsored projects in Sengeshong—including building art schools, renovating family workshops and galleries, holding ICH expos, art competitions, and even a Guinness World Records event—have grabbed the attention of tourists, art merchants, and affluent Han patrons to the village across the Guchu River east of Gasar.

Without any obvious advantage, Gasar residents strive to find their "niche" in the battle for economic fortunes. Some Gasar painters, including a good friend of Jampa, have shifted from art making to planting pear trees. A year earlier, this friend of Jampa had borrowed RMB 50,000 from the local bank and rented a piece of land for his pear orchard.[32] This year he borrowed another RMB 80,000 from the bank and opened a beverage factory, squeezing his fruits to make pear juice—one of Rebgong's native products (Ch. *tu te chan*) promoted by the local government. Would the white petals falling on women's hair and Buddhist scriptures give this painter-turned-entrepreneur enough blessing to make money and pay back his interest by the end of this year? While the three of us used to hang out at Jampa's house in previous years, Jampa and I rarely saw this friend after he started his pear business—he was too busy running between different places, socializing and entertaining businessmen and government officials who could help him squeeze money from his orchard.

Later in the day of the *cho kor*, I learned from the *chu dak* and monks that villagers had collected over RMB 6,500 in auspicious money that afternoon. Every participating household, or more precisely, women participants from that household, received RMB 50 as a reward. This left a few thousand yuan for the village monastery, for its renovation project later in the year. This might not seem like much, but an example from Tshe ring skyid (2015) can help us situate what the few thousand yuan means to Gasar village monastery and its residents. Tshe ring skyid is a local resident from Gasar. She reports that in 2009, the village monastery made a deal with a Chinese company to build a gravel plant down by the Guchu River, utilizing stones, gravel, and sand from the part of the river belonging to Gasar (Tshe ring skyid 2015, 255–56). As the village monastery controls that area, the Chinese company promised to pay RMB 5,000 every year to the monastery and continued operating its plant on the riverbank for a decade. Using this number as a reference, the few thousand yuan that Gasar women collected for the village monastery on their *cho kor* was about half of the annual patronage the monastery received from the gravel company, from whom Gasar residents had to buy sand and stones, which they had taken freely from the river in the past.

The encounters on the village road helped me to see that the unexpected visit of the art dealer and Drolma's *cho kor* were not entirely separate events. When Jampa questioned Drolma—"Who said you could decide?"—he knew perfectly well that Drolma would never try to make a decision about his art business. Unlike Pema Tso, Drolma did not venture into the art market. The cup of tea and her appropriate response to the art dealer's questions were parts of women's "gendered spatial practices" in their everyday lives at home (Makley 2007, 137), even as, or especially as, Drolma had taken on the new role as a thangka painter. Yet Jampa might have also realized that he had probably never had full control of his art business either. By going to town to apply for government funding, Jampa missed his chance to meet with the art dealer. Had he also missed his chance to meet more clients by living in Gasar, a village that keeps up its art making tradition but falls outside the government's current development plans? Had he missed his chance to make money from squeezing pear juice by sticking to thangka painting? The frustrations of male painters like Jampa push them to run faster and farther on the village road, which has led to many "broken" families and a "lost" village because many men in the village no longer have time to engage in *cho kor* or many other communal events.

On a village road where trucks carry stones and gravel from the village river to other construction sites, where art dealers come and go to find desirable thangkas to be featured in urban galleries or shops, where husbands return from business banquets instead of pilgrimage, what do women try to stop with their own bodies? The wheels of cars? Drivers' pocket money? Or the ticking of the clock, which is taking away the place they call home? In her analysis of circumambulation in Labrang Monastery, less than one hundred miles from Rebgong, Makley (2003) points out that the circumambulation Tibetan women practice in their daily lives is a form of both resistance and compliance. Although circumambulation is the most important way for Tibetan laywomen to achieve self-improvement, women *choose* to avoid the most sacred of spaces and times as a way to maintain the physical and ideological distinction between the center and the periphery. It helps to reconstruct "male ritual authority" (Makley 2013, 610), which has been threatened by the development of ethnic tourism and the marketplace, which have both commoditized Labrang in profound ways.

Like Labrang women, those from Rebgong have to play the role of the feminine hinge for their families and the village. Many married painters like Drolma, trapped by the canvas, shoulder the frustration of their husbands or other male family members who feel disadvantaged in the new economy. Women bandage the family's economic wounds by picking up a paintbrush. Meanwhile, they readily let their painting be disrupted by their other economic, familial, and social obligations. Because of women's presence in the village's communal life, the name list of families' gift registers—for girls' coming-of-age rituals, elders' sixtieth birthday celebrations, or funerals—will not dwindle even as men are increasingly absent from these life cycle events that bind the community together.

By circumambulating the houses, the village monastery and temples, the wheat and barley fields, the growing numbers of pear orchards, the riverbank and the gravel plant, women not only ask for protector deities' blessings but also reinforce the sense of home. By standing in the middle of the village road and asking for auspicious money, women collect a toll for the profits made from their time, their labor, and *their* village. They use their bodily experiences to reclaim the village's sovereignty, which is threatened in both residents' material and spiritual lives by current social changes, including the commodification of Tibetan thangka paintings. If Rebgong women painters ever had an iconographic representation, she should be holding a paintbrush in her hand, but her back would probably be bent under the weight of a baby, a bag of grain, and twenty pounds of Buddhist scriptures—hope, nutrients, and merits—things that keep the village alive and well.

Empowerment Redefined

Just like the skit in the live broadcasting show that was not a faithful reflection of Tsomo's story, Rebgong women painters find that their own aspirations and hopes are often overlooked. Women's struggles in their professional and personal lives are sometimes tweaked to mesh with both the gendered (and hagiographic) image of Tibetan women in the popular media and an official rhetoric that promotes the overly economic-focused notion of development.

Telling the tale of a modern queendom, Tenzin Jinba describes a similar dilemma of Tibetan women in Danba County. Rejecting the "Valley of Beauties" label, Suopo village leaders strive to emphasize its women's esteemed social and political status as well as women's exceptional leadership—a "queendom" discourse (2014, 65–67). Although there is no woman leader in the village, Suopo headmen back up their claim by citing the story of three local women who were village leaders in the 1950s and 1960s and were sent to Beijing and received by Chairman Mao. In fact, historically, Suopo women did not have major political power, nor do they enjoy any leadership now. Tenzin Jinba points out that the three women had to take on the role as village heads simply because political and social movements at that time had forced most young men to take positions outside the village. Although Suopo women today feel marginalized in many aspects of their local social lives, Suopo men keep singing the praises of "women leaders" to fight against the sexualized image of minority women in the booming ethnic tourism. Meanwhile, they also fabricate a myth of a historical "eastern queendom"—as a selling point—in order to distinguish themselves from nearby villages featuring the physical beauty of Tibetan women.

With this "confusing diversity of visions" (Behar 1995, 2), can Rebgong women painters find their own voices or, in this context, their own brushstrokes through thangka painting? In our conversations surrounded by stretched canvases, carefully ground pigments, and piled-up paintbrushes, many women painters told me that their favorite image in thangka painting was Tara. Some described "joy from the bottom of the heart" that they experienced while painting her image.[33] When female painters say they like to depict the various manifestations of Tara, what can we read from such a statement? What has made some Tibetan women devote their lives to painting thangkas despite the constraints and challenges? Beyond economic returns, could women painters find other forms of empowerment through making the image of Tara, the Buddha, and other deities?

In Rebgong most monks and laypeople I interviewed consider everyone as having an equal opportunity to engage in meritorious works (Tib. *dge las*), regardless of the practitioner's gender, age, or occupation. However, this view may conform to the "confident exegeses," criticized by Makley (2003, 610), of the egalitarian nature of Buddhism (see Makley 1997; Martin 2005; Lopez 2018). To defend the diminishing sense of "Tibetanness" in contemporary China, Tibetan women are expected to be "respectful, humble, silent, and deferential" and to occupy ritually lower status than Tibetan men (Rajan 2014, 154), even from the perspective of some activists who support Tibetan women's empowerment (Rajan 2015, 133). On the other hand, because Tibetan women spend more time on mundane work, such as farming, childcare, household chores, and helping neighbors, women generally have less time than men to engage in merit-making activities. Moreover, within a society that places monks at its pinnacle and laywomen at the bottom (there are no local nunneries), Tibetan women are often excluded from the most sacred spaces, such as the inner core of a monastery or certain holy sites on a sacred mountain (Makley 2007, 173; Huber 1999, 124).

At the surface, Namgyal's initiative in accepting female apprentices to learn thangka painting coordinated well with the government's agenda of cultural development. Yet having spent over twenty years in a monastery, Namgyal wanted painting to do more than improve Tibetan women's income. Like a few monks in Rebgong who have expressed their pity for Tibetan women, who could only realistically hope to be reincarnated into a female body (see Makley 2003, 614), Namgyal hopes that thangka painting, compared to alternative economic options afforded to Rebgong women, could offer more opportunities for Tibetan women to accumulate merits, improve their karma, and ultimately "have a better rebirth." As a consequence, Lhamo, the female painter who chose to stay in art school, told me she does not care who has commissioned a thangka painting, what the painting is made for, or whether she could keep any artwork of her own. Through painting thangkas, Lhamo expects to achieve the upward mobility for her next life by viewing images of the sacred and depicting them—an unprecedented opportunity of religious merit making.

In the past few years, Lhamo and other female apprentices in the art school painted the image of Green Tara (Tib. *sgrol ma ljang khu*) for clients from various places. Green Tara is one of the most popular subjects of thangka painting commissioned or purchased by non-Tibetans in China. According to Lhamo, some Han clients appreciate the aesthetic beauty of the thangka of Tara; some perceive and worship the cult of Tara in Tibetan Buddhism as the equivalent of Guanyin in Chinese Buddhism; and a few sophisticated clients have been guided by their guru or by diviners to commission a thangka of Tara for their particular religious needs.[34] Despite the fact that Rebgong thangkas are commissioned or purchased for various reasons, most Rebgong painters attend to the rules of Buddhist iconography and follow the religious protocols associated with the making of a Buddhist image. Lhamo and other female apprentices usually recite the six-syllable mantra (*om ma ni pad me hung*) and/or the ten-syllable mantra of Tara (Tib. *om ta re tut ta re tu re swa ha*) while painting her images.[35] One female apprentice at the art school told me that when she had to walk alone in the dark night, she always called Tara's names and chanted her mantra, which made her feel the goddess was near enough to protect her.[36] "Do you know how much assurance and joy I have while I am painting thangkas of the Tara?" the apprentice said to me. "She is right in front of me and gives me all the protection I need. I feel very safe."

In today's Rebgong, most thangka painters, including women, practice Tibetan Buddhism in their daily lives and show their highest respect to religious objects, whether they are Buddhist scriptures, dharma instruments, or thangka paintings. Like the female apprentice who feels much protection by painting the image of Tara, Rebgong *lha zo* view thangka paintings as agentive objects in which Buddhas, bodhisattvas, and deities are present. In the art market, while auxiliary aspects such as decorative patterns or the size of a painting can be tailored to the budget or individual preference of the client, it is the painter's foremost responsibility to make the iconography, composition, and religious practices associated with a thangka painting correct. If a thangka is appropriately painted and consecrated and later venerated by others, it will bring merits to the *lha zo* not only for this life but, more important, for her next life.

There is another layer of empowerment in Rebgong women's art making practices. By convention, thangka paintings are commissioned to meet the particular needs of the client. The painter thus becomes an important medium, through whom the manifestation of the deity, the protection and blessings, are able to reach out to the person in need. Hence, to a woman *lha zo*, painting a thangka of Tara for another villager or a Buddhist patron is significantly different from calling Tara's names or reciting her mantra when the painter herself needs the deity's blessing to conquer fear, illness, or difficulties. Since an image is the result of personal or collective knowledge and intention (Belting 2014, 9), a thangka is not simply an art commission; it is also a commission of the painter's karma or agency when she exercises her virtuous nature by using her paintbrushes to help a person in need.

Many women painters might not fully conceptualize the religious benefits and empowerment generated from painting thangkas when they begin to participate in art making. Many families sent their daughters to learn thangka painting following the government's program to alleviate poverty through art production. Certainly, in today's Rebgong, some women participating in thangka production are still largely driven by economic concerns, such as Pema Tso, who tends to consider herself an entrepreneur doing thangka business, or by other incentives, such as Tsomo, who longs to see the outside world. However, as many Rebgong women painters improve their artistic skills and gradually become involved in the entire process of thangka painting, they become more familiar with the fundamental virtues and taboos and other religious discourse of art making, which in the past was exclusively controlled by male painters. Women's participation in thangka painting does not necessarily diminish the religious value or the authenticity of Tibetan thangka art. On the contrary, through making Buddhist images and navigating the art market, some Rebgong women find a new pathway to connect with their religion and history and to reclaim their religious identities, which have been omitted from the official rhetoric of thangka painting.

Meanwhile, as male painters are pushed by an increasingly competitive market to travel farther away from home, Rebgong women painters not only shoulder additional familial and social obligations but also play a major role in keeping the notion of village intact and alive. Women are pulled between the family's needs for natural reproduction and cultural reproduction. Although not all Rebgong women who engage in art making are able to run their own studios or become professional artists in their own right, women's participation in art making is unprecedented. Despite villagers' misunderstandings, market discrimination, or the distorted image of women painters fabricated by the government, many female *lha zo* in Rebgong continue making art out of their devotion to Tibetan Buddhism, art, and the most valuable place to them, which they call home.

When I asked Drolma if she knew that thangka painting was a meritorious act, she told me that *lha zo* enjoyed a respected social status in Rebgong, especially before the emergence of the new markets. I then asked her if she thought she could accumulate religious merits through painting thangkas like male painters do, and Drolma, apparently recalling our joke about men and *cho kor*, laughed and said, "I guess it works for women too."

A Safe Journey Home

On the last day of the New Year celebration, the year of the Water Dragon, the heads of Drolma and Jampa's *tso wa* decided to throw a dinner party for all the wives. The *tso wa* leader reserved a few tables at a Muslim restaurant in town and waited at the gate to receive everybody. Drolma and Jampa invited me to go with them. Their children stayed at home with Ama in the village. Like Drolma, most wives came with their husbands. Women put on their "town look"—down jackets, skinny or flare jeans, and heels. I noticed that Drolma also wore makeup that night, which was quite unusual. Like other public events in the village where men and women each occupy their own space, at the restaurant the men sat together at two tables, while the women, myself included, sat at the other two. Holding a cup of barley spirit, the leader of the *tso wa* stood up and made a toast: "We are here to thank all women in our *tso wa*. Without your hard work at home, on the farm, your care for the elders and children, it would be impossible to have the quality of life we are enjoying now. To our heroines!" The women burst into laughter. They gave the leader generous applause and finished the wine in their cups.

The drink was pleasant. The food was delicious. As the party spirit grew, women and men, remaining in their seats, took turns singing—praising the snowy mountains, the mighty river, the beautiful village, and loving mothers. The *tso wa* leader brought his cup and visited every table to make a toast. When he finished his ritual at my table, he quietly pulled me aside and said: "Our men in the *tso wa* collected some money to hold this party for our women. You see, it makes our women so happy. Would you also like to make a donation?" Though I was sitting among the women, I recognized I was also a beneficiary of *their* women, who not only fed me with *go re* but also with their stories. Following what other men did, I gave the leader RMB 100.

The dinner party lasted until midnight. Empty barley spirit and beer bottles piled up on the table. Before we left, women hurried to put leftover food into plastic bags to take back home. Some couples decided to stay with their relatives in town for the night. Other determined ones, including Drolma and Jampa, waited for a taxi on the town street for over half an hour without any luck. Sonam, one member of the *tso wa*, kindly offered to take people back to the village in his minivan. Fifteen of us squeezed into his van, a vehicle with capacity for eight. I was not surprised that Drolma had to sit on my lap but was amazed that Jampa managed to smoke with two men on his lap. Outside town there was not much light on the road but a lot of snow. One of the van's headlights stopped working, and Sonam, who was probably a bit drunk too, kept slipping to one side of the road until he almost hit the curb, which terrified all his passengers. He assured us it would be okay.

As the wheels rolled, one woman in the van started to chant "om ma ni pad me hung." Other women, including Drolma, followed her. Jampa pinched out his cigarette and joined in the chanting with other men. Sonam slowed down the car, two hands on the steering wheel. The amulets dangling from the rearview mirror, one mini-thangka of the Four-Armed Avalokiteshvara and one photo print of the eighth Shartshang Lama of the Rongwo Monastery, danced gracefully to the tune of the chanting. With the moonlight so dim as to only shed blessings on the tips of the mountains, the sound of Guchu River guided our way. Like golden fish, we were carried by the peace and harmony promised by the sacred mantra, flowing smoothly to the north on an empty village road.

Only at night can one hear the breathing of the river and the heartbeat of the mountains. They witness the first flakes of snow and the thawing of streams, the women's *cho kor* in spring, and the drumming, dancing, and offerings burned with the Tibetan Wind Horse (Tib. *rlung rta*) at the Lurol festival to pray for a good year. They witness the cycle of the seasons and the circle of lives. They witness the expansion of the village road, which has taken many residents too far away from home to hear the river or the mountains calling. But tonight they witnessed wives and husbands coming back from a dinner party in town. They heard the chanting of *om ma ni pad me hung* in a crowded van going ten miles per hour on a quiet village road, like the song of those who returned home from their pilgrimage in the past. The chanting was disrupted by street dogs barking from their sleeping places in front of the village monastery, on the south edge of Gasar. We had a safe journey home.

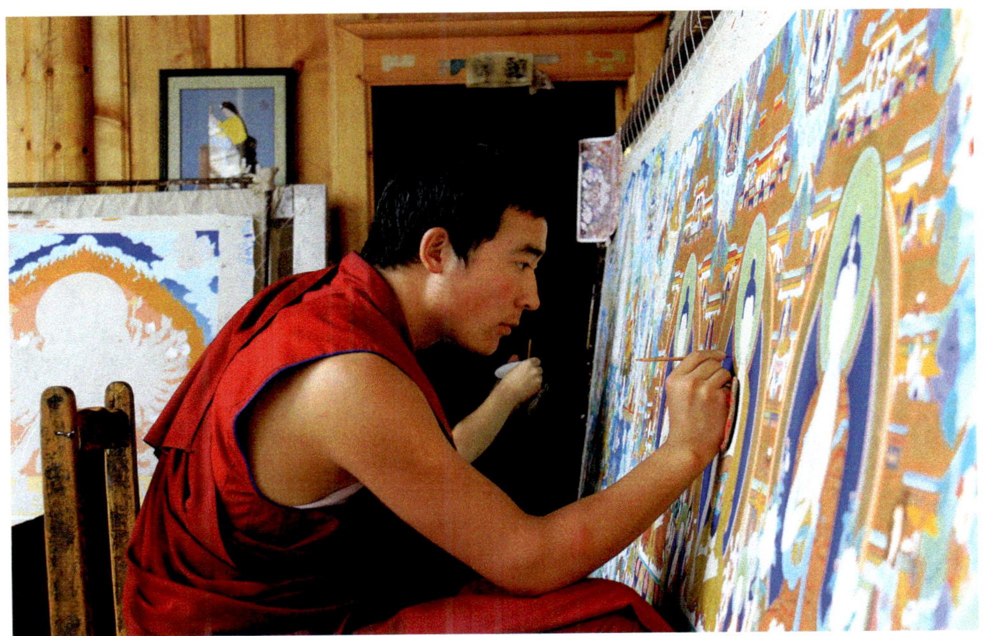

PLATE 1 A monk painter working on a thangka in his teacher's home studio in Rebgong, 2012.

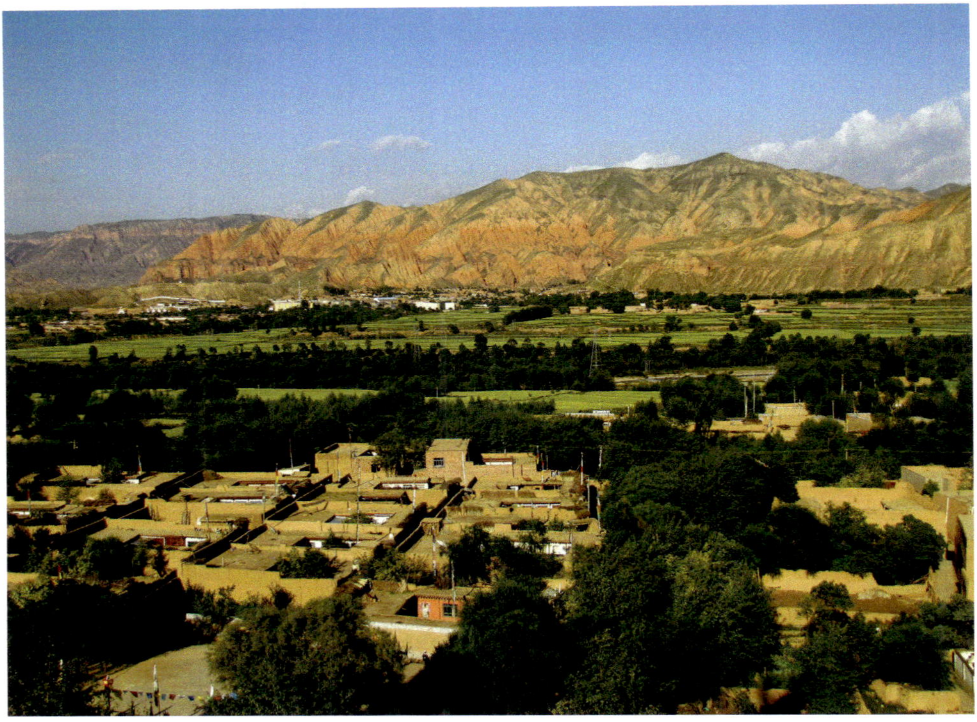

PLATE 2 Partial view of Gasar village and the valley of the Guchu River, 2011.

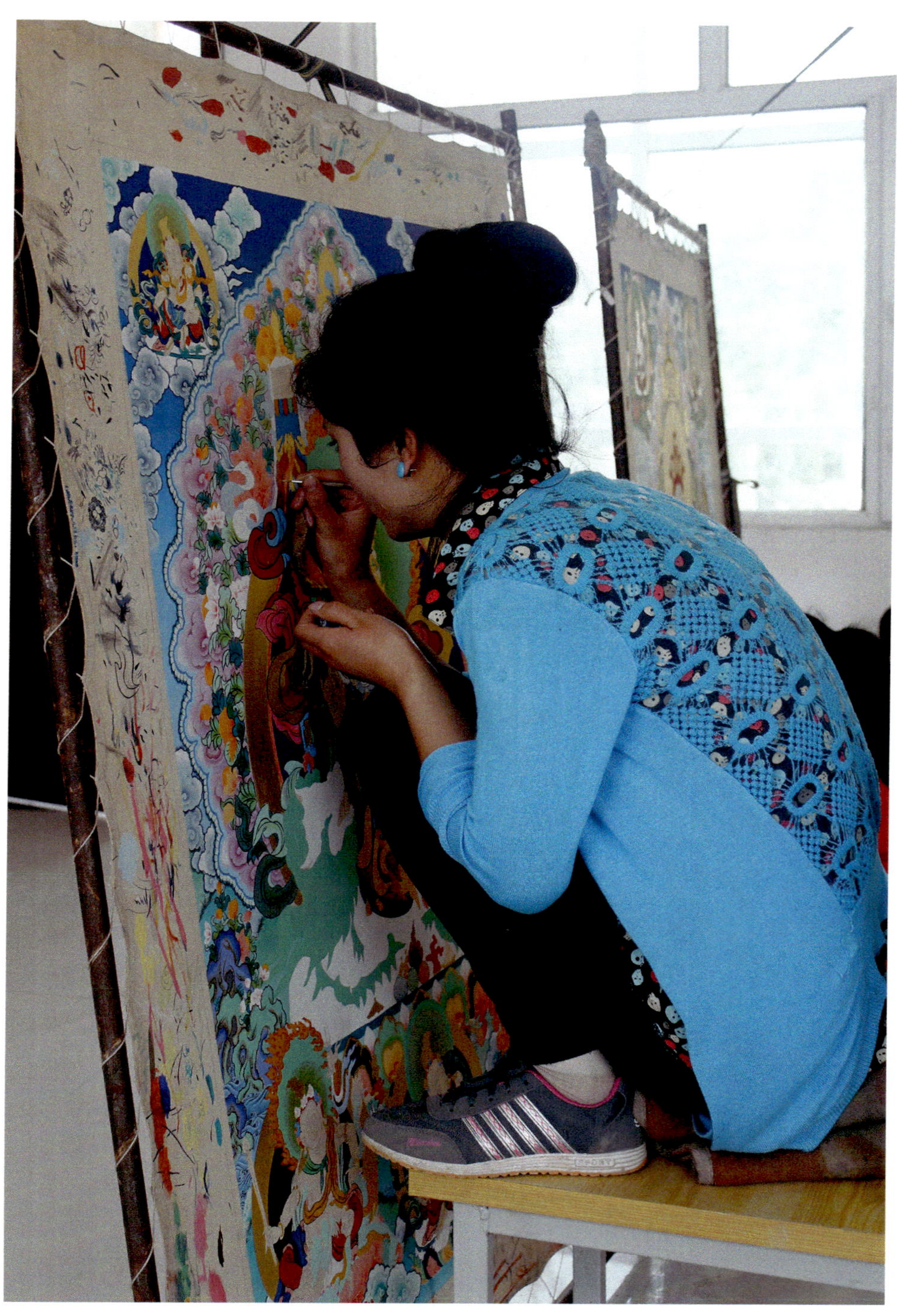

PLATE 3 A female apprentice in a local art school, 2013.

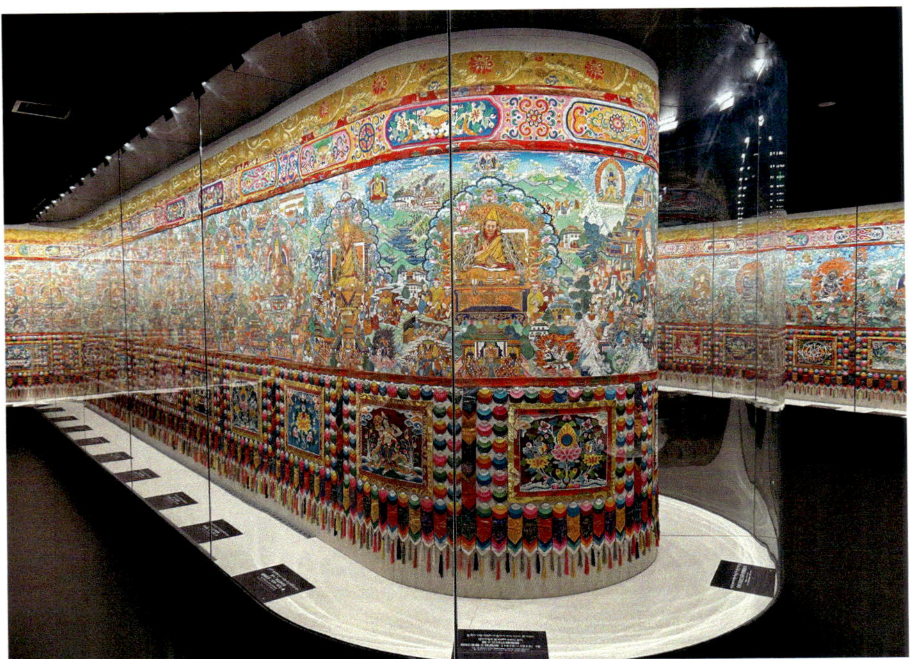

PLATE 4 *The Great Thangka* displayed at the Tibetan Culture Museum in Xining, Qinghai, 2024.

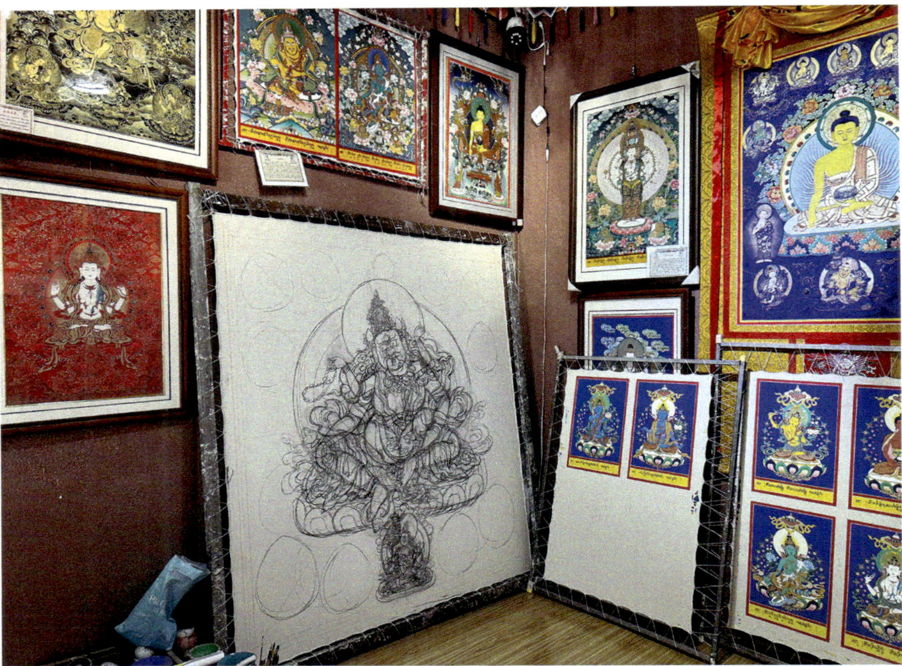

PLATE 5 In a *lha zo*'s art shop in 2024, the artwork in progress shows the charcoal sketch of Yellow Jambhala, a thangka commissioned by the village monastery, surrounded by his other thangka paintings for sale.

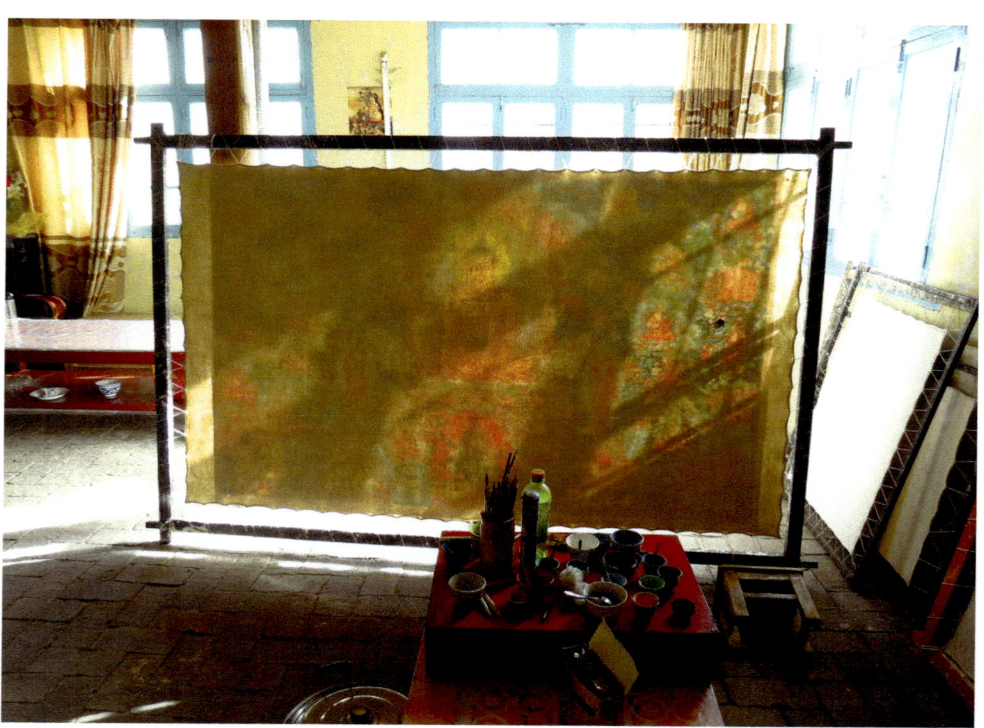

PLATE 6 A painter pinned a printed poster on the back of his canvas (*center*) to copy the content and composition of the thangka (designed by a renowned painter in Rebgong), 2011. This method speeds up production and is especially useful when the content of the painting is complex.

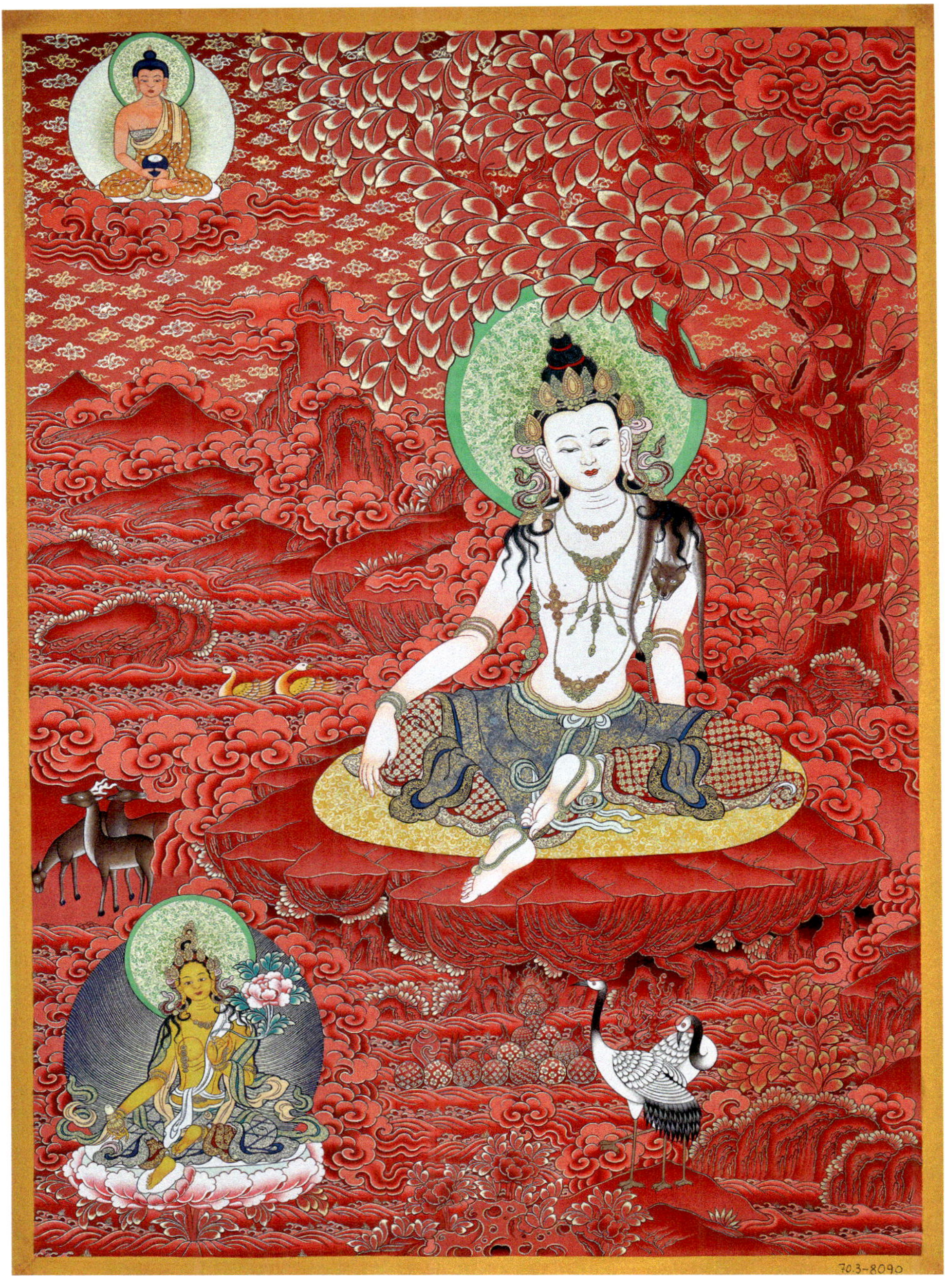

PLATE 7 Lutso's thangka painting *Avalokiteshvara with Mind at Rest* (2019), now in the Tibetan collection of the American Museum of Natural History (70.3/8090). Photo by Mourrice Papi, 2021. Courtesy of the American Museum of Natural History.

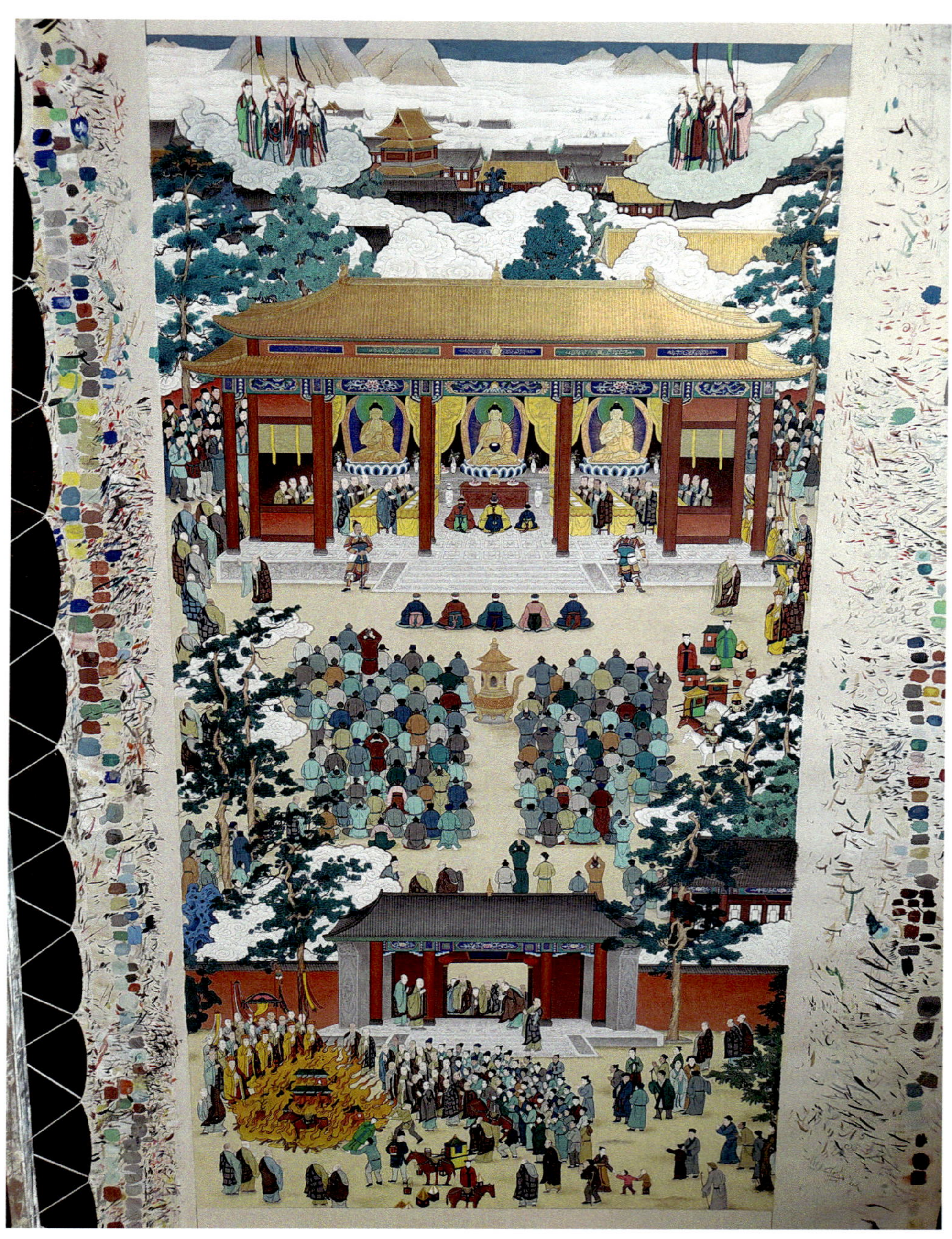

PLATE 8 Tashi Gyatso, Chodrak, and Fan's painting depicting the Water and Land Retreat held in Xiantong Temple (artwork in progress). Photo courtesy of the artists, 2022.

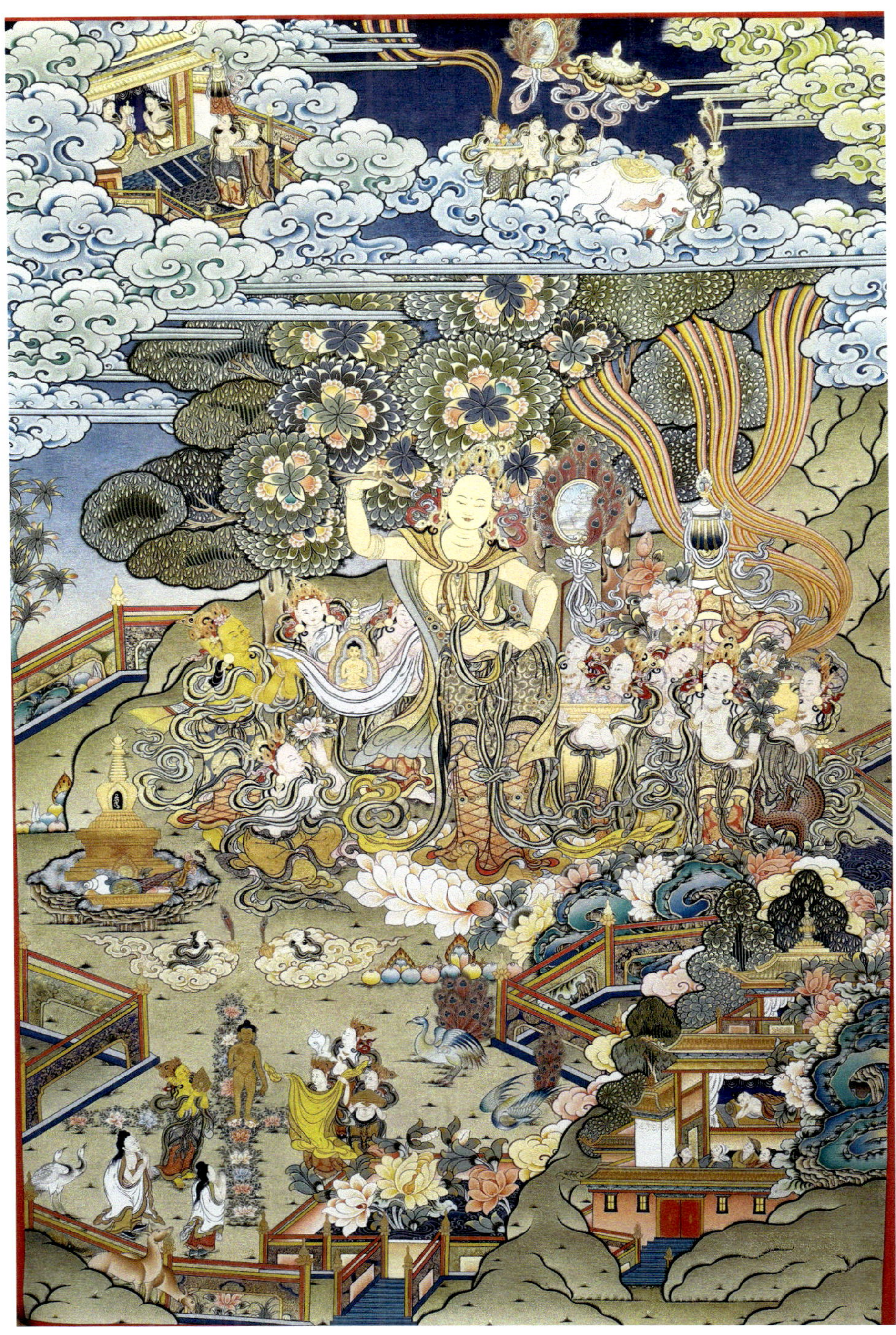

PLATE 9 Tashi Gyatso's thangka painting depicting the life story of Buddha Shakyamuni, the first scroll in the set of nine paintings. Photo courtesy of the artist, 2010.

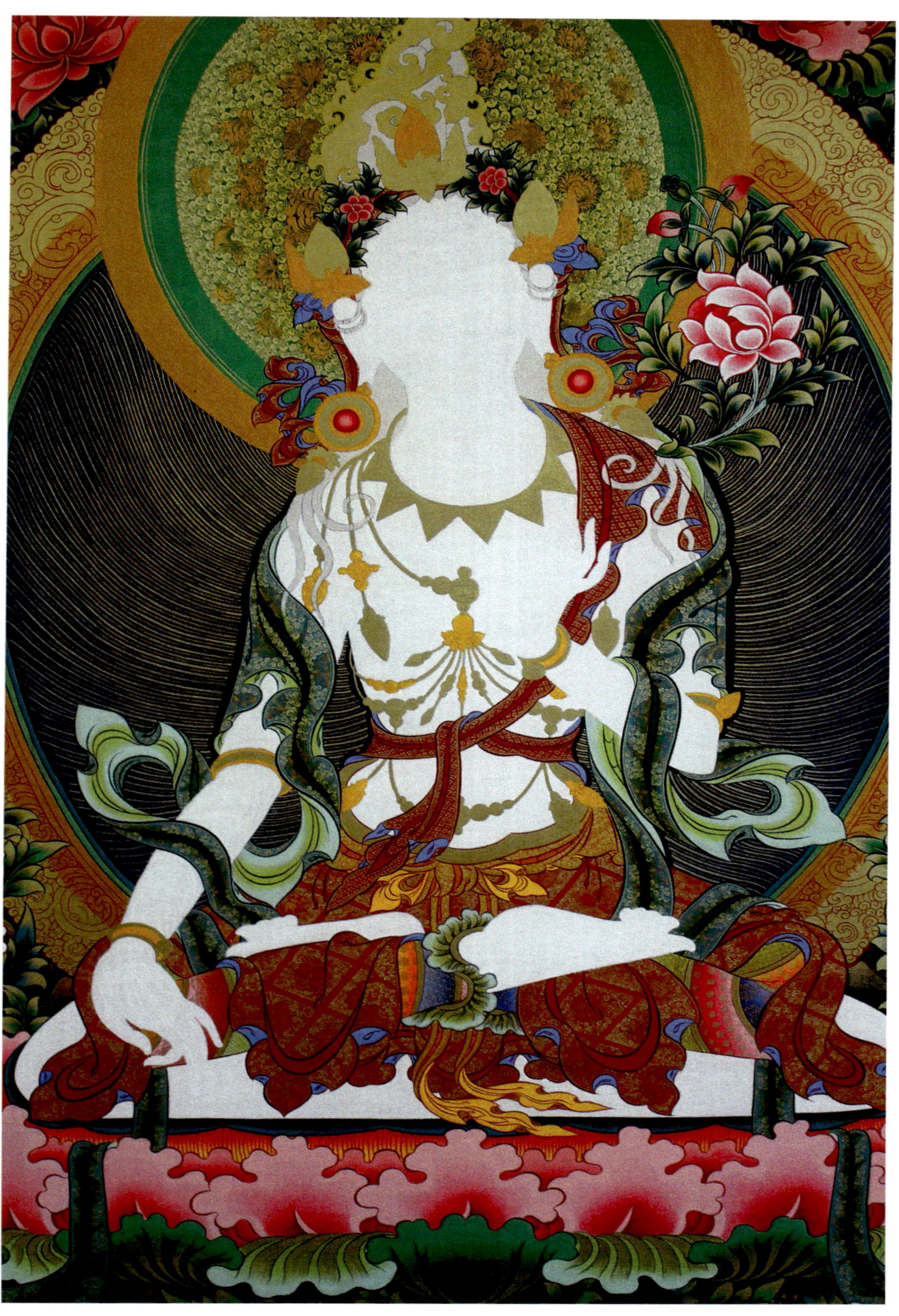

PLATE 10 An unfinished thangka depicting the White Tara painted by Lutso when she was an apprentice in the art school, 2013.

CHAPTER 4

The Travels of a Thangka

In a five-star hotel in Beijing in February 2019, Lutso pulled out a roll of thangka paintings from a poster tube and carefully unfolded them in front of the owner of an art gallery. She had made this trip to foster new connections in the art world. "This is a red thangka of *Avalokiteshvara with Mind at Rest*, my recent artwork," Lutso said, pointing at the one on the top.[1] The background is vermillion—in Tibetan this type of thangka painting is known as *mtshal thang*—and the pigment is made from red coral stones, carefully ground and mixed with a specific type of animal glue. In the painting Lutso posed Avalokiteshvara off-center under a Bodhi tree in a meditative posture. His primordial teacher, Buddha Amitabha (Tib. *'od dpag med*), is on the top left, with Vasudhara (Tib. *nor rgyun ma*), the deity associated with wealth, on the bottom. Cranes and deer stroll around Avalokiteshvara. The auspicious treasures float above the water in front of him (plate 7).

After this Lutso laid out her other paintings on a small desk: thangkas of White Tara, Manjushri, Buddha Shakyamuni, and so on. The gallery owner looked at the paintings with great interest. She took photos of them with her iPhone from time to time. After a while, the gallery owner raised her head and asked Lutso: "Your thangkas are nice. But others can also paint what you've done. Why are yours different? What makes you unique?" Lutso was puzzled. She looked at me as if I might have answers.

Having accompanied a few male painters from Rebgong on their gallery visits in Beijing and Shanghai, I had gone through similar situations. From Lutso's puzzling look, I sensed there must be some misunderstanding between the gallery owner and Lutso, about uniqueness or creativity in the context of Tibetan thangka art. The gallery owner might agree with the philosopher Walter Benjamin, who thought the "aura" of art lies in its uniqueness and originality, whereas the endless reproduction of copies destroys the value of art. This canny gallery owner might also have been speaking on behalf of her affluent Han clients, who routinely seek out the novelty that has characterized Western or modern art production; some of these clients also rely on thangka paintings, or Tibetan Buddhism in general, to project social or economic distinction (Osburg 2020).

The gallery owner acknowledged the fact that Lutso is one of the few Tibetan female thangka painters in Rebgong, but she was not too excited about it—neither the religious authenticity nor the gender politics were likely to help the gallery owner sell enough artworks to cover the rent in this five-star hotel. I tried to rephrase the gallery owner's question in a more specific and constructive way. "She wants to know your specialty, what you are good at," I whispered to Lutso.

"I see," Lutso said quietly, seeming to relax a little bit. She pointed to the detailed golden lines and meticulous patterns on the deities' halos and clothing and said: "I am good at the gold lining. Look, these are my own designs." The gallery owner took another look at those details, tapping the gold lines with her fingers. "You do have talent," she nodded.

I first met Lutso in 2013. At that time she was one of the few Tibetan women who had received professional training in thangka painting as men did. Six years later, Lutso opened a thangka studio in Rebgong, the first Tibetan woman to operate a studio and train her own apprentices. Lutso's experiences are unusual. Unlike most women painters in Rebgong who work with their husbands or stay in art school, Lutso had chosen a pathway without marriage and without support from any art institution. How does Lutso pursue a career path as a professional *lha zo* and navigate in a market that has been dominated by men? More importantly, what does operating a thangka studio mean to Lutso, and in turn, how does her practice reshape the meaning of Tibetan thangka art?

Lutso, like other women painters in Rebgong, constantly struggles with three interconnected layers of constraints: the state's overarching agenda of cultural development; the market biases discriminating against the participation of village-based female painters; and the gender and cultural expectations for Tibetan women in the village. Consequently, Lutso has various motives, struggles, and choices as a *lha zo*. The career of her thangka painting *Avalokiteshvara with Mind at Rest* intertwines with her life experiences as she navigates different markets and enters into competing regimes of value (Appadurai 1986; Myers 2002). Through painting thangkas and training her own apprentices, especially female *ge truk*, Lutso is able to support her family, empower other Tibetan women, and reinforce her religious identity across very different social spheres.

The Divination

Fifteen years before her gallery visit in Beijing, Lutso and her father visited a diviner (Tib. *mo pa*). Lutso was in the sixth grade and lived with her parents in Thokya village. She said she did not like school but really loved painting. She had even won a prize in a children's art competition in town. She kept on thinking about dropping out of school and becoming a professional thangka painter.

At that time Tibetan women in Rebgong were not allowed to learn or to paint thangkas. Lutso's father was a migrant worker. He was very open-minded, compared to other people in the same village, possibly because he spent most of his time traveling and residing in China's urban centers. He was supportive of his daughter's painting dream. Nevertheless, he still wanted Lutso to continue school with the hope that even if she could not graduate from college and get a job at a government office, she could at least attend professional school and become a nurse or bank accountant.[2] To him, such professions seemed more modern and secure than being a *lha zo*. Moreover, like many other parents in the village, Lutso's father worried that the apprenticeship would take too long, after which his daughter might not be able to find a desirable husband. However, he did not force Lutso to stay in school. He left her daughter's fate to a diviner.

The *mo pa* was a well-respected old man in the village.[3] The diviner took out some Buddhist scriptures and asked about Lutso's birthday. The air was intense around the table. There was the conflicted father, who wanted to support his daughter and her painting dream yet knew it would be difficult for Lutso to become a thangka painter because of the social pressure in a conservative village. There was the diviner, likely facing for the first time a Tibetan girl who wanted to paint thangkas. Finally, there was the young Tibetan woman, who so fearlessly chose to become a *lha zo* yet nervously looked at the few pages of the scripture—her fate was still at men's mercy.

The room was quiet, until the diviner closed the scripture and said, "If she wants to paint, let her paint."

Lutso first told me this story in 2013, when she was in her early twenties and was an apprentice in Namgyal's art school, one of the first schools in Rebgong to accept female students. She was admitted to the painting school because her father and Namgyal used to be middle school classmates. At the painting school, Lutso kept a simple routine. She got up around seven in the morning and stayed in front of the canvas and painted until sunset; after dinner she usually practiced iconographic models on a sketchpad for another hour or two.

Lutso liked art school, where she had nothing to worry about except painting. From Namgyal, Lutso learned not only painting techniques but also teachings from Tibetan Buddhism and Tibetan histories. According to Lutso, this kind of knowledge was not accessible to most Tibetan women, including her female relatives in the village. Lutso loved chanting scriptures with Namgyal, who used to be a monk, and hearing him tell stories about religious subjects or historical figures as he made corrections on apprentices' sketchpads. Although she heard people in the village questioning her parents—"Your daughter is as tall as her mother. Why don't you find her a husband?"—her father let her stay in school without pressing her into marriage. At the end of each year, students in the art school earned some money from their *ge gen* in paid apprenticeships. Lutso used the cash to buy food and gifts for her relatives during the New Year celebration. It made her very proud. Lutso hoped that she could stay in the painting school as long as she wanted. Such a wish turned out to be unrealistic.

A Good Tibetan Daughter

Lutso had become a wife and a mother of a one-year-old before she could sit down and think about a painting of her own design.

I visited her apartment in town in 2018, when *Avalokiteshvara with Mind at Rest* was just a sketch on canvas. The face of Avalokiteshvara was left empty. Before his eyes were painted, usually the last step of a thangka painting, we were not able to judge the quality of the thangka. In the bedroom-turned-studio, Lutso told me this painting was not a commission for anyone. Avalokiteshvara is one of her favorite bodhisattvas in thangka art. Lutso had never painted his meditating posture before. Besides wanting to try something new and exercise her painting skills, she intended to have one virtuoso piece to showcase her artistic achievement—for occasions like her visit to the gallery in Beijing or art exhibitions—since painters cannot keep commissioned thangkas for themselves.

Lutso had left art school in 2014. While Namgyal recognized her talents and wanted her to stay a few more years to advance her learning, Lutso decided to leave for Beijing, where she could make better money and help her father pay his debts. In Beijing, through a relative's connection, Lutso painted thangkas as a wageworker for a gallery featuring Tibetan art. She told me she missed the time spent in Beijing because on top of the well-paid salary and varieties of entertainment available in the metropolitan area, she saw career opportunities. She had once been interviewed on a TV program produced by an official channel in Beijing. Her coworkers encouraged her to socialize with the newspeople or to look for clients, using this interview as a promotion. However, unlike Leshe, who was able to stay in Beijing and open his thangka shop after the Olympic Village event, Lutso left behind her network and opportunities in Beijing, including that five-minute interview, and returned to Rebgong largely because her parents wanted her to get married and have children.

Lutso was the older daughter in the family. Her younger sister was still at school. When it came to fixing the house, planting or harvesting the field, her mother always called her. Lutso felt obliged to help while her father was away working in other cities. She felt she was the only person her mother could count on—and nothing would make her mother feel more secure than Lutso getting married and settling down in Rebgong. However, having a baby imposed greater economic insecurity on Lutso. Her husband is a fine painter himself. Lutso said that if they painted together, they could produce an excellent piece of thangka painting. However, after the baby was born, Lutso had little time to paint. While her husband painted with apprentices in his thangka studio, another apartment they rented in the same building, Lutso stayed with the baby and could only paint mini-thangkas (Tib. *tsa ka chung chung*) when the baby took naps—she usually finished a mini-thangka in a day or two. "It's really not exciting to paint mini-thangkas, but they sell fast. I can make some pocket money from mini-thangkas to buy diapers or baby food," said Lutso.

Lutso's conundrum was by no means unique. While male *lha zo* embrace the aspirations brought by the new market and expand their travel all over China, painting fixes most Tibetan women in the village or at home, where their time and labor for child rearing, household chores, agricultural work, and communal events are expected and crucial. Even though some women, including many of Lutso's classmates in the art school, have received years of training in thangka painting, their art making careers are cut short by their marriage and subsequent obligations to the family and the village. When Lutso needs to help out her mother in the village, her day is spent on child-care, feeding, washing, cooking, farmwork, household errands, and helping neighbors. A routine that repeats and continues, like the turning prayer wheel on the roof of the house, it goes on and on.

Lutso never blamed her father for causing her to leave art school or Beijing. Although he spent most of the time working away from home, she felt close to her father because "he knows a lot." If Lutso needs to make a decision, she talks to him. When I visited Lutso in her apartment in 2018, her father was taking a break from work and helping Lutso look after her son. Lutso finally had some time to work on a regular-sized thangka and figure out a design of her own. I looked at her sketch of the *Avalokiteshvara with Mind at Rest*—the elaborately crafted patterns on deities' halos and clothing, Lutso's creative touch, caught my eye. I said to her, "It must be sold at a high price when it is finished." Lutso nodded and said: "I hope I can make a lot of money. I hope I can support the family one day so that my dad won't need to work so hard."

A Woman Painter in the Art Market

Back in my office in New York, I checked the time, 10:30 a.m. Lutso, who was in Rebgong, might not have gone to bed yet. Laurel Kendall, curator of Asian Ethnology at the American Museum of Natural History (AMNH), had proposed to collect one thangka painting from Lutso, as an example of the contemporary practice by a woman *lha zo*. I thought of *Avalokiteshvara with Mind at Rest* but was unsure if it had been "sold" already. I called Lutso via WeChat.

"Yah, what's going on, *a ce* [Tib. Sister]?" Lutso always answered my call like this.

"Do you still have the thangka *Avalokiteshvara with Mind at Rest*?"

"Yes, I do."

"Do you think it's possible for the museum to purchase it for our Tibetan collection?"

"Oh, it sounds good."

After a few seconds, Lutso asked, "*A ce*, is it a good thing to be collected by a museum?"

I laughed but silently, on the other end of the line, knowing that there must be hundreds of thangka painters who dearly want to get their paintings into a museum collection (let alone a collection in a world-famous museum), for their works to be recognized, preserved, and displayed or to obtain a certificate of some kind.

In my recent visits to Rebgong, I sensed an intensified competition among local art makers. Under the government's agenda of cultural development, numerous painters are trained in home studios, art schools, and government-sponsored accelerated programs. In 2006, when Rebgong art was listed as a national ICH, the official count of thangka painters was about two thousand; the number had increased to more than twenty thousand in 2022.[4] It is no longer possible to meet clients "by chance," as monk Rinchen had met his Shanxi patron in 2011. Thangka painters in today's Rebgong have had to spend more time painting, explore various marketing strategies, or travel farther to China's urban centers to promote their work. In Sengeshong, summer usually means busy "business hours," when tourists from around China and from abroad come to Rebgong, especially during the celebration of Lurol festival. Some painters made wooden signs carved with "Rebgong artist family" (Ch. *re gong yi ren zhi jia*) or "Excellent thangka artist" (Ch. *jie chu tang ka yi ren*) in Chinese and hung them in front of their home gates. Some painters wore their hand-painted mini-thangkas around their necks or hung them on the rearview mirror of their cars. Once a tourist revealed any interest to these thangkas, the painter would start chatting and selling. I was also told that some painters, more aggressive than Pema Tso, even forced tourists to their home to look at their paintings.

Although many local residents gave a snort of contempt to such behaviors, every young painter faces the challenge of finding clients and establishing her or his business network after leaving the *ge gen*. According to male painters I have talked to, one needs to watch for painting competitions and cultural expos held in the prefecture or in Qinghai, where painters often demonstrate their artistic skills, obtain official accreditations, and get to know potential clients, including gallery owners, private collectors, and non-Tibetan Buddhist practitioners. When there is a vote for any official title or certificate—for instance, the "representative ICH inheritor"—a candidate needs to gather as many votes from their fellow villagers as possible. It would be ideal for a *lha zo* to appear on a TV show, have one's name and painting in the news, or be featured in the blog or vlog of an internet celebrity with millions of followers.

Beyond these endeavors, there are endless banquets, a "ritual" among businesspeople to maintain and develop one's social network in China (Osburg 2013; Bian 2018).

For Lutso it is unthinkable. Although she is one of the few Tibetan female *lha zo* in Rebgong, this identity did not win her any advantages. Like those male painters in Dharamsala who describe feeling "awkward" if a thangka is painted by a woman (McGuckin 1996, 39), some male painters in Rebgong, with a long-held notion of patriarchy or even out of jealousy, told non-Tibetan clients that women's painting is not efficacious or authentic. "Men breathe fire out of their mouths. Women breathe blood. How could women's thangkas be as effective as men's?" a male painter once said to me, in front of a few tourists who had wandered into his thangka shop. The market became an even more challenging place for Lutso after she made the decision to leave her husband, a few months after her trip to the gallery in Beijing, because she did not want to fight with her in-laws, who constantly urged Lutso to move to their village home and become a "normal housewife." Without her husband and his studio, Lutso not only had to recruit her own apprentices but also find new clients and compete with male painters.

With the rising popularity of Tibetan Buddhism among non-Tibetans in China, some male painters, such as monk Rinchen, Leshe, and Norbu, have sought out patronage from clients in the intermediate market. Beyond projecting ethnic identity by selling Tibetan Buddhist objects, male painters who engage with intermediate audiences use art making and networking to authenticate their religious identity and contest the state-led commodification of Tibetan thangkas. However, the intermediate market is much less accessible, if not completely off-limits, for female painters. Female painters travel less than male painters do and rarely socialize with clients. Visiting a gallery in Beijing is an exceptional opportunity for Lutso but not at all unusual for her male counterparts.

Lutso told me that it was very inconvenient for a Tibetan woman to go out and socialize with clients or attend art events organized by the government. She avoided social gatherings or business-related banquets, where collaborations were forged but the atmosphere might turn, or be assumed to turn, sexual (Zheng 2006; Osburg 2013). Moreover, Lutso felt her behavior in the market was always under the scrutiny of other villagers: people spread the rumor that she must have been taken advantage of by an official to win an art competition or gossiped that she had tried to hook up with a "wealthy man" when a male gallery owner from another province in China came to Rebgong and wanted to see her paintings. "People talked about it as if I were dating with the male gallery owner. In fact, we were eating in a restaurant with all my apprentices at the dinner table!" Lutso complained. Being very careful about her public profile, she met most of her clients and accepted commissions online. When someone ordered her thangkas, she discussed the design of the painting and the price with the client via text messages and sent out the artwork by express mail.

Lutso, who was much less experienced than her male counterparts in the art market, was unclear about what "museum collection" means to the career of a painter when I first mentioned it to her. Her visit to the gallery in Beijing was unproductive, as the gallery owner subsequently closed that site and shifted her marketing focus to Chinese contemporary art. Lutso returned to Rebgong with *Avalokiteshvara with Mind at Rest* and kept the painting until I called her. Now her patron, I explained to her that being collected by a museum could boost her professional profile and possibly bring her more clients.

"*A ce*, I don't know how to thank you. You've helped me a lot," Lutso said to me over the phone, "but if you were a man, people would have gossiped that we had some sort of secret 'exchange!'" We both laughed out loud.

A Reimagined Social Space for Women

A few months later, I returned to Rebgong with a check from the museum, and Lutso led me to her new thangka studio in town (figure 5). It is a very small apartment. Lutso rented this place after she split with her husband and her mother agreed to take care of her son in the village. The apartment only has two rooms, one used as a painting studio, the other as the bedroom for Lutso and her two female apprentices. Her male apprentices sleep on two temporary metal beds in the living room. The walls of the painting studio are stacked with canvases mounted on wooden or steel stretchers. Lutso and her apprentices sit in front of the canvases and paint under the generous sunshine coming through the window. All pigments are put on a tiny table in one corner of the room. The space is so limited that if someone would like to stretch her back, she will bump into someone else's back or canvas.

In this studio Lutso returned to the routine she had followed when she was in Namgyal's art school—except that she is now the *ge gen*. She and her apprentices get up at around seven in the morning and spend most of the

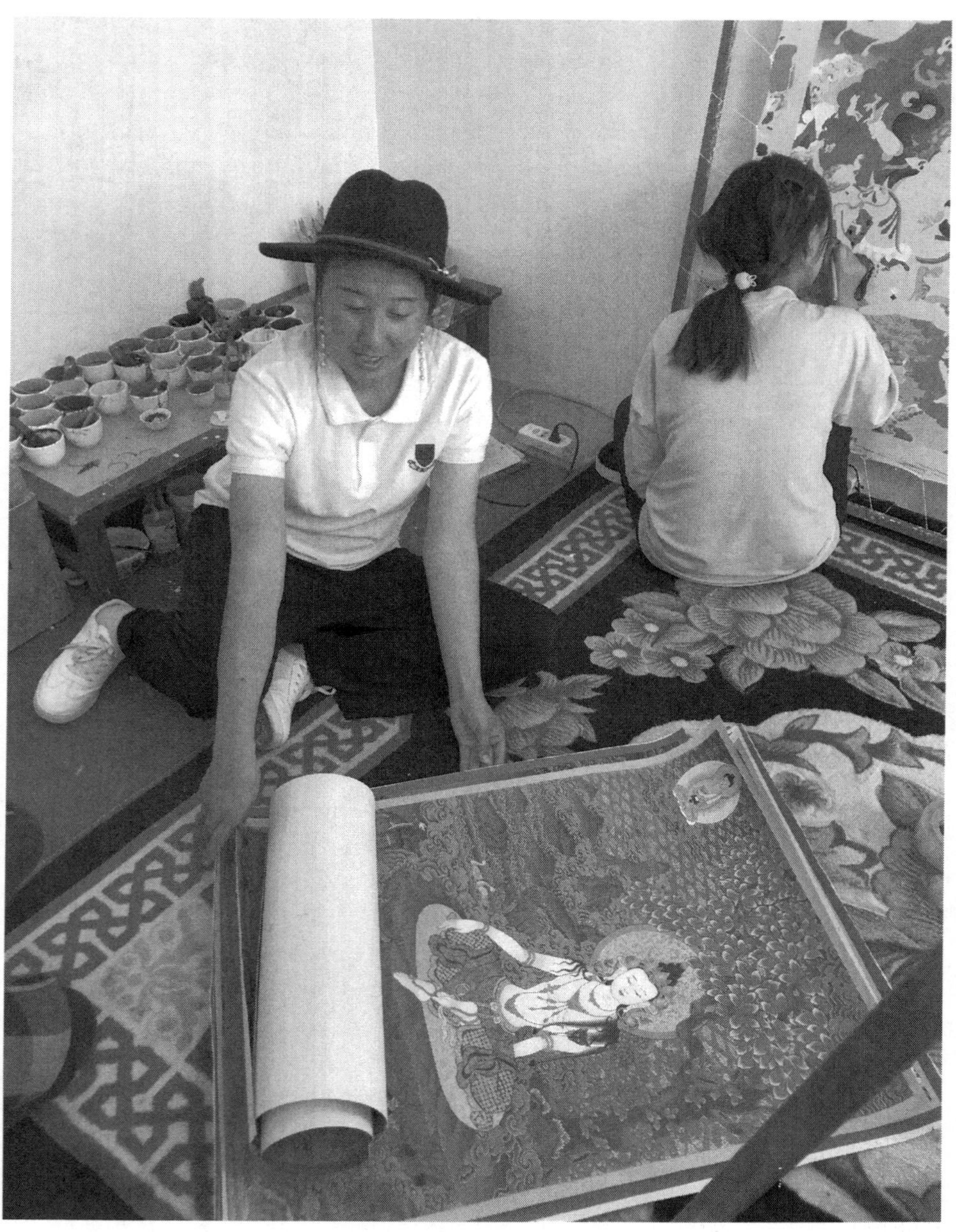

FIGURE 5 Lutso unfurling the thangka painting *Avalokiteshvara with Mind at Rest* in her studio in Rebgong, 2019.

day in front the canvases. They take one day off for every ten days working on thangka painting. During the break Lutso visits her mother and son in the village and buys them food, toys, and clothing. Lutso seems satisfied with what she is doing.

Over the years Lutso repeated a similar expression—"I feel most happy and satisfied when I am painting"—when I met her in the art school; when she was able to work on a regular-sized thangka, *Avalokiteshvara with Mind at Rest*, for the first time after her childbirth; and when she sat with her apprentices in front of the canvas in her own thangka studio. Besides accumulating religious merits, there is another level of empowerment in Lutso's art making practices. Notably, a *lha zo* produces functional images for others. Since thangka paintings are commissioned to meet the particular needs of the patron, the painter becomes an important medium, through whom the manifestation of the Buddha and deities, the protection and blessings, can reach out to the person in need. Lutso explained to me that reciting prayers or mantras during the painting practice is more of a way to help her better visualize the deity, bringing merits to her patron, than to engage with the deity's practices, accumulating merits for herself. "I feel satisfied because I am able to help others," said Lutso.

Like many male painters, Lutso gets most of her commissions from non-Tibetan clients. She recites prayers or mantras while working on a painting and takes most of her paintings to a local monastery for consecration (Tib. *rab gnas*) before she sends them to her clients. Lutso also accepts commissions from local residents, mostly from Tibetan women. For instance, Lutso painted a thangka of Green Tara (Tib. *sgrol ma ljang khu*) for a pregnant woman from her village because Tara is believed to have a positive influence on childbirth (Beyer 1988, 289; Makley 2003, 612). In the beginning of her own pregnancy, Lutso also painted the Green Tara and donated the thangka to the newly renovated village shrine. According to the village head, this was a meritorious thing for Lutso and her baby because her Green Tara thangka would bestow blessings to villagers who circumambulated and made offerings to the village shrine.

Lutso particularly welcomes Tibetan women to her studio to learn thangka painting from her. From her own experiences, she knows that women apprentices often feel intimidated in male painters' studios and are likely to discontinue their studies before they have acquired all the painting techniques. Some parents have told Lutso that precisely because she is a woman, they agreed to send their daughter to her thangka studio, as they considered it "inconvenient" for a girl to spend so much time with a male *ge gen*. Without any prior experience, Lutso's female apprentices start from doing pencil sketches on paper and proceed to do some simple coloring on the commissioned thangkas. In a few years they are expected to draw sketches of main deities on canvas, to do gold linings, or even to open the eyes (Tib. *spyan 'byed*) for deities—the last step currently done by Lutso or assigned to her most experienced male apprentices. Besides painting skills, her two female *ge truk* have observed and learned from Lutso's experiences—"possibilities a Tibetan woman could have"—as Lutso participates in the art market and balances her family and career as a female *lha zo*.[5] "If they stay with me long enough, the girls will be able to open their own thangka studios," said Lutso, "like what I have done." In that sense Lutso's studio materializes the reimagined social space for her female *ge truk*, whose choices remain circumscribed by gender and cultural norms in this society.

"An Independent and Stubborn Woman"

Although Lutso did not form any type of collaboration with the gallery in Beijing, the experience forced her to think about the question of "uniqueness" as she operates her own thangka studio. In the eyes of many non-Tibetan clients, thangka art is rarely seen as something creative or evolving. On one hand, this problem is indicated by what Clare Harris has called the "timelessness," or "agelessness," of Tibet (Harris 1999, 17). Harris criticizes those culture brokers who make Tibet into an imaginary entity, emphasizing its great physical and temporal distance from the West (also see Lopez 2018). While this romantic image boosts the value of objects placed in the collections of Western museums, private collectors, and art dealers, it denies the agency of Tibetans who live and create in contemporary Tibet. On the other hand, the religious value of Rebgong thangka art has been replaced by its commercial and aesthetic value when it is promoted on the national art market. Some popular images, such as Yellow Jambhala (the god of wealth), Four-Armed Avalokiteshvara, and Green Tara, have been repeatedly shown in state-organized expos, exhibitions, or TV programs and have become Tibetan "motifs." These images are therefore in high demand from non-Tibetan clients who are unfamiliar with Tibetan Buddhism or Buddhist art. In this new context, the uniqueness of Rebgong thangka art is conveyed with an emphasis on the rarity of natural mineral pigments or simply on its status as an ICH recognized by UNESCO.

Instead of being completely constrained by rules of iconography and composition, a thangka painter can have a certain amount of freedom in painting, for instance, to design nonreligious content such as plants and decorative patterns, to adjust colors, or to create scenarios from Buddhist texts that have not been depicted before. A phone call I had with Lutso in 2021, two years after she opened her thangka studio, suggests that she had become more confident as the *ge gen* of the art studio. "Several years ago, if you showed me a thangka of another painter and commissioned the same thing, I would just replicate the exact same image for you," said Lutso, "But now, if you show me a thangka by another painter, I can tell you where they did a good job and where they did a bad job. I would know how to improve on it." These could be small improvements such as adding flowers to the background and redesigning gold details or more substantial changes to the composition of the painting or the combination of colors. According to Lutso, her clients, new and old, usually approve of and like her designs.

On the other hand, the creativity that goes into the content of the painting requires a considerable amount of knowledge of Tibetan Buddhism. "Her painting skills are good, better than many male painters," *ge gen* Namgyal commented on Lutso's artwork in a conversation with me in 2019. "But as for the creativity with respect to religious contents, she needs more work," said her former teacher. I began to understand why Namgyal had wanted Lutso to stay in the art school longer—it was not just for the brushwork techniques she could hone but, more importantly, for the knowledge of Tibetan Buddhism and Buddhist art Lutso would otherwise have little opportunity to learn. For one thing, such knowledge is largely taught in monasteries.[6] Besides Namgyal, not many thangka teachers emphasize the learning of Tibetan Buddhism; fewer are interested in teaching female apprentices Buddhist scriptures. Moreover, graduating from the art school or leaving one's teacher means the apprentice will have to spend more time on "business"—establishing her network with clients, fulfilling patrons' commissions, and training her own apprentices—instead of nurturing her creativity in art.

Lutso has not received any commissions from monasteries so far. This does not necessarily mean that monasteries discriminate against women's paintings. According to Namgyal, monks may find it difficult to explain to women painters the religious content—female painters are good at replicating existing iconographies, tweaking small, nonreligious parts such as flowers and clouds—but when it comes to the religious content, for instance, whether the dharma instrument held by the arhat is appropriate for a particular scene, women painters usually have no idea. Namgyal had to tell his female apprentices what exactly needed to be painted when he took them to a monastery to work on wall paintings or scrolls. Although not every male painter has substantial knowledge about Buddhist scriptures, compared to women, men have easier access to learn from monks in the monastery and better opportunities to attend dharma assemblies, some of which exclude women. Moreover, there are specific tantric deities (e.g., Yamantaka and Palden Lhamo) whom women are forbidden to depict. It is not surprising why a monastery would hesitate to commission paintings from a thangka studio led by a female *ge gen*.

Lutso thinks it's unrealistic for her to go back to Namgyal's art school, as she needs to make money to support her family. She also insists that once an apprentice has left her *ge gen*, she should not go back again because the teacher will have new *ge truk* so the returning apprentice becomes a burden. On holidays Lutso brings gifts to Namgyal and his family. Namgyal has invited Lutso to pick up free mineral pigments and gold leaves from his art school whenever she needs. Lutso initially refused. When she finally agreed to take pigments from Namgyal in 2020, as her supply was disrupted by the COVID-19 pandemic, she insisted on paying him. "An independent and stubborn woman," Namgyal labeled Lutso, the female apprentice who made him proud.

Lutso is aware of her weakness in thangka art. In her studio she and her apprentices spend time reading Buddhist scriptures, as she did with Namgyal in art school, and visit her monk relatives to consult with them about the religious content of a painting that she is uncertain about. Lutso does not choose quantity over quality when she operates the art studio, despite the rising market demand and competition among local painters. Although Lutso never expects to achieve the level of knowledge or painting skill Namgyal has, she hopes that in the future she can paint stories and scenes that are rarely depicted, especially subjects associated with female deities and their various manifestations that have religious significance for Tibetan women.

The Journeys of a Thangka

THE VILLAGE

Before I left Rebgong, I spent a few days with Lutso and her family in the village, where Lutso helped her mother with barley harvesting. This is the place where the Tibetan girl refused to accept gender roles and made an unconventional choice—to become a professional *lha zo* before there was any art school or family workshop in Rebgong that publicly accepted female apprentices. Lutso might have been inspired by her father, a migrant worker who had spent most of his time in big cities and brought back stories illuminating the idea of a modern life, where women seemed to have the freedom of choosing what they wanted to be. Fortuitously, Lutso's choice of becoming a thangka painter was confirmed by a diviner. Yet she found that far from gaining greater freedom, she and many other female painters were trapped by the canvas. While a paid apprenticeship seems desirable to many families in Rebgong, women painters' art making is often compromised by their familial and social obligations, especially after they get married and have children. These constraints are heightened by the translocality of Tibetan men—many of whom, like Lutso's own father, are often away, working in China's big cities—and by an increasingly competitive art market that disadvantages village-based women and discourages their participation.

The painting *Avalokiteshvara with Mind at Rest* was probably depicted at a time when Lutso's mind was hardly at rest. Her new roles at that time, as a wife, a daughter-in-law, and a mother, as well as her regular responsibilities as a "Tibetan daughter," had prevented her from working on a regular-sized thangka for over a year, whereas the work of her husband or her father was largely undisrupted. The mouths waiting to be fed imposed stronger economic pressure on her. Nevertheless, with the same determination that had made her a *lha zo*, Lutso refused to be satisfied with painting mini-thangkas or taking on an auxiliary role assisting her husband's art making. I don't know if painting the meditating posture of Avalokiteshvara helped Lutso obtain a peaceful mind, but from this painting, Lutso has reasserted her identity as a professional *lha zo*—a married Tibetan woman with a one-year-old could paint like male painters do and make the painting a virtuoso piece—a battle she has seen as her destiny since the oracle of the diviner.

THE AIRPORT

I left Rebgong for Beijing with Lutso's painting in a poster tube. At the airport in Xining, I stood in line with other people waiting to get through the security gate and looked around. The airport was filled with tourists carrying all kinds of souvenirs: boxes of yak jerky, elaborately packaged caterpillar fungus, colorful wool scarfs, as well as turquoise stone necklaces and mini-thangkas hung around their necks. I was far from the only one who carried a poster tube. On the plane, another passenger tried to fit his long poster tube into the overhead bin—his was wrapped with a beautifully printed tag, "Ethnic treasure, Rebgong thangka" (Ch. *min zu jing pin, re gong tang ka*).

Such a tag has been added to Rebgong thangka art as a promotional device, affirming the works' status as a cultural resource to boost the local economy. When Lutso took *Avalokiteshvara with Mind at Rest* to the gallery in Beijing, her artwork was only appreciated as a piece of commodity art awaiting a marketable narrative—a narrative appealing to many secular consumers but distant from the core beliefs of many residents in Rebgong. Moreover, although self-improvement (including acquiring thangka painting skills) is encouraged among Tibetan women today, many Tibetan residents, activists included, emphasize the "unity and harmony of families" in order to defend the core of Tibetanness—such belief often reinforces Tibetan women's immobility and their periphery status in their familial, social, and religious lives (Rajan 2015).

Although painting is an important means for Lutso to meet her family's economic needs, especially after she left her husband, her artworks have gone beyond their monetary values. Painting gives Lutso a new opportunity to accumulate Buddhist merit and reconfigure herself as a social and religious actor. She is empowered by depicting an image of the sacred. She further empowers other women through accepting female apprentices and painting for Tibetan women in the village. Even without equivalent marketing or networking opportunities available to many male *lha zo*, Lutso is able to reclaim her religious identity and create a reimagined social space for other women through art making.

THE MUSEUM

In the fall of 2019, I brought Lutso's thangka, *Avalokiteshvara with Mind at Rest*, back to the American Museum of Natural History (figure 6). The painting entered the museum collection with value beyond its exceptional artistic quality—telling a story of how the personal, the social, and the religious intersect with one another through the lens of gender.

With written and visual materials documenting the "life history" of this thangka, the painting announces itself as a living practice, rejecting the idea of a "timeless" Tibet or a dying tradition of Tibetan art—an impression that could have been fabricated by some exhibitions of Tibetan art in Western museums, including some permanent exhibits at the AMNH.[7] To depict Avalokiteshvara without a commission is unconventional. However, when

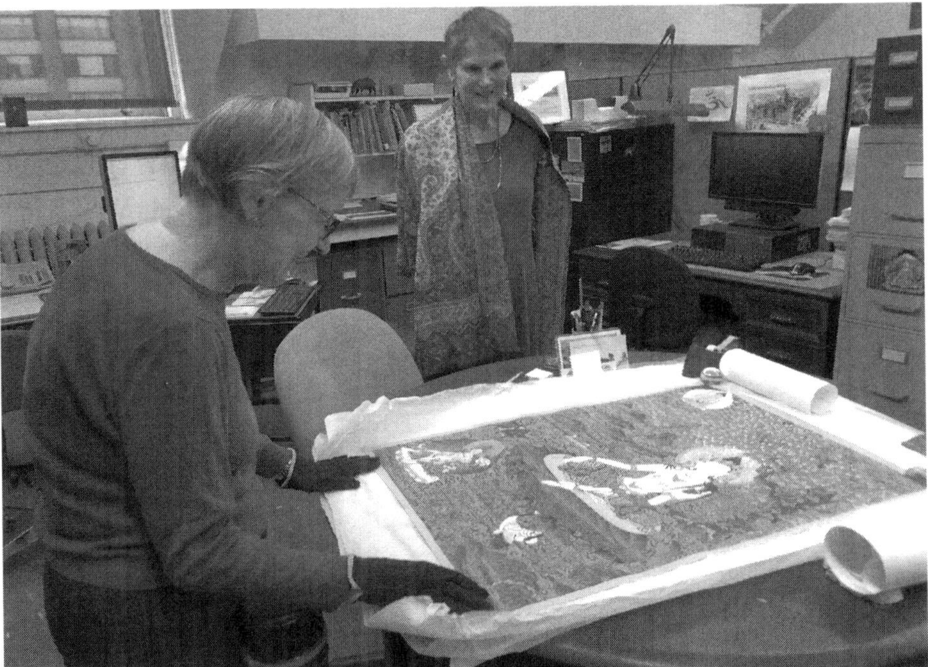

the museum decided to collect this painting, Lutso had it consecrated in a local monastery—an act that invites sacred beings to reside in the image as living essences, so people who later view and venerate the work will receive religious merit. Lutso's thangka painting provides an important example for audiences, especially Western audiences coming from a non-Buddhist background, to understand that Tibetan thangkas—as well as statues, masks, and shaman paintings produced in some other Asian places—are things made to be ensouled and have a special relationship with devotees, who are still making and using them today.

Lutso's artwork also captures an unfolding practice over time and highlights the significance of women's participation in art making in Rebgong. As I highlighted in the previous chapter, Rebgong female *lha zo* are mastering the male domain of art making and producing images with important religious value. Lutso has acquired a full complement of thangka painting skills and is capable of accepting commission on her own and training both male and female apprentices. Through making Buddhist images, Lutso and many other women painters in Rebgong find a new pathway to connect with their religion, history, and culture and, to various extents, to reclaim their ethnic and religious identities. Because of this, Lutso was able to complete the thangka of Avalokiteshvara, whose eyes are full of dignity, benevolence, and peace, and to bring the deities' protection and blessing to other people with her artistic skills—the responsibilities of a *lha zo*.

On the fifth floor of the museum, I unfurled the painting in front of my colleagues. I was reminded of how Lutso, in her studio during my last visit, took out the painting of *Avalokiteshvara with Mind at Rest* from a poster tube she kept in her bedroom. As she was unfurling the painting in front me and her apprentices, I caught the conversation between Lutso and one of them.

"Where will this painting go?" a male apprentice asked.

"To New York, the museum where *a ce* is working," Lutso said.

"Next time we want to see it, we will have to buy a ticket," the apprentice joked.

Everyone laughed.

"We can always paint another one. A better one," said Lutso.

CHAPTER 5

Artisan or Artist?

In 2013, a month before his show in a private art gallery in Shanxi, monk Rinchen was busy sorting things out. Having difficulty describing himself for the show, he asked me,

"Which one sounds better to you, *tang ka yi shu jia* [Ch. thangka artist] or *tang ka hua shi* [Ch. thangka painter]?"[1]

"Both sound fine to me. I address you as a *hua shi* [Ch. painter] most of the time, though," I said.

"Maybe 'artist' is better for this exhibition," said Rinchen, "a 'painter' sounds like a carpenter."

"*O le*, I see what you mean." I nodded.

"How about *seng ren yi shu jia* [Ch. monk artist]? Serious clients would prefer a thangka painted by a monk," added Rinchen.

A week later, Rinchen showed me a photo of the exhibition poster. Text reading "re gong seng lü yi shu jia" (Ch. Rebgong monk artist) appeared beneath his portrait.[2]

In the contemporary European and American art world of museums, galleries, collections, and criticism, the value of art depends heavily on individual creativity.[3] Many non-Western arts, when entering the global market or acquiring the status of "high art" in places like the British Museum or the Museum of Modern Art (MoMA) become "art by appropriation" (Errington 1998, 78)—not displayed as what they really are (e.g., their ritual functions or their meanings to local people) but framed to fit the imagination of their cosmopolitan audiences. Non-Western arts made for religious or ritual use, including Tibetan Buddhist images, are usually viewed as artifacts instead of art.[4] In this interpretation, if there is any creativity in Tibetan art, it is found in the works of individual artists who break with tradition (Gonkar Gyatso 2003; Höfer 2011; C. Harris 2012), not in ritual art shaped by the collective knowledge of religious texts, liturgical practices, and specific protocols of art production and distribution.[5]

Although religious art could be regarded, in Nelson Graburn's (1984) sense, as "functional/traditional art," this characterization should not hinder deeper exploration. Do thangka paintings, like Catholic statues (Kalb 1994; Kendall et al. 2013) and temple masks (Geertz 2004; Kendall 2021, 60–64)—things fabricated today to a high level of sophistication—not qualify as art because they are made for utilitarian and sacred purposes? Do the nineteenth- or twentieth-century Eurocentric views still get to define what "art" is or to reject Tibetan thangkas as art because of their seemingly conservative nature of production? Does producing a functional image necessarily eliminate the art maker's opportunity to exercise creativity, project identity, or pursue aesthetic distinctiveness through art making?

Rebgong thangka painters' agency and originality work in diverse arenas, including the Buddhist and monastic tradition, the state's Intangible Cultural Heritage paradigm, and the "money-mediated spirituality" of non-Tibetan clients. In these places, thangka paintings are understood differently (e.g., as art, craft, or high art), giving Rebgong painters multiple ways to define themselves. Anthropological works on art, especially on non-Western art, have reminded us that "art," "craft," or "artifact" are not descriptions of objective truths but contextual labels—they are socially constructed and often flexible categories (Errington 1998; Kisin and Myers 2019; Phillips 2022). Rebgong thangka painters can therefore present themselves and their work strategically to various audiences, demonstrating that thangka is art, craft, or sacred object depending on the context.

In the dominant representation of Tibetan art in China, Rebgong *lha zo* are either imagined as copyists of ritual objects or as craftsmen transforming religious paintings into art commodities for sale on the tourist market. Accordingly, their paintings are valued for the manual labor or natural material involved in the work. In addition to the official rhetoric, such a misperception is also reinforced by a combination of consumerism and the search for spirituality missing in the rapidly urbanizing China. Nonetheless, Rebgong art tradition is not established or sustained by copying existing images. Neither is the artistic value of a thangka simply judged by how closely it replicates a masterpiece. In Rebgong some painters fight against the view that reduces Tibetan thangka to a craft, while making and exhibiting their work in response to the "pure gaze" of non-Tibetan audiences (Bourdieu 1984, 3), who simultaneously look for spirituality and creativity in thangka art. Some other *lha zo* rely on their painting skills, knowledge of Buddhism, and thoughtful use of visual language to create scenes that exist in Buddhist scriptures only as text. The latter is exemplified in the innovative works of Tashi Gyatso and Chodrak, particularly in their recent project *Water and Land Ritual Paintings* (Ch. *shui lu hua*), commissioned by a monastery in Mount Wutai (Tib. *ri bo rtse lnga*) in Shanxi.[6] These examples help us rethink the concept of creativity and expand the scope of the "anthropology of art"—an intellectual space not only accommodating innovations by people whose art is framed on the walls of modern art museums but also encompassing works with important religious, cultural, and aesthetic significance for both local and global audiences.

The Imagined "Artisan"

Monk Rinchen had good reason to think carefully about how he should be described for the show in Shanxi. In the past, Rinchen had seen disappointed museum visitors who quickly passed through a thangka exhibition and mumbled, "These paintings always repeat the same thing." Rinchen had also met some non-Tibetan art dealers who did not care about the creator of a thangka painting as long as the painter "could reproduce popular thangka images" and "his price is good."[7] The encounters had informed Rinchen that many non-Tibetans viewed thangka painters as artisans or craftsmen, equivalent to carpenters (Tib. *shing bzo pa*)—people who live from specialized skills and manual labor. True to some extent, this view is also biased—Rinchen had tried to avoid such a characterization. In contrast to Kant, who thought art was different from craft because art "could turn out purposively (be successful) only as play," though not without "mechanism" (2000, 183), painters like Rinchen definitely refused to regard Tibetan thangka as a kind of craft.

"When you visited Kumbum Monastery or Qinghai Lake, have you seen the key chains of Tibetan knot or miniature yak toys sold at tourist stalls? Many Chinese think Tibetan thangkas are the same—*lü you ji nian pin* [Ch. tourist souvenirs]. If you bought a consecrated thangka at one stop and took it to the bathroom at the next, it would be horrific to us Tibetans. That's the difference,"

Rinchen explained to me. "We are not simply making handicrafts. There are deep meanings and strong karma associated with thangka painting."[8] Rinchen would be glad to know that two European art historians may fully agree with him on this and acknowledge that "the very fact of creating images that host the divinities makes them 'artists'" (Tythacott and Bellini 2020, 4). In that regard, calling himself an "artist" or asserting "monk" in his title is not entirely a promotional strategy, albeit an effective one. What Rinchen tried to communicate with Shanxi audiences is the religious significance of thangka art as well as the social and cultural meaning behind the act of art making—all had been increasingly missing from the official representation of Tibetan art.

In 2008 Leshe participated in the one-month *Ethnic and Folk Handicraft Exhibition* (Ch. *min zu min jian shou gong yi zhi zuo zhan*) held in Beijing's Olympic Village. Leshe brought with him a few canvases, paintbrushes, and a box of pigments from Rebgong. He was assigned a place in the exhibition hall. His everyday work was sitting in front of the canvas and painting thangkas. The exhibition hall was frequented by Olympic athletes. Domestic and foreign tourists, as well as children brought by parents looking for an educational experience, also poured in. Besides painting, Leshe answered questions, explained painting techniques, and shared his personal story with visitors—acting like an ambassador of Rebgong art. However, the unrest and protests in Tibetan regions earlier that year made it extremely sensitive to exhibit Tibetan religious art in public, let alone at the Olympic Village. On the other hand, the state was in need of events like the *Ethnic and Folk Handicraft Exhibition* to show ethnic harmony and national unity, a gesture Charlene Makley and others would call "national exhibitionism in a new global era" (Makley 2010, 127; Denton 2005; Shepherd 2009). Under such circumstances, a safe "script" of Tibetan thangka art would be one that emphasized painting materials and artistic techniques while minimizing the religious or historical context of Tibetan art. This was what Leshe (and other ethnic minority artists) had been instructed to do by the event organizer. On this global stage, Leshe performed the role of an artisan, an ethnic minority from the "Golden Valley," an inheritor of an old tradition.

Ten years later, the official script of Tibetan art had not changed. In fact, the "artisanal" status of thangka painting was engraved in the title of a major exhibition held at the National Art Museum of China (Ch. *zhong guo mei shu guan*) in Beijing. In 2018 the National Art Museum and Qinghai co-organized the show, *Paintings from the Snowy Realm, Dreams Built by Artisanal Hearts:*

Qinghai Thangka Painting Art Exhibition (Ch. *xue yü dan qing, jiang xin zhu meng—qing hai tang ka hui hua yi shu zhan*).[9] On the introductory panel, thangka painters were praised for their "artisanal spirit" (Ch. *gong jiang jing shen*), while thangka art production was recognized for its pragmatic merit in alleviating the poverty problem of several rural regions in Qinghai. The forty-eight thangka paintings included in the exhibition were created by thirty-one painters designated as "National or Provincial Arts and Crafts Masters," highlighted to museum visitors in addition to the artists' name and birth year. Next to each thangka scroll, there was a small label giving the artwork's title, the painter's name, and the year the artwork was completed. In one exhibition room, a few glass cases contained a variety of mineral pigments used in thangka painting, different types of paintbrushes, along with a detailed description of the painting process. Audiences without prior knowledge of Tibetan Buddhism or Buddhist art would likely be impressed by the aesthetics and delicacy of the artwork but leave the show wondering why a wrathful deity (Six-Armed Mahakala) is placed with the Buddha or, above all, what these paintings are for.[10]

Nevertheless, the official narrative of thangka art resonates well with the popular imagination of Tibetan art in contemporary China. Although the production of craft is often associated with "repetition, tradition, discipline, and the focus on achieving a predefined end product," these characterizations "can take on either positive or negative connotations depending on whether craft is being juxtaposed against industrial mass production or modern art" (Wong 2013, 148). Winnie Wong's research in Dafen village (Shenzhen), where painters make replicas of Western masterpieces upon commission (e.g., by museum gift shops, warehouses, or art dealers), demonstrates that the quality of Dafen's oil paintings is never judged by the closeness to the originals. Instead, Dafen's art production fulfills the "market demand for authentic handwork," desirable for "its closeness to modernist artistic values summarized in the masterpiece of Vincent van Gogh" (151). Like tourists who visit rural ethnic regions looking for a distant "other" or a pure past (Schein 2000; Chio 2014; Oakes 2016), many non-Tibetan consumers of Rebgong thangka paintings imagine an artisan, who embodies the manual work and traditional knowledge lost in the modern industrial life, as well as the spirituality left behind by a rapidly urbanizing China.

When I searched for Rebgong thangka on a Chinese e-commerce company's website in 2021, I was surprised to find a photo I had taken in 2012, showing a

Rebgong monk painter working on a thangka painting, on the home page of many online shops of Tibetan art (figure 7). The photo was included in an essay I had published on a social media platform in China. I suspect these online shops "adopted" the image from that article (or later copied each other), without, of course, acknowledging either the painter, the photographer, or the publisher. What I find intriguing is the fact that several different shops uniformly chose this image as their cover photo. The exuberant color of the image would certainly be an attraction to many online shoppers, just like offline tourists and consumers who embrace the colorful ethnic minority culture depoliticized and commoditized on China's flourishing marketplace (Jinba 2014; Blumenfield 2018). The painter's action—holding a paintbrush and working on an unfinished thangka—as well as the level of concentration revealed on his face confirm the keyword *handmade* (Ch. *shou gong* or *shou hui*) repeatedly emphasized in shop descriptions. This characterization translates to a monetary value at least ten times more than that of a mechanically reproduced thangka image. Alternatively, instead of featuring the so-called artisan, some other shops post photos of ground mineral pigments up front, sometimes accompanied by an image of historical murals or antique thangkas—"the colors are still vibrant after hundreds of years," justifying why a thangka painted with natural pigments has to cost over RMB 10,000 (about USD 1,584).[11]

Interestingly, the online merchants who are fond of the image of the monk painter have neglected not only the story of my essay (about how the monk painter's *ge gen* strove to build an art school) but also other images included in the essay, for instance, photos of lay painters and women painters. Many non-Tibetan merchants of Buddhist paraphernalia in the Tibetan market in Chengdu display their knowledge about Buddhism or their own faith in Buddhism to build trust with clients, for instance, by burning incense in the shop, telling stories about their guru, or sharing information about their vegetarian diet (Brox 2019). Such packaging "involve[s] wrapping commodities in veils of authenticity" (114). Although cyber merchants may not be able to communicate with their clients as much as Chengdu shopkeepers do in person, showing the image of a monk is an effective and essential tool to add religious or spiritual value, hence extra economic profit, to the artwork on sale. In their practice, religiosity is used as a Tibetan motif and appropriated—what exactly Tibetan Buddhism is or teaches does not matter as much as how it appears.[12] As long as the image of the art maker conforms to the popular imagination of Tibetans as pure and faithful, his artworks are considered "authentic."

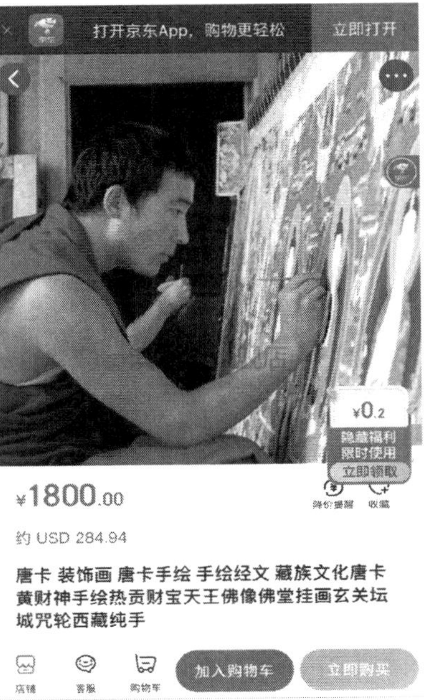

FIGURE 7 The screenshot of an online thangka shop's home page in 2021, using my photo of the monk painter without permission (plate 1).

Consumers' imagination of the artisan denies the painters' aspiration for modernity (Su 2020, 176). Gary Larson's 1994 cartoon is an apt summary of this irony: upon spotting "anthropologists" approaching from afar, the "primitives" rush to put away their modern devices—lamp, television, VCR, and phone. Not only do the primitives know what the anthropologists are looking for; they also respond by performing what the anthropologists expect—the "static vestiges of the past."[13] This is exactly how some Rebgong thangka painters react to today's art market. One painter told me that he locked his Xerox machine in a cabinet in his painting studio. Although he only used it to make photocopies of art books for his apprentices, he was afraid if his clients saw the Xerox machine, they would interpret him as simply coloring the photocopies of others' art—a form of mechanical reproduction. For the same reason, another painter would rather go to the printing shop in town to make photocopies than keep a copy machine at home. "Because you just don't know when an art dealer or a visitor shows up at your home studio," he said.

Along with the Xerox machine, many painters have also learned to hide their aspirations and desires, in order to appear "unpolluted" by the forces of

modernization. At an art show, a painter (innocently) told one of his clients
that he wished to make a lot of money through painting thangkas so that he
and his family could buy an apartment and move to the city. The client, an
affluent middle-aged woman, looked at him with contempt and said: "What's
good about the city? So much pressure. So much pollution. Why do you rural
folks always want to move to the city? Do you think you can paint the same
thangka after you squeeze yourself into a 'pigeon's nest' [Ch. *ge zi long*, a nick-
name for a tiny apartment]?" What she did not know was that this painter was
already painting from a "pigeon's nest"—his rented studio in town was no
more than 130 square feet and accommodated two other apprentices. Having
learned his lesson, the painter, in conversation with future audiences, sealed
his mouth about the urban apartment (that he eventually purchased in Xining after a few years of saving) and performed the "good artisan" by uttering
his wish was "to preserve the tradition of thangka art." This fits the bill for
general audiences, just like the image of the monk painter—an artisan frozen
in time. No consumer has to know when the monk painter completed that
thangka, how much he was paid by the dealer, if he ever returned to secular
life, or where he bought himself and family an apartment the day he decided
to leave the Golden Valley.

Audiences from the intermediate market, although more knowledgeable
about Tibetan Buddhism, still do not necessarily comprehend the desires
and concerns of thangka painters. After monk Rinchen returned to Rebgong from Shanxi, he told me his show had been successful. He met several
celebrities, including entrepreneurs, singers, movie stars, and contemporary
artists—many of them were followers of Tibetan Buddhism. At the opening
event, some of the visitors commissioned thangkas from Rinchen for their
specific purposes of practice and meditation (e.g., particular mandalas that are
rarely asked for by tourists). Moreover, Rinchen encountered new questions
beyond whether the thangka had been consecrated. One entrepreneur asked
Rinchen if he had a certificate in any form from the monastery he belonged
to. Rinchen was at first confused, saying: "I shaved my head and changed
into monk robes at the age of twelve. I have been living in the monastery ever
since. Why would I need any certificate?" He later learned that this entrepreneur had met some fake monks, secular people who pretended to be Tibetan
monks and held praying sessions to cheat the entrepreneur's offering, including money. Another client, who had commissioned several thangka paintings
from Rinchen after attending his show, approached him cautiously and said:

"Rinchen, you are very talented. I may invite you to my place someday. But you should never get yourself involved in those riots in your region." Rinchen knew he was referring to the incidents of protest in Rebgong in previous years.

Like art collectors and patrons of Tibetan Buddhism in the West, intermediate audiences in China look for "a kind of therapy" in thangka art or "the illustrations for a self-help manual for the unenlightened" to defeat the malaise of urban life (C. Harris 2012, 20). Some intermediate audiences in China turn to the spirituality and moral authority of Tibetan Buddhism in order to project social distinction, while the consumption of luxury commodities has failed to do the work (Osburg 2020). For both audiences, the art they commission and the artist or monk they sponsor have to be "true" and "safe." For that matter, Rinchen invited the first entrepreneur, who asked for a certificate, to come to Rebgong and see for himself. But Rinchen did not tell the second client that he chanted Buddhist scriptures not only to pray for peace during those difficult times but also for village fellows who had been hurt or lost their lives in the unrest. Some audiences asked Rinchen why he introduced himself as an artist. "An artist makes art for others," Rinchen responded. "When I paint thangkas, I think about how to help others."

High-End Thangka in Shanghai

On a sunny summer morning in 2012, my mother and I were on our way to a private art gallery in one of Shanghai's most expensive neighborhoods. Thondup, a thangka painter from another county near Tongren, had invited me to his exhibition. My mother, who had an interest in Buddhist art though she did not engage in any practice or teaching of Buddhism, was curious enough to come with me.

I first met Thondup at Jampa's home in Gasar village earlier that year. Thondup was trained as a clay sculptor by his father but maintained a strong interest in painting. When he turned sixteen, he came to Sengeshong and Gasar to learn thangka painting. Thondup got to know Jampa through friends and stayed with him for two years. Unlike Jampa's other *ge truk*, Thondup was only a few years younger than Jampa. Both of them loved singing and drinking. Besides laughter catalyzed by alcohol, their bond grew stronger through backing each other up in fistfights on the town streets. Nonetheless, Thondup insisted on calling Jampa *ge gen* or *shi fu* (Ch. teacher) most of the time. After Gasar, Thondup traveled to Gansu, where he not only made paintings and sculptures but also became a sort of an art dealer specializing in Tibetan Buddhist art. As one can imagine, some of Jampa's thangka paintings found their destinations through Thondup's hands.

During the New Year celebration, Thondup came back to Rebgong. He brought Jampa gifts as well as the news about his upcoming show in Shanghai. Jampa lit a cigarette but did not respond immediately upon hearing about Thondup's show. Thondup must have felt uneasy, for he kept twisting the lid of his insulated mug.

"What's in your mug?" Jampa threw out the question, breaking the awkward silence.

"Oolong tea." Thondup took a sip.

"That's shit. Here, take the beer." Jampa pushed a bottle of Tsingtao in front of Thondup.

"It is only afternoon—let's drink later," Thondup said, taking another sip of his oolong.

"Rongwo gonpa." Jampa slapped his own thigh. "You sound like those useless urbanites!" Both of them laughed.

"When are you going to organize an exhibition for me?" Jampa asked, after finishing his cigarette, in a tone that was hard to distinguish between joking and serious.

Thondup responded: "*Ge gen*, I've told you I am now making these *gao duan* [Ch. high-end] thangkas. The audiences are different."

Later in the evening, Jampa told me that Thondup had hardly helped him sell any thangka paintings in recent years. Thondup gave him excuses like "the clients were different" or Jampa's paintings "were not in his clients' taste." Jampa characterized Thondup as "selfish" because Thondup "only thought about his own business." Jampa had expected this former apprentice and good friend to be more grateful or helpful; after all, not only had he taught Thondup painting skills, but he had also supported Thondup's art business in Gansu in the beginning. "Thondup made quite a bit of money by selling *my* paintings," said Jampa. "Otherwise, he could not expand his business like this or meet so many clients."

Nevertheless, before Thondup left for Sengeshong to visit his other friends, he agreed to take a few thangka paintings from Jampa and "try [his] best to sell them." When Thondup invited Jampa to his show, Jampa refused, saying that he would need to help with the farmwork then. "But she should go," Jampa pointed at me. "She studies thangkas. She'd be interested in seeing your high-end thangkas." Thondup, of course, happily exchanged phone numbers with me and promised to send me exhibition updates. As Thondup started his car, Jampa yelled to him, "I will ask her to see if you exhibit my paintings under your name!" Both of them laughed and waved goodbye.

Four months later, I recalled Jampa's words as my mother and I were getting close to the gallery. Again, I was unsure if Jampa said it as a joke or he really meant it—did Jampa think Thondup would appropriate his work? Why did Jampa feel uncomfortable about Thondup's show in Shanghai? What were Thondup's high-end thangkas, which spoke to a different audience than Jampa's paintings?

"Welcome, my friends," Thondup greeted us as we entered the gallery.

The interior of the gallery was spacious, filled with the smell of Tibetan incense. Thondup's thangka paintings were spaced out comfortably on the cream white walls of two exhibition rooms. Between the two rooms, we caught sight of a simple and straightforward exhibition title, *The Solo Exhibition of Himalayan Artist Thondup* (Ch. *xi ma la ya yi shu jia dun zhu ge zhan*), in both Chinese and English, painted in gold against a frost-blue wall. In front of the title wall, a low coffee table was surrounded by several cattail cushions (Ch. *pu tuan*) on the floor. Thondup was sitting cross-legged on the cushion and reading a book as we came in. Knowing that my mother had not been to Tibet nor did she practice Tibetan Buddhism, Thondup offered to walk her through the exhibition. The first room exhibited thangka paintings of the Buddha, bodhisattvas, celestial deities like Tara and Jambhala, and religious teachers including Guru Rinpoche (Padmasambhava) and Tsongkhapa. The other room was for "more advanced disciples," in Thondup's words, showing paintings of tantric deities, dharma protectors, and mandalas. Except for a label next to the title wall briefly introducing Thondup as the artist, there were not many texts for viewers to read. Thondup patiently explained the content of each painting to my mother.

"What do you think?" asked Thondup, turning to me. I gave him a nod observing, "It feels different from other thangka exhibitions I've seen." Thondup laughed and said: "Jampa does not understand it. He thought I would hang his painting on the wall and put my name under it, didn't he?" I asked him what he meant by high-end thangkas. Thondup stopped in front of the painting of the Green Tara. I could see Thondup had inherited some of Jampa's style—the deity's forehead was a bit longer, with two eyes farther apart, than how she was depicted by some other *lha zo*. "We are not supposed to change the iconography of the deity. It is written in Buddhist scriptures," Thondup said, "but as artists, we can think how to employ the subtlety of color to make the deity more divine." In other words, Thondup had updated Jampa's color palette. For this Green Tara, Thondup had chosen a darker shade of green—close to teal—as contrasted to Jampa's lighter emerald green to paint the body of the deity. He put the deity against a dark-blue head halo and a same-colored background, instead of using Jampa's sky blue. Moreover, Thondup used significantly fewer gold details than Jampa did in decorating the deity's halo and apparel.

"Do you know what is the problem with Jampa as well as many other painters in Rebgong?" said Thondup. "They have used too much gold." Thondup explained to us that Rebgong painters liked to say that one prominent feature of their regional style was the delicacy of the gold details. Over the years, the use of gold had been inflated. Clients or tourists who did not know much about Tibetan Buddhist art were easily sold by the shining or metallic finish and considered them "precious." Unfortunately, in Thondup's opinion, the overuse of gold details had obscured the texture and subtlety of the mineral pigments. "If you look at old thangkas, there are not many gold details. But their use of mineral color is mindful and sophisticated," Thondup said. "That's what makes the images long-lasting and divine." Thondup also criticized the use of bright or light colors in many Rebgong painters' work (including Jampa's).[14] In his opinion, many painters did not think carefully about how to use real colors; instead, they covered everything with gold details. The careless combination of bright colors and gold decorations, in Thondup's words, "has downgraded thangkas to *nian hua* [Ch. New Year paintings] or *min su hua* [Ch. folk paintings]."

At that moment, a young man came into the gallery. He addressed Thondup as *shi xiong*—a Chinese term that in some cases means they are disciples of the same Buddhist teacher (Osburg 2020, 75), or it could simply mean they both practice Tibetan Buddhism. Thondup introduced him to us as Mr. Gu, who had studied in France for six years and now operated a publishing company in Shanghai. Thondup invited us to sit around the coffee table and boiled water to make tea. While waiting, Gu told Thondup that he had met his guru, who said some of his disciples would be interested in seeing Thondup's thangkas. "You know what the guru told other *shi xiong*?" Gu said. "He said, if you want to invest in art, invest in Tibetan thangkas; they not only rise in value like modern art, but they also bring you and your family merits and protection." Thondup nodded, making a praying gesture to show his gratitude. As Thondup skillfully poured the amber-colored oolong into our cups, he said, "There is another reason why I call it high-end thangka."

Thondup pointed his fingers around and said: "Look at this place. This is Shanghai's most expensive district. It costs a fortune to operate an art gallery here. Everything sold in this gallery has to be marketed to high-end clients." According to Thondup, his high-end clients were wealthy people in China, in some cases including foreign nationals but rarely Tibetans. Thondup's Rome was not built in one day. Since he had previously operated as an art dealer in Gansu, he had been deliberately establishing networks with *kuo lao ban* (Ch. wealthy entrepreneurs) from different places in China. Thondup would agree with Caple (2020) and Osburg (2020) that many of these rich people practice Tibetan Buddhism—in particular, the wealthiest are often disciples of the most-venerated guru. Although Thondup's ethnicity is Mongolian in the official record, he often identifies himself as Tibetan since he speaks Tibetan, practices Tibetan Buddhism, and makes Tibetan religious art. With his Mandarin skills—certainly a plus—he conveniently became the liaison between some religious teachers and their affluent disciples.

This was how Thondup got to know the owner of the gallery in Shanghai as well as Gu and his guru. It also explained why most paintings in his show were tagged with a five-digit price in RMB. "Jampa doesn't understand it," Thondup repeated his remark. "We can't sell Tibetan thangkas as tourist souvenirs. They are precious to us Tibetans. We need to make it expensive and high-end." I glanced at the books Thondup kept on his coffee table, *Art Collection*, *Art Today*, and a recent catalog of an auction house in Beijing—Thondup had done his homework. "When I invited *ge gen* Jampa to my show, I wanted him to see what I am doing, to see the market," Thondup said. "Jampa and many other Rebgong painters compete by lowering their price and think it will attract clients. It's shortsighted. Jampa should learn how to network." In that sense, the gallery was operated as a clubhouse. The show was targeted to a specific group of people—the wealthy non-Tibetans who practiced Tibetan Buddhism—and excluded tourists, middlemen, and general audiences like those who go to the thangka show in the National Art Museum.

In Thondup's practice, as well as in monk Rinchen's case, the exhibition and circulation of Tibetan thangka paintings is only part of a larger social practice in contemporary China, where art, wealth, beliefs, and social status intersect with one another (Yü 2012; Osburg 2013, 2020). Unlike Maori art that might "have been 'invented' through museums" (McCarthy 2013, 176) or Australian Aboriginal paintings that are made as "efficacious performances of an identity and of rights that the viewer/recipient should recognize" (Myers 2002, 5–6), Tibetan thangkas are not specifically produced, or "invented," for high-end non-Tibetan consumers.[15] Artworks in Thondup's show are not secularized either, in contrast to many government-organized exhibits or expos. The authenticity of Tibetan thangkas, pursued by Thondup's audiences, is not simply evidenced in the artist's brushwork or the quality of pigments but is essentially endorsed by word of mouth within a social circle. Thondup's circle consists of people who have the privilege to sit on an elevated platform in the shade during a Tibetan monastery's dharma assembly, while local Tibetans sit on plastic sheets on the ground (Osburg 2020, 78).[16] The information and material objects circulated within this network are mediated by people like Gu's guru, who occasionally gives his disciples advice on investments, as well as by painters, art dealers, and counselors like Thondup who have various interests in this game.

Although the religious value of Tibetan thangkas is essential for Thondup and his clients, the audiences' pursuit of authenticity does not necessarily mean they see (or intend to see) Tibetan thangkas like Rebgong residents do. The eyes of a "cultivated individual" recognize the qualities of high art with aesthetic dispositions shaped by their own education, usually heavily influenced by Western aesthetics (Bourdieu 1984, 4–5). Like the sophisticated African traders in Côte d'Ivoire who manipulate their objects to fit the expectations of Western collectors (Steiner 1995) or Maroon wood-carvers in French Guiana who create narratives of symbolism that confirm Western audiences' imagination (Price 2007), Thondup, both a painter and art dealer, knows exactly what his high-end clients are looking for—the "cultured habitus" (Bourdieu 1993, 257)—and tailors his thangka paintings (and his exhibition) to their aesthetic taste.

I do not know if Thondup appropriated Jampa's paintings during his early years in Gansu, but by the time he held a show in Shanghai, Thondup had already replaced Jampa's "folkish" art with a cosmopolitan representation of Tibetan religion and art. In Thondup's exhibit, there was no need for a lengthy description of what Tibetan thangka is (his patrons were informed) or when Rebgong thangka became a national or international ICH (which his patrons might find irrelevant). Labeling himself as a "Himalayan artist," Thondup positioned himself in a larger artistic circle beyond the community of regional thangka painters. Of course, the incense, cattail cushions, and freshly brewed oolong helped too, which boosted him to a higher level of the social circle—African traders in Côte d'Ivoire or shopkeepers in the Tibetan market in Chengdu know it well.

After I returned to Rebgong, Jampa was interested in knowing about Thondup's exhibition. "No, I don't think he appropriated your paintings for the show." I gave it to him straight. Jampa laughed. I described Thondup's exhibition and told him what Thondup meant by "high-end."

"He thinks we use too much gold, doesn't he?" Jampa asked.

"For the taste of his clients," I responded.

"You know what?" Jampa joked (or not). "I think it is because he himself is not good at painting gold details—he only stayed with me for two years!"

Water and Land Ritual Paintings

In my conversation with Tashi Gyatso and Chodrak, brothers and *lha zo* from Sengeshong, they often mention the phrase *lha bzo dngos ma zhig* in Tibetan or *zhen zheng de yi shu jia* in Chinese, which can be roughly translated as a "true artist." To them neither the label "ethnic craft" nor "high-end art" could fully illuminate the future for Rebgong thangka paintings. Painters like them believe that innovation in Tibetan thangka has always been part of the art making practice, instead of a response to the government's requests or the market's preference. Rebgong *lha zo* have certain room to exercise their creativity "but not for its own sake," as creativity or innovation is understood in European or modern art (Linrothe 2001, 16). The creativity of *lha zo* in thangka painting is not necessarily at odds with religious protocols either (Jackson and Jackson 1988, 40–42; Linrothe 2015). Tashi Gyatso and Chodrak's recent project *Water and Land Ritual Paintings* exemplifies how painters define the notion of art beyond the framework of ICH or commodification and suggests rethinking the concept of creativity in the context of Buddhist art.

In 2017 the abbot of Xiantong Temple at Mount Wutai first mentioned to Tashi Gyatso and Chodrak the idea of commissioning a set of *Water and Land Ritual Paintings*. This set of ritual paintings is used in the Water and Land Retreat (Ch. *shui lu fa hui*), or the Liberation Rite of Water and Land (Ch. *shui lu pu du zhai hui*), one of the most elaborate rituals in Chinese Buddhism (Dai 2009; Bloom 2013).[17] Ostensibly a Buddhist ritual, the Water and Land Retreat offers devotees an opportunity to "save their ancestors, rebalance the relationship between humans and ghosts, and ensure the stability of their connections to the cosmos more generally" (Bloom 2013, 13–14). Therefore, the images used in the Water and Land Retreat not only depict the Buddha and Buddhist deities but also assimilate figures from Daoism, Confucianism, folklore, and this-worldly people.[18] Because of Mount Wutai's prestige and the merit-making nature of this ritual, an increasing number of devotees from all over China participate in the Water and Land Retreat held in Xiantong Temple annually. Xiantong Temple had a set of the *Water and Land Ritual Paintings*, which was made in the 1980s when religious institutions and practices were recovering from the Cultural Revolution. The abbot, however, was not satisfied with the painting because the artistic quality was rough and many of the contents were incorrect.

The abbot had sought a couple of Han painters to do the work. Their sketches were unsatisfying as well, largely because they did not know much about the religious meaning of the images. These painters had to copy existing images; thus, their work inevitably contained mistakes or negligence that the abbot had tried to avoid. The abbot found it very hard to explain to these painters what he expected to see on canvas, since he knew little about painting while these painters knew little about the Water and Land Retreat or Buddhism in general. The abbot turned to Tashi Gyatso and Chodrak, who had been making mural paintings, thangka scrolls, and sculptures for various temples at Mount Wutai. In particular, they spent a few years working on the life story of Buddha Shakyamuni, a set of fifty-four thangkas commissioned by Tayuan Temple in the late 2000s. The abbot of Xiantong Temple was impressed by the brothers' artistic skills and, more important, by their ability to visualize religious texts on painting in a faithful and thoughtful way. The abbot showed Tashi Gyatso and Chodrak the *Water and Land Ritual Paintings* he had and told them he expected them to do better. The brothers at first hesitated, unsure if they could produce liturgical painting for practices in Chinese Buddhism. When the abbot told them that "not many painters today could command such a work," they accepted the commission.

Back in Rebgong, Tashi Gyatso and Chodrak realized they had accepted an unprecedented challenge. Although the content and composition of *Water and Land Ritual Paintings* have many similarities with Tibetan thangka paintings, certain figures and aesthetic details in Chinese art were new to them. As the Water and Land Retreat had spread widely across China (e.g., to Sichuan, Yunnan, Zhejiang, and Shanxi), the practices and images associated with the ritual had developed regional variants too. It made the conformity between the image and text less clear (Bloom 2013, 23–25), or at least not as rigid as the iconographic and iconometric rules in producing Tibetan Buddhist art. To make things worse, many old paintings, murals, statues, steles, and scriptures had been lost, especially during the Cultural Revolution. Besides the set of paintings made in the 1980s, the abbot of Xiantong Temple could only provide the brothers four collated volumes of the *Water and Land Ritual Protocols* (Ch. *shui lu yi gui hui ben*; hereafter "the *Protocols*"), with the last volume giving the guidance on making *Water and Land Ritual Paintings*.

Tashi Gyatso and Chodrak recruited another pair of hands—their Han apprentice Fan Qingji (b. 1984, known as Fan), who came to Rebgong in 2011 and has been staying with them and learning thangka painting ever since. Fan had a professional degree in art and specialized in Western oil painting. He worked for an animation company for some time before he came to Rebgong and became obsessed with Tibetan thangka art. With both a diviner's approval and Fan's determination, demonstrated through quitting his animation job, Tashi Gyatso and Chodrak accepted Fan as their *ge truk*. Fan is a talented student, also hardworking. Although Fan was a little too old to start thangka painting from scratch, he caught up quickly and had mastered the painting skills after seven years in Rebgong. Just when Fan thought he had freed himself from his previous training in Western oil painting and found a rebirth in Tibetan art, his *ge gen* presented him with the project of *Water and Land Ritual Paintings*.

The three of them studied the *Protocols* together, especially the last volume, in which religious figures and compositions of the paintings were described. In Fan's words, the *Protocols* read more "like a roster"—it gave the names of all kinds of beings and their places (Ch. *pai wei*) on the painting but very little information about "what they look like, what they wear, what their personalities are, or what their relationships are with other figures in the ritual." Whereas Fan perceived *Water and Land Ritual Paintings* as group photos, like those taken at a conference or a graduation ceremony, Tashi Gyatso and Chodrak wanted stories incorporated in the painting. Fan soon realized the task was far more complicated than what Tashi Gyatso had initially told him, not just "like painting the *Wheel of Existence* [Tib. *srid pa'i 'khor lo*] in thangka." Tashi Gyatso had said so probably because he did not want to discourage Fan from participating. But on the other hand, making something like the *Wheel of Existence* was the brothers' initial estimation when they accepted this commission from the abbot. The brothers now needed to make a decision: they and Fan could make a set of *Water and Land Ritual Paintings* relying on their knowledge of Tibetan Buddhism and Tibetan art—so the final product would be in Tibetan style. Alternatively, they could venture into a new terrain of liturgical art making but work with the same level of sophistication as they paint Tibetan thangkas, which requires reading Buddhist scriptures, researching different art styles, and redesigning the entire set of seventy-six paintings. Tashi Gyatso and Chodrak chose the latter.

With Fan's help, his *ge gen*'s bookshelves were quickly overwhelmed by new additions such as *Shanxi Painted Sculptures* (Ch. *shan xi gu dai cai su*), *The Manual of the Mustard Seed Garden* (Ch. *jie zi yuan tu pu*), *The Collection of Dunhuang Wall Paintings* (Ch. *zhong guo dun huang bi hua quan ji*), and *The Five Hundred Arhats by Kano Kazunobu* (Ch. *shou ye yi xin: wu bai luo han tu*). They also searched for possible images associated with the Water and Land Retreat online, from museums' digital collections, libraries, academic publications, and auction house catalogs.[19] Because the images from different sources varied greatly in style and quality, Tashi Gyatso and Chodrak did not think they could simply copy or adapt any existing painting.[20] The brothers decided to make their own design. Based on the *Protocols*, Tashi Gyatso, Chodrak, and Fan organized the figures into different groups and sketched the image of individual figures by referring to previous paintings and sculptures of a particular group (e.g., Guanyin images, arhat paintings, Confucius's portraits). This had forced them to do intensive research on Chinese art and to scrutinize Tibetan thangkas and Chinese paintings in a comparative perspective (figure 8).

In this process, Tashi Gyatso and Chodrak made several adjustments in their painting style. For instance, the scale of a Tibetan deity is usually larger (according to Tashi Gyatso, the height is about eight and a half heads) than a Chinese deity (whose height equals seven and a half heads), which is closer to the proportion of a real person. The stomach and pelvis of Tibetan deities are also wider than their Chinese counterparts. Tashi Gyatso and Chodrak believe that religious images need to evoke faith, conviction, and enthusiasm from viewers who worship them. Therefore, they adjusted the iconometrics they used to paint Tibetan deities and adapted the body proportion to be closer to the aesthetics of Chinese devotees.[21]

The use of color was another area for which the three artists made technical adjustments, though they still drew from the same set of mineral pigments applied in thangkas. While many Rebgong painters prefer the technique of

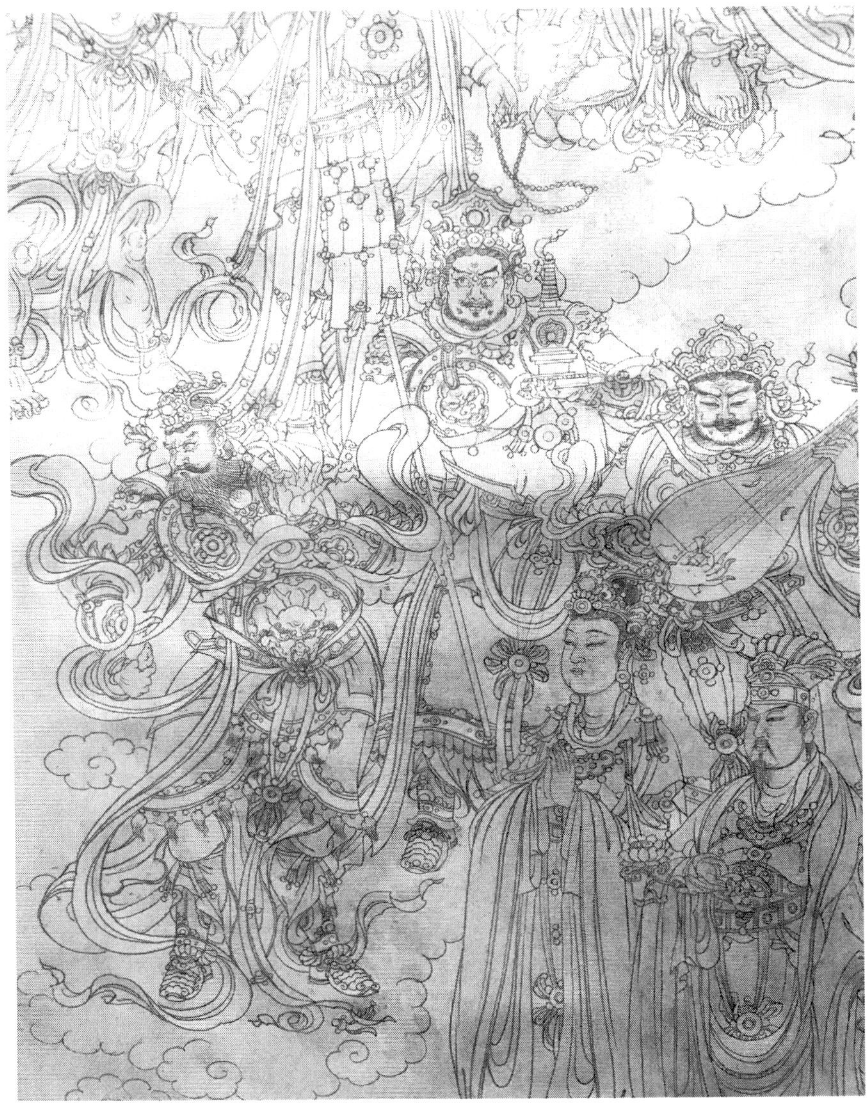

FIGURE 8 Tashi Gyatso, Chodrak, and Fan's pencil sketch on canvas for the Water and Land Ritual paintings, 2018.

dry shading (Tib. *skam mdangs*) in coloring sky and landscape in thangka paintings—applying dye washes to a dry surface, one layer over another—Fan increasingly used wet shading (Tib. *rlon mdangs*), "the gradual blending of two adjoining areas of wet paint," to color trees, lands, and clouds in their *Water and Land Ritual Paintings* because it gave "an unbroken, smooth field of colour" (Jackson and Jackson 1988, 98). Tashi Gyatso and Chodrak might have agreed with Thondup, the high-end artist who considered the use of gold as excessive in Rebgong thangka paintings. Tashi Gyatso and Chodrak restrained the amount of gold embellishments in their *Water and Land Ritual Paintings*, yet they incorporated the technique of adding gold details, using a darker shade of the color, instead of gold, to delineate floral or decorative patterns on clothing and ribbons. It gave the final product a sophisticated look and maintained its splendor (Ch. *zhuang yan*).[22]

Besides technical adjustments, the three artists also had some leeway to exercise their creativity in designing the content and composition of their *Water and Land Ritual Paintings*. Unlike some people' understandings that the scripture or the *Protocols* prescribe every detail in a painting, in some cases an artist's creativity is welcomed or even expected, as indicated in the scripture. For instance, in the fourth volume of the *Protocols*, the page describing the "Thirteenth Seat in the Lower Hall" (Ch. *xia tang di shi san xi*) explains:

> For this seat, it feels regrettable to only write down the names and places instead of to paint them. The *Water and Land Retreat* is a spectacular event. We need to carefully arrange objects and perform rituals according to the rules for the *Retreat* to be rigorous. Painters are instructed to produce three paintings, illustrating where the main altar is, where the inner alter is, and other settings of the monastery. The paintings should also include the monks, who perform chanting, incense burning, and candle lightening, as well as other personnel who assist the ritual. The painting should help the patrons who view them strengthen their faith and veneration. The image can be tailored to specific monasteries, with the painters' skillful arrangement of details.[23]

In one scroll for the "Thirteenth Seat in the Lower Hall," Tashi Gyatso, Chodrak, and Fan situated the scene of the Water and Land Retreat in Xiantong Temple, with clothing and architectural features roughly indicating the

Song dynasty (plate 8).[24] In the center of the painting, they depicted Xian-tong Temple's Grand Hall (Ch. *da xiong bao dian*). Inside the hall, two groups of monks are seated on each side, chanting Buddhist scriptures, while the patron (the back view of an emperor) and his family sit in front of the statue of Buddha Shakyamuni, Buddha Dipankara, and Buddha Maitreya. The top part of the painting depicts heavenly maidens riding on auspicious clouds and listening to the Buddhist teaching. Two human guards stand outside the gate of the Grand Hall. The ministers and devotees sit or kneel in the outdoor square. After the chanting and teaching, the monks circumambulate the Grand Hall and eventually walk out of the enclosure. The bottom part of the painting illustrates a scene of monks chanting Buddhist scriptures while laypeople pray and burn votive offerings.

In this scroll the three artists did not fully engage in either the scattered perspective used in Tibetan thangkas or the linear perspective used in Western oil paintings. According to them, they referred to the composition of the Qing dynasty painting *All Dharma Converge to One* (Ch. *wan fa gui yi tu*)—the viewpoint extends from the Grand Hall in the middle of the painting to distant mountains and clouds depicted at the top.[25] In specific parts of the painting, they largely adapted the techniques of Zhang Zeduan (1085–1145) in his panoramic painting *Along the River during the Qingming Festival* (Ch. *qing ming shang he tu*) and Sun Wen (1818–1904) in illustrating the scenes from the novel *Dream of the Red Chamber* (Ch. *hong lou meng*).[26] In this way they could clearly show to the viewer how objects were arranged and how rituals were performed, as expected by the *Protocols*.

Another challenge was to illustrate the procedure of this elaborated ritual within the bounds of three paintings. Tashi Gyatso and Chodrak applied a narrative style known as synoptic narrative in this scroll, which depicts a single scene but with characters appearing multiple times in various places to convey the meaning that multiple actions are taking place.[27] This was not the first time Tashi Gyatso and Chodrak had illustrated a synoptic narrative. In the thangka depicting the life story of Buddha Shakyamuni, Tashi Gyatso skillfully arranged three stories together on one scroll, including the Buddha's descent from the Tushita heaven, entering the womb of his mother, and being born in the Lumbini garden (plate 9).[28] On the top of the painting, Tashi Gyatso depicted the scene in which the Buddha came down to the earth in the form of a white elephant. With rainbows descending from the sky and traveling through a tree, our view is directed to the bottom right of the painting, where Queen Maya, Shakyamuni's mother, conceived him as she dreamed of an elephant entering her right side. Queen Maya appears again in the middle of the painting, standing and grasping the tree in the garden, giving birth to Shakyamuni. The child, fully formed, emerges from Maya's right side in a sitting position. He appears the second time on the bottom left of the painting, in a walking position, taking seven steps generating a path of lotus flowers. Although the sequence of events is not always clear in synoptic narratives, especially to viewers without any background knowledge of the story being shown, the choice of such a style is proper in depicting both the life story of Buddha Shakyamuni and the *Water and Land Ritual Paintings* since the images are meant to accompany the teaching of Buddhist scriptures.[29]

It took Tashi Gyatso, Chodrak, and Fan a year to sketch a few designs and send them to the abbot of Xiantong Temple. The abbot was very pleased with their work and planned to hold a consecration ceremony at Mount Wutai for the paintings upon their completion. The compensation offered by the monastery for this commission was similar to the brothers' other monastic commissions for their thangka paintings. As Fan put it, doing an innovative project like this was like "burning money" because the research behind the art making not only required buying books but also involved traveling to other places to observe mural paintings or museum collections and inviting scholars and specialists to Rebgong to review their work. Tashi Gyatso and Chodrak used the income from "selling" thangkas to affluent patrons to nurture their monastic commissions, including this creative project.

As the three artists proceeded with this project, they became more confident and excited. One initial worry of Tashi Gyatso and Chodrak was of possible criticism for Tibetanizing ritual paintings in Chinese Buddhism. This worry was less about political discourse than about reinforcing the misperception that Rebgong painters were specialized artisans who painted everything like thangkas. Tashi Gyatso and Chodrak learned from their *ge gen* Jigme Chokyong (Tib. *'Jigs med chos skyong*, 1901–88), a monk *lha zo* who had painted for the ninth and the tenth Panchen Lama, that being a *lha zo* means much more than making painted scrolls. A *lha zo* has the responsibility to produce the image of the sacred that brings merits and power to the patron in need and evokes faith and virtue from viewers. To do so, artists are not necessarily constrained as to the medium, material, or art style they can use. But it is very important for thangka painters to understand the religious teaching and to develop the image from the religious text by relying on their sophisticated art skills. This is how Tashi Gyatso and Chodrak understand the meaning of the true artist.

The *Water and Land Ritual Paintings* gave Tashi Gyatso and Chodrak an opportunity to step out of the realm of Tibetan art and carefully study Chinese art and even Western art. Fan also learned from this process that his past training in Western oil painting was not meant to be forgotten but to be connected to other styles and traditions. On some evenings Tashi Gyatso and Chodrak asked Fan to hold workshops for all the apprentices by showing them slides of artwork from different genres, not only Chinese bird-and-flower paintings but also the work of Henri Matisse, Pablo Picasso, and Piet Mondrian. Fan occasionally explained the differences between Tibetan thangka and Chinese painting by demonstrating the sketch they had done for *Water and Land Ritual Paintings* using a projector. Tashi Gyatso and Chodrak wanted their *ge truk* to know other types of art, not necessarily to command one but to position their practice within broader art history.

For the same reason, in their art school, the boundary between Tibetan and non-Tibetan art was still carefully maintained. While Tashi Gyatso and Chodrak chose to use a variety of low-saturation colors in their *Water and Land Ritual Paintings*—a color palette close to paintings produced in the Song dynasty—they insisted on following the Tibetan rules of mixing and arranging colors for thangka paintings. Although Tashi Gyatso and Chodrak were burdened with various responsibilities, they tried to keep their morning routine—reviewing and correcting sketches their apprentices had done the past evening and telling stories or reciting scriptures associated with the image while making the corrections. They were aware that any careless mixing of art styles could bring bad karma to both the patron and the *lha zo*. Just like Shawo Tsering, who came back from Dunhuang realizing the importance of Rebgong's regional art tradition, Tashi Gyatso and Chodrak held tightly to that tradition. They knew it was their foundation from which to explore art making in other realms with the same level of sophistication and excellence as they painted thangkas.

The "True Artist"

Over the past few decades, anthropologists have offered their critiques on the definition of *art* by recontextualizing non-Western arts circulated and displayed beyond their local communities. For instance, Clifford's "art-culture system" (1988) seems increasingly problematic because in this system, "to qualify as art, an object cannot be collective but must be expressive of a more sublime characteristic that subordinates other properties to individual creativity" (Myers 2004, 6). It causes controversies if we see Australian Aboriginal paintings not as results of individual creativity but as materializations of people's relationship with their landscape and history (Myers 2002) or acknowledge the fact that male wood-carvers in Guiana have to fabricate an innovative interpretation for the art traditionally made for their wives and lovers but now admired by Western consumers (Price 2007). We can also question who is entitled to deliver the "serious speech" in the tradition of Indian paintings and the evaluation of artwork (Bundgaard 1999).

Far from being "dead" (Errington 1998; C. Harris 2012, 10), the regional art tradition in Rebgong is carried on by contemporary *lha zo* and constantly evolves over time. As we can see from *The Great Thangka* or Thondup's show in Shanghai, art making in Rebgong does not strictly follow the protocols of monastic patronage, nor is it entirely dictated by the government. The destabilized category of art causes much ambiguity for Rebgong *lha zo* (as it does for anthropologists) as they try to define themselves in their practice of art making and exhibition. Being situated in these "plural ecologies" (Weller and Wu 2021), Rebgong painters find various ways to negotiate space for art making in accordance with their own understandings of art—the heterogeneity I illustrate in this book is an important aspect of art making in today's Rebgong.

It is usually easier to define art by what it is not than articulating what it is. To monk Rinchen, thangka art is not a souvenir or a piece of home decor purchased or distributed at will. What makes it art is the religious meaning, or karma, associated with the painting. Although Rinchen is able to fight against many misperceptions of Tibetan art by finding or cultivating clients in his own way, he chooses to play the role of a safe and true painter whose works are worth collecting or commissioning. Like Rinchen, many other painters resist characterizing thangka painting as an ethnic craft; instead, they internalize the popular imagination of Tibetan thangka or thangka painters in their practice (Schein 1997; Luo, Oakes, and Schein 2019), such as hiding their Xerox machines and zipping their mouths about their economic incentives in art making. Thondup makes a more ambitious move. While he is certain that none of his high-end clients would be so careless as to put a thangka painting in the bathroom, he wants to make sure they understand that a thangka is precious to Tibetans. Therefore, he makes the artwork expensive, in the sense that the painting lacks a folkish flavor and the price is high. Thondup might not be the best painter in terms of artistic achievement, but because the art world "has never been driven by purely aesthetic considerations" (Price 2007, 613), Thondup nonetheless views himself a successful artist. He is able to boost himself and his artworks to a high-end social circle not by demonstrating unparalleled art skills but by packaging and networking in the realm of money-mediated spirituality.

As in other cases of ritual art making (Kendall, Yang, and Yoon 2015; Geertz 2004; Kendall 2021), the complex protocols of art production make Rebgong thangka art seem innately conservative, leaving little room for individual creativity. Moreover, the ICH discourse disproportionally emphasizes the preservation of the art form, thereby reinforcing the misperception that thangka painters are merely copyists. But some Rebgong *lha zo* challenge this perception and push us to rethink the notion of creativity in the context of Buddhist art making. In Buddhist art, innovations are not necessarily at odds with the religious function, as long as creativity does not come "at the expense of the religious intentions of the artist and patron or the functions of the work of art in its totality" (Linrothe 2001, 16; also see Kieschnick 2003). When Tashi Gyatso and Chodrak point out that innovation has always been part of the art making practice, they mean that beyond technical improvements, a painter should be able to imagine and create a visual representation for the story or scene that exists in the scripture only as text. This is exemplified in Tashi Gyatso's thangka painting depicting the life story of Buddha Shakyamuni as well as in the *Water and Land Ritual Paintings*. Such a level of creativity requires a painter not only to be familiar with Buddhist iconographies and iconometric rules but also to have substantial knowledge of religious texts to be able to depict figures in action, arrange the composition, and utilize the appropriate narrative style.

History replicates itself in an interesting way. Although the *Water and Land Ritual Paintings* are used in the ritual of Chinese Buddhism, Tashi Gyatso, Chodrak, and Fan were able to produce a set of works with the same level of sophistication as their thangka paintings. Like what Shawo Tsering and his fellow painters accomplished in Dunhuang eighty years ago, again it seems that only Rebgong *lha zo* can decipher the message embedded in Buddhist scriptures and visual images and translate them back and forth in skillful and thoughtful ways (or "shan qiao," as indicated in the *Protocols*). Nonetheless, Rebgong artists' accomplishment should not be celebrated as an example of individual creativity as venerated in the European or the modern art world. Tashi Gyatso and Chodrak understand the depth of their roots. The brothers' art journey was initiated during the art renaissance in Rebgong and was nurtured by both monastic patronage and predecessors like Shawo Tsering and their *ge gen* Jigme Chokyong. Rebgong's choice of not taking the same route as Garze's New Tibetan Painting as well as its later participation in the ICH discourse also ensure that some aspects of the art tradition are preserved and transmitted. Although commodification and secularization seem to have reconfigured Rebgong thangka art in powerful ways, new patrons—like monk Rinchen's Shanxi patron, Thondup's high-end clients, and Tashi Gyatso and Chodrak's affluent collectors—have, to various extents, sponsored the religious aspects of thangka painting and artists' innovation in Buddhist art making.

Besides contesting the Western notion of creativity, the practice of Tashi Gyatso and Chodrak also challenges the definition of tradition, or how the ICH discourse has defined the boundaries between tangible forms of cultural heritage. In that sense Tashi Gyatso and Chodrak have taken a step further than Shawo Tsering. Through working on their *Water and Land Ritual Paintings*, Tashi Gyatso and Chodrak opened themselves up to other forms of art making, by observing, studying, and comparing images from various sources and taking advantage of modern technologies. It helps them situate Tibetan thangka art in art history more broadly as well as to know their uniqueness and constraints as artists. While many modern artists consider religious protocols as imposing restrictions on art making, artists like Tashi Gyatso and Chodrak, who are equipped with profound religious knowledge and sophisticated visual language, rely on such structures to free their creativity—the qualification of a true artist.

CHAPTER 6

The Life of a Painting

A passage from Pema Tseden's short fiction leads us to the Tibetan world of death and memories and indicates the role of art making in people's spiritual lives: "The next day, the tulku invited seven monks from nearby monasteries to chant scriptures for seven days and seven nights. After that, the old stone carver never appeared in Lobsang's dreams. Sometimes, on a night when the moon was big, round, and bright, when drunken Lobsang went home alone, he could hear someone was chiseling mani stones from afar, silent, like a ballad without words" (2014, 30).[1]

Not all Rebgong thangkas leave the community for the external or intermediate markets or monasteries near and far. Some paintings are made, used, and kept within lay communities in Rebgong, exemplified by thangkas made for the deceased family member—the *kye go* (Tib. *skyes sgo*) thangka, or "thangka for rebirth."[2] The *kye go* image is crucial in Tibetan death rituals; it is "the second main reason for the commissioning [of] *thang kas* in the Tibetan world," pointed out by Tibetologist Erberto Lo Bue (2017, 9).[3] In Rebgong, where the *kye go* thangka is often executed by the deceased person's own family member(s), or in some cases by relatives or close friends in the same village, the making of *kye go* thangka itself is an important aspect of mourning. To produce an efficacious *kye go* image and to hold an appropriate funeral— essentially a communal event in Rebgong—becomes particularly important when more and more of the elderly have passed away "unexpectedly" outside their village homes (e.g., because they were in a hospital for medical treatment or had moved away from the valley).

Encounters with *kye go* thangkas in Rebgong lead us to consider an often neglected area in the anthropology of art: the production and distribution of the so-called traditional or functional arts. Even when *lha zo* produce for their "own people," the physical material, the painter's artistic skills, the workshop's reputation, and the art maker's intention each play a crucial role in making an image that works.

At a time when Buddhist and monastic authority are being challenged by social, economic, and political changes taking place in Tibetan communities, when art making in Rebgong is commoditized and secularized by the state, and when the spiritual power of lamas and monks is increasingly appropriated by non-Tibetans who follow and practice Tibetan Buddhism, the making of *kye go* thangkas, together with practices associated with death and mourning, has special connotations for residents in Rebgong. In Pema Tseden's story, the sound of stone chiseling is a call to people's beliefs and hopes. For Rebgong *lha zo*, that call is manifested on their canvases. Painters' practices in producing *kye go* thangkas as well as the building of family shrine rooms, or *cho khang* (Tib. *mchod khang*), where *kye go* images are kept, demonstrate their under-standings of efficacy and complexity in their response to change. The *kye go* thangka is not only a painting that assists funeral rites, but it is also an image that stores personal stories, family memories, and local histories, kept and viewed by local residents as an "anchor" (Kipnis 2021, 92) when many things around them are changing.

The *Kye Go* Thangka

It was the coldest summer for Jampa. When I saw him in July, Jampa was wearing a black down jacket. He sat on the floor in his living room. Next to him was a canvas mounted on a stretcher, with a few sketched lines in charcoal—he was painting a thangka. It was not just any thangka but a *kye go* thangka. Jampa was making this painting for Ama, his mother, who had died a few days earlier.

Ama's death came as a surprise to all of us. She was still young, in her midfifties, and in good health. In previous years, when we performed *cho kor*, she was able to carry a full load of Buddhist scriptures on her back and cir-cumambulate the entire village. According to Jampa, Ama started complaining that her stomach hurt in late spring. Jampa took her to visit both the Tibetan medicine specialist in town and to the prefecture hospital. After a series of examinations, they were told that Ama's condition was not good and that they should seek better diagnosis in Xining. With help from a relative who worked in the prefecture hospital, Ama was admitted to a hospital in Xining, where she was soon diagnosed with pancreatic cancer. Jampa stayed in Xining to take care of Ama while she was hospitalized for treatment. But in less than two weeks, Ama's condition had deteriorated. Very soon, death claimed her.

Jampa immediately took Ama's body back to Rebgong. He asked a lama in the village monastery to divine the cremation time as well as the content of Ama's *kye go* thangka, which would be consecrated and used at the *gong dzok* (Tib. *dgongs rdzogs*), a funeral rite held forty-nine days following Ama's death.[4] The cremation, assisted by monks and male villagers, was held outside the village soon after Jampa took Ama back to Rebgong. After the cremation, Jampa took Ama's ashes back home and invited a group of monks from the village monastery to chant scriptures for her. Relatives, neighbors, and families in the same *tso wa* came to help with cooking for the monks, lighting butter lamps, offering purified water, turning prayer wheels, and reciting prayers. The monks chanted scriptures at Jampa's home for seven days. After that, Jampa took Ama's ashes to the village monastery, where the monks continued chanting for her for another fourteen days. The day when I returned to Rebgong and met Jampa was the last day of the monks' chanting at his home. Jampa had just started to sketch the *kye go* thangka.

According to the lama's divination, the central figure on Ama's *kye go* thangka was a tantric deity, who has profound healing and purification powers. Following the lama's advice, Jampa put the Medicine Buddha (Tib. *sangs rgyas sman bla*) above the main deity, with the Shartshang lama of the Rongwo Monastery and the tulku of Gasar's village monastery on each side of the Medicine Buddha. Because this thangka was dedicated to his mother, Jampa chose to paint the three deities of long life—White Tara (Tib. *sgrol dkar*), Amitayus (Tib. *tshe dpag med*), and Ushnishavijaya (Tib. *rnam rgyal ma*)—below the main deity. In the funeral rites, lamas and monks who chanted scriptures in front of the *kye go* thangka not only recruited deities to help purify Ama's karmic sins but also reminded her to follow the deities and religious teachers who could guide her on the journey toward a good rebirth.

Painters in Rebgong exercise tremendous care when painting a *kye go* thangka. Any negligence or mistake not only affects the efficacy of the painting but also delays the painting progress—it is crucial for the deceased that the *kye go* thangka is completed within forty-nine days, the transitional period between death and rebirth. Yet this is challenging for most painters. Jampa did not remember when he had last slept or if he had slept at all. As the only son in the family, Jampa had to take care of everything: bringing Ama's body back from Xining, arranging the divination and cremation, inviting monks, preparing objects and offerings to be used in the funeral rites, and of course, chanting scriptures for Ama whenever he could. Drolma, Jampa's wife, was exhausted too. Squeezing time between chanting, cooking, cleaning, child-care, and receiving guests, Drolma helped Jampa prepare the canvas, applying one layer of gesso over another, polishing the surface with a bowl until it became smooth as silk. But when Jampa picked up a charcoal and started drawing, he found the lines blurring in front of his eyes. His eyes were red and burning, probably from too much crying or sheer exhaustion. Jampa put down the charcoal and closed his eyes, leaning his head against the pillar in the middle of the living room. He started reciting prayers, but tears fell again.

Funeral as a Communal Experience in Rebgong

From the very beginning of my fieldwork, Rebgong interlocutors, lay or monastic, told me over and over how difficult it was to be reborn as a human. "The chance to return to the next life as a human," said a painter, "is extremely low, even lower than the opportunity for a blind turtle living deep in the ocean, who only takes its breath on the surface once every century, to by chance put its head into a floating yoke when it pops up from the water for air."[5] Stories like this instruct people to avoid harmful deeds and accumulate virtue through acts of charity, such as donating to monasteries and building stupas, to ensure a better rebirth.

All schools of Buddhism consider that the indulgence in this-worldly plea-sure and material possession spurs suffering, which binds individuals to the endless cycle of death and rebirth (Skt. *samsara*, Tib. *'khor ba*, Ch. *lun hui*). Enlightened beings are freed from such a cycle, entering the transcendent state of nirvana (Tib. *mya ngan las 'das pa*, Ch. *nie pan*), the final goal of Bud-dhism. The unenlightened ones are drawn by their karma, the cause and effect of actions, into a new life in one of six modes of existence: as a hell being, a hungry ghost, an animal, a human being, a demigod, or a god (Germano 2007; Lopez 2018). Tibetans call the forty-nine days' interim period between death and rebirth *bar do* (literally "between two").[6] During this transitional state, the deceased becomes conscious about their death, encounters confusion and frightening apparitions, and is eventually liberated from samsara (though this is very rare) or finds rebirth. Charlene Makley describes a good Buddhist death as "a chosen, well-accompanied, and divinely protected journey of the consciousness (Tib. *rnam shes*) through precisely timed stages of separation from the body and the household" (2018, 227). It takes a village to achieve this (Craig 2020, 228).

The living family members have to rely on monks as essential agents to help the deceased embark on her or his future journeys. The food and offerings made to monks will be transferred as merits to the deceased (Lopez 2004, 330). Monks assembling at the funeral recite prayers and chant scriptures to offer the deceased guidance and purification (Makley 2018, 228). This reciprocal nature of the relationship between the monastics and the laity is not just established for any specific event but is maintained and nurtured in everyday life (Makley 2007, 150).[7] Lay families regularly take the responsibility of cooking and cleaning for their monks as well as contributing labor and money to the maintenance and renovation of the village monastery. In turn, monks are expected to offer prayers and protection for the laity—death is a particular case in which monks' intervention is necessary and crucial. At various stages of the funeral, monks not only offer guidance and purification to the deceased but also act as patrons to "[host] deities on behalf of the deceased and for the specific communities the dead leave behind" (Makley 2018, 226). Because of this, no rural family in Rebgong, as far as I know, has ever sought alternative ways to hold the funeral, as happens in some other rapidly urbanizing areas in China (see, Kipnis 2021; Weller and Wu 2021).

In Tibet *lha zo* also play irreplaceable roles in assisting at funerals. A *kye go* thangka or statue is necessary and essential at the *gong dzok* (the ritual held on the forty-ninth day after the death) because monks need to summon deities and religious teachers, who are *present* in the image after consecration, to guide the deceased. "Without a *kye go* thangka, the deceased would get lost," said one Rebgong painter. Worse still, the lost soul would likely become an unruly ghost wandering around and causing trouble. Even during the Cultural Revolution, when almost all religious practices and Buddhist arts were banned, some painters, including Namgyal's father, took great risks and secretly made *kye go* thangkas for neighbors who had lost their loved ones. When in need, Namgyal's father brought a candle and a canvas to the inner room of the house and covered the windows with wooden boards. After Namgyal came back from school, his father instructed him not to tell anyone he was home or let any stranger in. Although the work produced under a dim light and in an intense atmosphere might not match the quality we see in Rebgong today, those *kye go* thangkas were treasured by the family, hung and venerated under the cover of night—they gave light for both the deceased and the living during the turbulence, when no one could predict the future.

In Rebgong's art making villages, it is usually convenient to have a family member, or members, execute the *kye go* image. But of course, families can commission a *kye go* thangka or statue from other village artists too, as long as the *lha zo* agrees to finish the work within forty-nine days. I was told there is a family in Sengeshong that has bad karma. For instance, the color of their thangka fades quickly or the surface of the painting cracks easily, even if they use the same materials as others. Villagers believe it is because during the Cultural Revolution, one of their family members did something horrific to the monastery and the monks. Although they paint thangkas now and constantly donate to the monastery, the sin of iconoclasm is not canceled out (see also Chen 2013, 220; Kendall 2021, 30–33). To paint a thangka with a cracked surface for an art collector might be an embarrassment, but to make a bad *kye go* thangka for a deceased family member would be a disaster. Therefore, this family commissioned *kye go* thangkas from other painters in the village, offering generous compensation in hopes of lifting their karma.

If the content of the *kye go* thangka is complex, relatives of the deceased may also recruit other painters to help work on the painting together. When Thondup's mother passed away, he was instructed to make a large thangka depicting the Buddha Shakyamuni and other deities. Thondup asked for help from *ge gen* Jampa, who is known for his proficiency and efficiency in making an image. Jampa paused the painting he was working on. He did the sketch and eventually "opened the eyes" for all the deities on Thondup mother's *kye go* thangka. Nevertheless, Rebgong painters consider painting the *kye go* thangka for their own deceased family member a crucial responsibility. Regardless of painting skills, living family members work on the *kye go* thangka as an essential way of mourning and assisting the deceased make the transition between worlds and between lives. When talking about thangkas made for "outsiders"—art merchants, collectors, or tourists—many painters emphasize the material or technique involved; sometimes they also comment on the aesthetics. But when it comes to *kye go* thangkas, painters care most about faith. "The faith will make it work [Tib. *blo dkar na don 'grub*]," a painter told me, "When I painted the *kye go* thangka for my deceased relative, I only thought about how to help them."

Because of this, Jampa insisted on painting Ama's *kye go* thangka on his own. But his work would not be possible without logistic help and social support from other villagers. As in other communal events, households in the same *tso wa* had at least one family member come to Jampa's home, bringing him *go re* (baked bread), tea bricks, and cash. According to Jampa's gift register, there were over thirty *tso wa* families who came and sent gifts, while a dozen more from other *tso wa and other villages* provided gifts and help for Ama's funeral. Ama's close relatives and friends (most of them elders) stayed at Jampa's house for several hours a day, chanting scriptures, making butter lamps, offering purified water, and turning prayer wheels. Some relatives and neighbors (most of them women) chose to practice the daylong fasting ritual (Tib. *smyung gnas*), during which participants did not speak to others, eat, or drink anything, instead reciting prayers in hopes of bringing Ama purification and blessing. Since household members of the deceased are not supposed to travel during times of mourning, relatives and friends brought Jampa copper bowls, cups, butter, *tsam pa* (roasted barley flour), and other offerings as well as the mineral pigments he would need for the *kye go* thangka. For Jampa, a painter who had just lost his mother, it might not be easy to have a focused mind to work on a thangka. But support from relatives and friends did alleviate the burden brought by Ama's sudden death and helped him concentrate on painting.

The Sound of the Mani Stone

Pema Tseden's short fiction *The Silent Mani Stone* was written at a time when Tibetan rural regions were going through significant social changes—urbanization, increasing mobility, commodification. Uncertainty and resistance to change, sometimes in the form of ghosts, are haunting the living and the dead.[8] Ghost stories not only "illuminate . . . the psychological relationship between repression and ghosts" (Kipnis 2021, 133) but also highlight the concerns of local Tibetans and the complexity of their response to change—things not immediately obvious if we only rely on interviews, direct observation, or news reports. Combining the analysis of both fiction (the ghost story) and ethnography (Jampa's experiences) helps us understand how realities should be read and regarded in a place where many things go silent—like "the ballad without words," as Pema Tseden puts it.

The Silent Mani Stone opens with the death of Lobsang's mother. One afternoon Lobsang, a notorious drunkard in the village, was inebriated and did not know his mother had died. This was certainly condemned by other villagers. Although Lobsang had witnessed his father's death from excessive drinking when he was little and swore never to drink, he broke that promise at the age of eighteen. After his mother passed away, about a month before the story takes place, he let himself become drunk almost every day, including the night when he heard someone chiseling a mani stone from afar.[9] The only stone carver in the village, a lonely old man, had also died a few days earlier. Since Lobsang had become a good-for-nothing drunkard, nobody believed him about what he had heard until he found a newly carved syllable on a piece of stone at the mani stone pile where the old carver had once worked. This stone had been commissioned by Lobsang's mother when she was still alive. She had regretted that her anger toward Lobsang's father had prevented her from holding an appropriate funeral for him, who had recently appeared in her dreams to beg her forgiveness. The old stone carver had only managed to finish the first two syllables before he himself passed away. But now the stone had a third syllable.

Lobsang took the stone to the tulku in the local monastery. The tulku examined the stone and began to worry that the soul of the stone carver would not depart but would continue to wander in the village. Before the tulku organized another ritual to send off the stone carver, the old carver appeared in Lobsang's dream and asked him to beg the tulku to let him finish the mani stone. The tulku agreed. When the stone carver eventually completed all six syllables, the tulku admired his work so much (calling it *gui fu shen gong*, "uncanny workmanship") that he wanted to commission another mani stone from the deceased carver. In Lobsang's dream, the stone carver said he was too tired to pick up his chisel; it would be impossible for him to carry out any more work. At that moment, Lobsang's mother appeared and told the stone carver that she and Lobsang's father would be willing to donate this piece of stone to the local monastery on behalf of the three of them (the deceased), an honor and even a better way of accumulating merits. The next day, Lobsang brought the stone to the tulku and told him what the stone carver and his parents had said in his dream. The tulku was delighted. He assembled seven monks to chant seven days and nights for the stone carver. After that the old man never appeared in Lobsang's dreams.

In the story Pema Tseden portrays a sense of loss, a repeating theme in his films and writings—the loss of the last stone carver and the unfulfilled wishes and promises. The deceased stone carver stayed in the village because he had an unfulfilled obligation and no one else could help him; he had no children and no apprentices, as young people were more interested in going to cities than acquiring his stone carving skills. Lobsang's mother passed away with regret because she was unable to help her husband find a better rebirth. Lobsang's father had never obtained forgiveness from his wife. Lobsang, too, had failed to keep his oath, succumbing to alcohol. In real life, what losses befall Tibetans living in Rebgong? Did Jampa have unfulfilled wishes too?

Two years before Ama's death, I attended the Lurol festival with Jampa's family, the annual ceremony held in the sixth lunar month to worship and entertain mountain deities and local protectors. At the ceremony, we met David, a tourist and writer from Europe who was trekking in Qinghai. Jampa invited David for dinner and a drink at home. The two of them talked happily for hours (with me interpreting) and regretted not having known each other earlier. When their spirits were high, David asked Jampa what was his biggest dream in life. Jampa responded, without hesitation, that he had sworn that one day he would carry Ama on his back and walk all the way to Lhasa for a pilgrimage. David was impressed, but before he could say anything, Jampa laughed and said: "When I made that oath, Ama was skinny. But now, you see, she has been eating well and put on a lot of weight. I am afraid I couldn't do it!" Everyone laughed. Back then Jampa, of course, said it as a joke. Deep in his heart, he believed that there would come a time when he and Ama would set off on their trip to Lhasa. Two years later, at Ama's funeral, Jampa reminded me of that conversation with David. "Many things in life are unexpected," Jampa sighed. "Now I will never be able to do it."

"You should always extinguish the candle and fire before you go to bed because you never know if you will wake up the next morning," a monk at Rongwo Monastery said to me, when we talked about how to prepare for the unexpected in life. Although prominent teachers like Tsongkhapa have advised us to be mindful of death, since all things we depend on for life are tenuous, very few people seem fully prepared when death actually comes, whether it is their own death or the death of their loved ones.[10] Jampa said Ama left without much worry, although she had asked Jampa not to drink too much. It was Jampa who found it particularly difficult to say goodbye. For him Ama was one of his most important anchors in life, an essential tie binding together his beliefs, hopes, and identity. The (idealized) image of a Tibetan mother (Makley 2007, 147–49), always selfless and nurturing, always waiting for her wandering son to return home, symbolizes stability when everything around her is changing. When that tie disappeared, Jampa's world collapsed.

In knitting together the stories of losses and unsettled spirits, Pema Tseden creates a profile of a drunkard and purposefully arranges several key moments of the story at the time when Lobsang is drunk (e.g., when his mother died and when he first heard the sound of stone chiseling). But Pema Tseden never tells us what motivated Lobsang to start drinking. Was it because of his father? Was it because he was lazy? Or was it because of his disappointment about life when everything around him was changing? From Pema Tseden's description, we know Lobsang indulges in drinking, but we also get to know him as a faithful and devoted Tibetan Buddhist who respects the tulku, monks, the mani stone, and anything that is "sacred." When he saw that a sheep had peed on a mani stone after the old carver passed away, since nobody was tending to the stone pile, he kicked the animal away, cleaned the stone with his shirt, and lamented that it was the "dharma ending age."[11] Writing about death and loss in contemporary China, Kipnis points out that "grief involves the loss of a social relationship that had served as an anchor. This loss disorients" (2021, 92). Such disorientation is Lobsang's drunkenness, the blurred and confusing visions of the future, the hangovers felt by many Tibetans who, like Lobsang, have experienced the loss of family members and the coming of strangers, the changing landscape of the people's hometowns, and the diminishing authority of Buddhist agents—lamas, monks, divine spirits, and such—in people's daily lives, and a feeling of helplessness in the face of such changes.[12]

In contrast to Pema Tseden's "last stone carver," Jampa and other *lha zo* in Rebgong do not seem to be the last thangka painters. Jampa was born in the time of the "renaissance" of Rebgong art (Linrothe 2001). Though Jampa has never been a monk, he acquired art making skills and Buddhist knowledge through the thorough training from his *ge gen* and from working on numerous monastic commissions in Rebgong and nearby regions. When Jampa was ready to run his own workshop, he was embraced by the boom of Rebgong's art market; from the late 1990s to the early 2000s, Jampa did not have to worry about looking for clients. Besides monastic commissions, orders from art dealers poured in, filling up his schedule quickly. With his income in those years, Jampa was proud to make generous donations, from hundreds to over a thousand RMB, to the village monastery and Rongwo Monastery. He not only repaired murals and statues in the village monastery but also frequently used his art making skills to help neighbors and friends prepare their rituals without charge. With the money left over, Jampa renovated his house, bought the latest model of motorcycle, and enjoyed drinking and karaoke with friends in town.

But this vitality did not last long. Jampa met intense competition when the market became crowded with freshly trained painters from government-sponsored schools and accelerated training programs. That competition was bitter when Gasar village, where Jampa was living, fell off the radar of the Protection Zone, whereas painters in some other villages had better chances for government support to open family-owned galleries or shops. Many *lha zo* have been pushed to seek their own economic fortunes, like Jampa, who went as far as Shandong to look for desirable clients. His travels meant less time spent with Ama, delaying their pilgrimage to Lhasa. His travels and economic pressure also postponed his plan to build a domestic shrine of his own design, on the north side of his house. After Ama passed away, Jampa stood in the courtyard of his house and stared at the empty space to the north. He said it looked like a hole in his heart.

Jampa could have chosen an easier way. When Thondup brought up the high-end thangka to his *ge gen*, Jampa was not unaware of the kind of clients Thondup dealt with. Yet Jampa was skeptical. Besides not thinking much of Thondup's painting skills, Jampa was also skeptical about those affluent non-Tibetans who follow and practice Tibetan Buddhism and frequently patronize Tibetan lamas and monks to hold teaching and prayer sessions "at their places." The "flying lama" phenomenon is not new. In the early 1990s, Western disciples of Tibetan Buddhism often bought plane tickets to fly their Tibetan teachers to their "elective" centers in the United States or United Kingdom, leaving Tibetan residents in India and Nepal to complain about "the 'brain drain' of Tibetan lamas to the West" (Bentor 1993, 114). Today Han disciples of Tibetan Buddhism compete for access to their gurus, leading Tibetan lamas affiliated with Han disciples to grumble that they "felt torn by the needs of their Han followers" (Osburg 2020, 78). In 2013 a monk in a local monastery told me that their tulku even asked the monks to restrict their travel to outside places and to spend more time on study and engagement with the local communities.

Like many painters in Rebgong, Jampa did not teach his children painting.[13] "I want them to go to school so they will have a brighter future than mine," said Jampa. Such a response echoes that of other Tibetans in pastoral communities in Sichuan who have changed their views on schooling over the past few decades (Gyal 2019). The resettlement program, the regulations on land use, and the booming of the "project economy" (Ch. *xiang mu jing ji*) in Tibetan communities since the early 2000s have largely transformed the subsistence economy into a cash-based economy.[14] Many Tibetan parents who are "concerned with the future" of their children choose to send their youngsters to school to learn Chinese, science, and economics (Gyal 2019), hoping they pass the college entrance exam (Ch. *gao kao*), graduate with a higher degree, and secure a government job or become an entrepreneur (Rajan 2015, 132–33; Washul 2018). Jampa attributed his "being left behind" to his lack of education. "If only I had gone to school," said Jampa to his children when they did not do well on school exams, "I would be doing much better than I am now." But when his children stepped on the paintbrushes piled on the carpet or had a hard time uttering the name of the deity he was painting, Jampa knew he could not rely on them to paint him a *kye go* thangka when the day came. He is deeply conflicted, seeing his own children being admitted to college (a few years after Ama's death) yet drifting farther away from his life, a life already losing its direction without Ama on his back.

At a time when religious practices or assemblies in Tibet have to be occasionally rescheduled or canceled due to regulations to "maintain the stability of the society" (Ch. *wei wen*) (Barnett 2012; Makley 2018, 226), both the monastic authority and the collective fortune of all patron communities—that is, local laities—are challenged. The appropriation of Tibetan Buddhism or Buddhist art by non-Tibetans makes Jampa uneasy. According to my conversation with roughly a dozen customers from the intermediate market in Beijing and Shanghai as well as Rebgong painters' reports, not a single non-Tibetan client has ever commissioned a *kye go* thangka for a deceased family member; most of them have never heard of it (*wang sheng tang ka* in Chinese). When more and more young painters, who are unable to recite the long mantra of Yamantaka but produce dozens of images of him every year for tourists and art dealers; when Jampa's apprentices don't have the patience to finish their study in his studio but leave early to operate their own thangka businesses; and when the mentalities of many painters around him shift from "painting for others" to "painting for money," Jampa finds Thondup's high-end thangkas disturbing. Like Lobsang in Pema Tseden's story, Jampa, from time to time, laments the moral decline in the village and that he is the one "left behind." When Jampa called the oolong-drinking Thondup a "useless urbanite," he enhanced his point by choosing beer over tea. Did Jampa, like Lobsang, choose alcohol so he could hear the silenced sound of stone chiseling—the calling of his beliefs and hopes haunting him under the moonlight?

That sound is furtive. In Pema Tseden's fiction, it happens only at night, when the moon is big, round, and bright. It only comes from afar and is only meant to be heard by a drunkard, a mind intoxicated by alcohol so as not to be disoriented by changes under the dazzling sun. Through Lobsang's drunkenness, Pema Tseden signals his refusal (McGranahan 2016) to accept changes that would leave so many unfulfilled wishes behind—"everything inconsistent, illogical, insensitive, dislocating, and disturbing" happening in Pema Tseden's homeland (Yü 2014, 139). Unlike the more direct and radical refusal revealed in Pema Tseden's film *Old Dog* (2011), in which a shepherd would rather kill his beloved Tibetan mastiff than sell it to the black market or see it stolen, his refusal in *The Silent Mani Stone* is subtle, quiet, yet powerful, also with a trace of hope.

The hope has driven the deceased stone carver who *chose* to stay in this world to complete what was unfinished. When the tulku wanted to send him off immediately, the stone carver called the tulku "narrow-minded" and argued: "I had been carving holy stones my whole life, accumulating tremendous merits. No matter what happens, I would not become an evil ghost to harm the village." His determination moved the tulku. The wandering spirit was therefore not seen as a threat but as an unprecedented blessing. Villagers brought food and offerings to the deceased carver, who worked in the darkness of the night; even the tulku attempted to commission a new stone from the ghost carver on behalf of the monastery. Although the villagers first failed to believe Lobsang—that he had heard a chiseling sound from the stone pile—when he was proven correct, he turned from a notorious drunkard to a person with "great virtue" because the tulku told villagers that only the most devout could first hear such a sound.

Jampa's painted canvas, like the sound of the stone carver's chisel, connected a confusing present to a once-reassuring tradition. Absorbing the profound changes, Jampa not only produced an efficacious *kye go* thangka to send off Ama, but he also painted his religion, beliefs, love for his mother, disappointment about changes taking place, and his hopes for the future on that thangka.[15] The painted scroll preserves these memories for Jampa, long after the funeral has ended—just like the drunken Lobsang, who continues hearing the sound of stone chiseling even when the stone carver no longer visits his dreams.

About three weeks after Ama passed away, Jampa and I returned to Xining. Jampa needed to take care of the paperwork associated with Ama's death in the hospital. The doctor had made an exception for him to take Ama's body back to Rebgong immediately after her death to observe necessary funeral rites in the village. Jampa had not paid the medical bill or signed the death certificate before he left the hospital.

Because of moving or seeking medical treatment in a hospital, nowadays, increasingly, Rebgong elders die outside the village. In Rebgong, if a person dies outside the village, her body may not be taken back to her village home because the unexpectedness of the death is considered inauspicious.[16] "The sudden death, a car accident or abrupt illness, could be a result of being possessed by evil ghosts, so things go out of control," one painter told me. Although some families manage to get their elders back to the village before death, others, like Jampa, must cope with the unexpected, including holding the cremation outside the village before bringing the ashes of the deceased, purified by monks at the cremation site, back to the village home. In the latter case, it is especially important that monks and villagers pray and chant for the deceased to reassure her that even though she died outside the village, she is surrounded by family and neighbors and supported by her monastic guardians. The *kye go* thangka is essential as it recruits deities and religious teachers the deceased person knew in this life—in Ama's case, the Shartshang lama and the tulku of the village monastery—who can guide the deceased through potential uncertainties or obstacles on her way to rebirth.

At the hospital, the doctor, a middle-aged Han woman, warmly greeted Jampa and gathered all the paperwork. I helped Jampa fill out the forms in Chinese, while the doctor asked Jampa about the funeral. She seemed relieved when she heard that the funeral rites had gone smoothly so far. The doctor turned to me and said: "He is a very filial son. Before he begged me to take his mother's body back to Rebgong, he had not slept for two days or maybe more. I don't know how he managed to go through all this!" The doctor refused to accept the "red packet" (Ch. *hong bao*) that Jampa had prepared for her, telling him to keep that money or donate it to the monastery on behalf of his mother.[17]

On our way back to Rebgong, Jampa pointed to the Yellow River (Tib. *rma chu*) and told me after the mourning, forty-nine days after Ama's death, he would cast Ama's ashes into the river. "But now," said Jampa, "I need to complete Ama's *kye go* thangka. Nothing else matters more than the painting."

The Family Shrine Room

Jampa finished the *kye go* thangka in time and held a smooth *gong dzok* for Ama. After that Ama's *kye go* thangka was hung in the domestic shrine room in Jampa's home. Another desirable option for Rebgong residents, in terms of accumulating merits, is to hang the *kye go* thangka in the monastery, where lamas and monks frequently purify and pray for the image. However, because of the sheer number of *kye go* thangkas produced locally every year, the monastery has to be very selective.[18] According to several painters I interviewed, the monastery only accepts paintings "of the highest aesthetic quality," since these paintings are displayed in monastic halls and seen by the public, including local residents and visitors. Moreover, a monk who was responsible for the maintenance of the hall in a local monastery (Tib. *sgo gnyer*) told me that the monastery worried about the thangkas being stolen or damaged, so he could only hang a limited number of scrolls from villagers.[19] On the other hand, many local residents, including Jampa, prefer keeping the *kye go* thangka of the deceased family member at home because the painting is one of the few material things for the living to remember the deceased. Scholars and curators who put up Tibetan shrine room exhibits in museums often overlook this fact.[20]

Alongside the concern that Buddhist paintings and statues are usually decontextualized as art in secular settings such as galleries and museums (Clarke 2015; Tythacott and Bellini 2020), an increasing number of museums in the West feature immersive displays—in this case, Tibetan shrine rooms—to encourage visitors to appreciate the religious art and objects from a more "authentic" perspective (Clark 2016; Tythacott 2017). For instance, the "Tibetan Buddhist Altar" in the Newark Museum of Art, originally constructed in 1935—the first in America—was redesigned and repainted by Tibetan artist Phuntsok Dorje and consecrated by the fourteenth Dalai Lama upon its completion in 1990 (Reynolds 1991, 5; Paine 2013, 41). Jacques Marchais built a Tibetan altar in her garden on Staten Island, New York, in 1947, the "Potala of the West" as she named it, intending to "invent [a] spiritually uplifting" environment with Tibetan objects she had bought and traded from "Oriental art markets" in the West (Harris 1999, 34–35). More recent shrine room exhibits opened, for instance, in the World Museum Liverpool in the United Kingdom, the Rubin Museum of Art in New York, and the Smithsonian's Freer and Sackler Galleries in Washington, DC.[21]

Although the shrine room exhibits have become increasingly popular among visitors, who immerse themselves in these spaces to meditate, contemplate, or simply slow down, such display easily reinforces the "orientalist" logic the curators originally intend to avoid (Clark 2016, 2; Tythacott and Bellini 2020, 18).[22] The dim light—achieved with simulated flickering butter lamps—the backdrop soundtrack of monastic chanting, and the lack of labels (or separation of labels from objects by placing them outside the shrine room or online), while fabricating the authentic feeling one has stepping into the shrine room in a real Tibetan home, make it very hard for general viewers to know what the exhibited objects are and how they are used (Gopnik 2010). Moreover, while some of the exhibits claim to showcase the shrine room of a "private household," we see little connection between the objects displayed and the personal, familial, or local histories behind them, nor can we necessarily distinguish a monastic or a noble shrine room from the one in a peasant's household or the altar in a pastoralist's tent. No exhibit, to my knowledge, has ever mentioned *kye go* thangkas or statues that are kept and venerated in Tibetans' domestic shrine rooms.[23] Although the shrine room exhibits are generally well received by Tibetan audiences and Buddhist disciples in the West, anthropologist Imogen Clark questions if Tibetans living inside China have any "opportunity to voice their opinions about such forms of representation" (2016, 16). Although Tibetan exiles seem to be satisfied with the Western exhibition practices, it could be a result of power inequality since Western support is essential to their political cause (Clark 2016; Lopez 2018, 11). To hear at least some of the missing voices, let's return to Rebgong.

In Rebgong the size of the family shrine room, or *cho khang*, varies with the design of the house and the economic situation of the family, but it usually occupies the center space of the house (figure 9). In the middle of the *cho khang*, there is a wooden shrine cabinet (Tib. *kun dga' ra ba*), often elaborately carved and painted.[24] In the cabinet, the family displays Buddhist scriptures (representing *gsung rten*, the "speech support"), the stupa (*thugs rten*, the "mind support"), and statues (*sku rten*, the "body support") of Buddha, deities, and religious teachers associated with the family's particular sect and linage practices. In front of the cabinet, there are offering tables (Tib. *mchod lcog* or *mchod stegs*) holding butter lamps, a silver mandala offering (Tib. *man dal*), purified water in copper bowls (Tib. *yon chab*), bowls of rice and barley, and an incense burner.[25] Some families also arrange offerings of butter cakes (Tib. *gtor ma*), conch shells (Tib. *dung dkar*), and flowers and fruits on the offering stands.

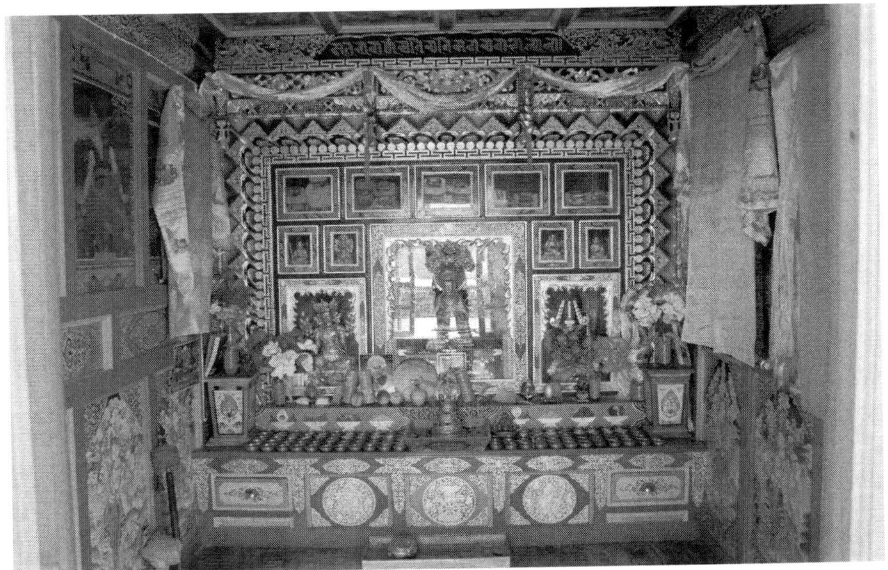

FIGURE 9 A family shrine room in Gasar village, 2012.

The taste of urban industrial life frequently slips through, as I have observed many families put cans of Coca-Cola, Red Bull, almond milk, and packaged snacks side by side with rice, barley, and *go re* (baked bread). Like the Korean patrons who are broadening their selection of food offerings (e.g., imported kiwis, champagne, and Pringles potato chips) in rituals of ancestor worship (Kendall 2008, 160), most residents in Rebgong welcome exotic offerings on their altar. My gift to Jampa's family, a box of pastries from Beijing, was put on their altar during the New Year celebration. On the offering table of some other painters, I have also seen a piece of amethyst, gold or jade Zodiac sculptures, and statues of Guanyin given by their non-Tibetan patrons or friends.

On the walls adjacent to the cabinet, scrolls of thangka paintings, including *kye go* thangkas, are displayed. The *kye go* thangkas hung in the family's shrine room can include not only those made for household members but also paintings for deceased *ge gen*, monk relatives, tulkus of local monasteries, or prominent religious teachers in the region. If there is space in the cabinet, the family can also commission a *kye go* statue for the deceased tulku or religious teacher and place it on one of the shelves. Likewise, a young monk who inherits the monastic dwelling from a deceased monk (often a relative) keeps and venerates the deceased's *kye go* thangka in his private shrine room. Besides *kye go* thangkas, some families follow the diviner's advice and make a thangka depicting the birth deities (Tib. *skye lha*) of all living household members together on one painting for their *cho khang*.[26] Thangkas commissioned to dispel illness or bad fortune are hung in the shrine room as well.

When I asked if the increasing number of thangkas stacked one on top of another on the wall would be a problem, Jampa and Tsering Gyal assured me that the paintings would not "fight" with each other, as in the case of some Korean shaman paintings (Kendall 2021, 50–57). "We'd love to display the paintings as if in a museum," joked Jampa, "but we only have so much space. It's okay if some part of the painting is covered by others." Tsering Gyal mentioned again the importance of *dad pa* (faith), pointing out that it all depended on the family's faith and its economic status—if a family could not afford to commission an image for a deceased tulku, they should not feel guilty about it as long as they remembered and prayed for him sincerely.

Families usually do not keep material possessions such as the clothing or jewelry of the deceased. Rebgong residents agree that the purpose of holding funeral rites and mourning is to help the deceased embark on her future journey, without any hesitation or worry left in this world, to eventually obtain enlightenment or find a desirable rebirth. The corpse of the deceased, vacated and purified by lamas and monks, is "ideally eliminated as a gift to hungry demons or animals" (Makley 2018, 227–28). But people do not necessarily "cut off" their deceased relatives.[27] At the beginning of my fieldwork, Jampa had warned me not to photograph old people when I visited their homes. He explained to me that Tibetans do not take photos of elders; some consider it rude, while others think it inauspicious.[28] So, when an elder passed away, there was often no photo of the person left for the family. "Just like Han or Americans who remember their deceased loved ones by looking at their photos," said Jampa, "we Tibetans keep their *kye go* thangkas in the shrine room. The paintings are made for commemoration and veneration."

Every morning the family members change the water offerings, light butter lamps, and pray in front of the images kept in the shrine room. The elders like to sit outside the shrine room during their leisure hours, turning prayer wheels and reciting prayers for both the living and the deceased. During the New Year celebration, the household head visits the local monastery with a register recording names of deceased family members (Tib. *bsngo yig*), to ask monks to chant scriptures and pray for those who have passed away.[29] Parents from time to time lead curious children into the shrine room, pointing to *kye go* thangkas and telling stories about their grandparents, father's *ge gen*, or the tulku of the village monastery, some of whom the children never met.

Building the domestic shrine builds family memories. Dorje, one of Tashi Gyatso's apprentices, started the renovation of his domestic *cho khang* in 2022, when he did not travel much due to the resurgence of the COVID-19 pandemic and related restrictions in China but had enough money that he and his wife (also an apprentice of Tashi Gyatso) had pulled together after a few years of saving. Dorje had been learning thangka painting for more than nine years before he traveled with *ge gen* Tashi Gyatso to Mount Wutai in 2018, to help with the renovation of monastic buildings. Before his trip to Mount Wutai, Dorje painted thangkas on flat surfaces almost exclusively, including the few times when he helped with the mural painting in local monasteries. During the two years at Mount Wutai, Dorje picked up architectural painting techniques from Tashi Gyatso and Chodrak. Although the color theory is largely similar between thangka and architectural painting, making pigments for architectures (usually on wooden surfaces, which require a different proportion of mineral powders, water, and glue in the mixture) and applying colors on three-dimensional objects were new challenges for Dorje. He practiced these skills at Mount Wutai and later applied them to his shrine project back home.[30] Dorje also designed his own altar, after observing various styles at Mount Wutai and in Rebgong. After Chinese carpenters from Gansu carved the wooden cabinet, pillars, and offering stands, Dorje and his wife took over the painting work and completed the project in three months.

Tsering Gyal once said to me, half-jokingly: "You urbanites show off your wealth by competing over who has the most luxurious car. We compete over who has the best *cho khang*." His painter friend immediately objected and said it does not matter how the shrine looks; the most important thing is that the family is sincere and faithful. However, they agreed that if a family could afford a BMW or an apartment in town but still kept a shabby shrine, it would be a disgrace. The renovation of the domestic *cho khang* often happens when the family is enjoying a good economic status and when the painter has a relatively stable work schedule. Norbu renovated his shrine after he came back from Beijing, while Tsering Gyal did his after two years painting in Shandong. By contrast, painters such as Jampa have to pause their plans to build or renovate a shrine room due to economic hardship, illnesses, or costly accidents.

According to Dorje, the cost of imported pinewood, carpentry, gold, and mineral pigments that he used for his shrine was approximately RMB 50,000 (USD 7,447), about three-quarters of his annual income. Dorje considered the finished project "just a medium-level shrine," responding to my praise for his exquisite work. Dorje pointed out that the mandala paintings on the ceiling and thangka images on the side walls were in fact produced by an inkjet wall printer. "If the wall paintings were a hundred percent handmade, like my *ge gen*'s shrine," said Dorje, "it would double or triple our cost and take much longer to make." Even if the Buddhist objects are mechanically reproduced or commercially fabricated, many Tibetan consumers believe that ritual actions (e.g., consecration) and faith labor (e.g., praying in front of a statue) can produce the "aura" or efficacy of religious objects, made in unconventional settings (Brox 2019). Dorje said he chose the printed images and arranged them on the wall according to the advice of his monk relative. A consecration ritual, performed by monks from the village monastery, was also held after scriptures, statues, and thangka scrolls (including *kye go* thangkas, which partly covered the wall paintings) were installed in this new shrine. Echoing other painters' comments, Dorje said, "After all, what you do in the shrine room is more important than how it looks."

I do not know how painters would respond if they saw "yoga raves" held in museums where Buddhist images may also be displayed or saw people attending champagne brunches at Jacques Marchais's Potala of the West.[31] But for Rebgong residents, the family shrine room is simultaneously sacred and intimate. It is not a space primarily designed for meditation practice, nor even just for accumulating merits, but also an enclosure "layered" with personal stories, family memories, and local histories.[32]

Before Jampa built his new shrine, he used the small room on the east side of the house as a temporary shrine. Ama's *kye go* thangka was also kept in that room after the funeral. In the beginning of my fieldwork, when I slept in the guest room adjacent to the temporary shrine, I could hear Ama's chanting every morning; she was the first to get up to change offering water and light butter lamps. After Ama passed away, it was Drolma who got up early to make offerings. Before the children went to school, Jampa led them to the shrine room, chanting the "The Refuge Prayer" (Tib. *skyabs 'gro*, Ch. *gui yi jing*) and the scripture to worship the Medicine Buddha as well as lighting butter lamps in front of Ama's *kye go* thangka.[33]

No matter whether a *kye go* thangka was produced in the hidden corner of the house during the Cultural Revolution or is carefully designed and made in a home studio in today's Rebgong, *lha zo* emphasize the importance of faith in commissioning and making the image. Even when a Buddhist image is fabricated in a conventional setting such as a family workshop and made for internal use, as in the case of *kye go* thangkas, art makers' and families' intentions and practices may also affect the efficacy of an image in important ways. Efficacy in Rebgong is more complicated than "does the painting have [spiritual] power?" (Ch. *ni zhe ge tang ka ling ma*), a question often asked by non-Tibetan consumers when they purchase a thangka painting. While many painters in Rebgong respond to such a question by confirming that the image has been consecrated, efficacy goes beyond whether the painting's iconography is correct or whether it can be venerated as the receptacle (Tib. *sku rten*) for the Buddha or deities.

Like Guanyin statues in Hong Kong, each thangka "has a life course that intersects with the stories of places, shrines, and people who have engaged with the icon" (Palmer, Tse, and Colwell 2019, 899). An efficacious *kye go* image not only assists the deceased in finding a good rebirth but also preserves personal, familial, and local memories. Painters' acts or thought, will, or intention are intertwined with the otherwise invisible forces that make the images work in these many ways (Gell 1998). In that regard, the making of a *kye go* thangka itself becomes an important part of mourning for the painter(s). The *kye go* thangka is also one of the few material things the deceased leaves for the living, produced within the window of *bar do* with communal support from both the monastics and the laity. For most Rebgong residents, the painting is later kept in the domestic shrine room, where it is viewed and prayed at by the family long after the funeral and mourning have ended.

In addition, we need to read the meaning and efficacy of *kye go* thangkas against the backdrop of current social, economic, and political changes taking place in Rebgong. A combination of Jampa's personal experiences and Pema Tseden's fiction suggests that the unexpected changes in life, the misfortunes, and the unfulfilled wishes are not simply karmic consequences a person has to bear (also see Makley 2018, 223). The "dharma ending age" invoked by Lobsang in Pema Tseden's story should be understood as some locals' critique

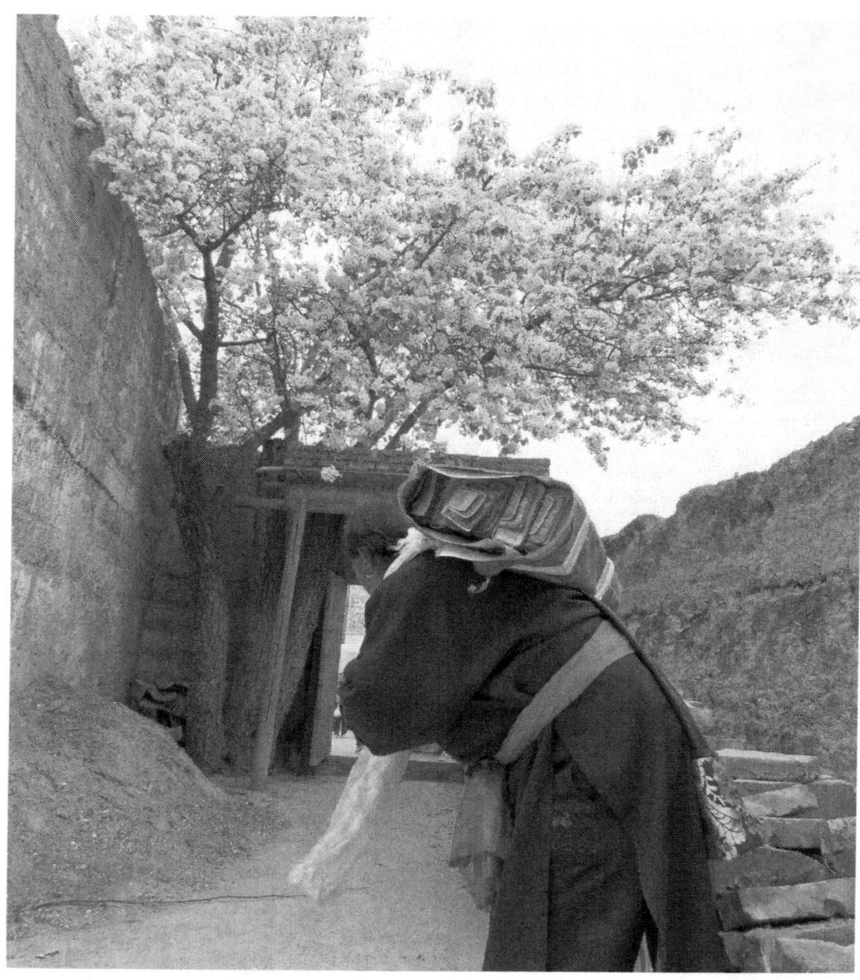

FIGURE 10 Ama carrying Buddhist scriptures and exiting the village monastery following other women on the day of the *cho kor*, 2012.

of the current economic development and social regulations that have challenged the Buddhist authority and the collective fortune of the community in rural Tibet. As in other rapidly urbanizing areas in China, these changes have resulted in many unsettled spirits, haunting the living both in their daily lives and in their perspectives for the future. Without Ama, the vision of the future is more clouded for Jampa as he observes the high-end thangkas, impatient apprentices, and even his own children, for whom the life of a *lha zo* is alien. Knowing that his children will probably not paint a *kye go* thangka for him, Jampa executes Ama's painting with great care and faith.

Nevertheless, people's response and resistance to change are complex. Many *lha zo*, including Jampa, do not passively accept everything happening around them. Jampa has applied for government allowances, traveled farther to find clients he approves of, involved Drolma in art making at home, and more importantly, indicated his refusal of Thondup's representation of Tibetan thangka and the appropriation of Buddhist efficacy by his high-end patrons. While Lobsang in Pema Tseden's fiction anesthetizes his mind with alcohol so he can hear that "silent" sound of stone chiseling, painters like Jampa materialize their politics of presence in artwork (Makley 2018), by continuing the practice of *lha zo* who consider sincerity or faith as most important to the image's efficacy. When Ama passed away in the hospital, Jampa negotiated and was able to take Ama's body back to Rebgong and proceed with the funeral apace. For Jampa it was crucial to hold an appropriate funeral and produce the *kye go* thangka on his own as well as to continue venerating Ama's *kye go* thangka in the family shrine. Art making therefore mediates the unexpected and other changes in life for painters like Jampa, even when the view of the future remains unclear.

A few years after Ama's death, I visited Jampa and Drolma again. In their family *cho khang*, I saw a few *tsa tsa* (Tib. *tsha tsha*), stamped mini figures made into the shape of the Buddha, placed on the offering table under the wooden cabinet. Jampa told me the *tsa tsa* were made of clay, mixed with the ashes of Ama's bones. He had made hundreds of them during Ama's funeral. After the mourning period, he and a monk from the village monastery brought the *tsa tsa* to the Yellow River. As the monk chanted and prayed, Jampa put most of the *tsa tsa* in the river as an offering. A few remaining ones were kept at his home shrine. "I cannot carry Ama on my back to Lhasa," said Jampa, "but I will carry her *tsa tsa* with me when I go on the pilgrimage and place them on top of the mountains."

Before I left Rebgong, Jampa asked me for a photo that I took during the *cho kor* in Gasar, when Ama was still alive, so he could copy it onto his hard drive. In that photo Ama stood in line with other women, carrying the twenty-pound scriptures on her back, smiling (figure 10).

Epilogue

Walking on the village road one afternoon, Tsering Gyal was in a mood to tell stories. "The first Shartshang Lama once had a dream," he began.[1]

In the dream, Manjushri handed him a paintbrush. The next day, Shartshang Lama asked around if anyone knew how to paint. Only a monk from Sengeshong knew about drawing, but he barely drew horses and trees. Shartshang Lama gave him the paintbrush and sent him to Lhasa to learn painting. After the monk finished his learning and returned home, he painted flowers on paper. The painted flowers attracted dozens of butterflies and bees. He painted a mural of Yellow Jambhala. A cat jumped right onto the wall because it thought the mouse on the deity's left hand was real! This is the "origin myth" of Rebgong thangka, if you ask me.[2]

As we circumambulated the eight stupas, Tsering Gyal continued:

Rebgong *lha zo* become famous because of our outstanding art making skills. But excellence comes from rigorous training and a lot of practice. You don't know how I learned painting when I was a kid, do you? I remember one winter, when it was very, very cold. My hands could not stop shivering. The lines I drew were shaky too. My *ge gen* had a ruler in his hand. Whenever I made a mistake, his ruler hit my hand . . . until I could control the paintbrush and my lines were smooth and steady. The *ge gen* also asked us to remember the proportion of each deity. But we were little kids. Who had the patience to sit there all day to study the proportion? One day when the *ge gen* was not home, we ran out and spent the entire afternoon playing on the riverbank, napping in the woods. When the *ge gen* came back, he got so angry that he made us draw the proportional grid and practice the iconography until midnight.

After a pause, Tsering Gyal said, "But I am now very grateful to my *ge gen*. If he had not forced me to study that hard, I would not be able to paint as well as I do today. The grids are imprinted in my heart, something I can always rely on."

To Tsering Gyal and many other Rebgong art makers, the proportional grid (Tib. *thig khang*) is more than a painting device. By repeatedly reciting "head 12 *sor*, neck 4, chest 12, stomach 12," the apprentice is grasping a certainty: no matter how big or small the Buddha's image is, the proportion of his body parts is always the same, as inscribed in the scripture (figure 11).[3] By constructing the iconometric grids on canvas, the painter builds her or his own "railings"—a support to the shaky hand, a navigation for the lost paintbrush, a reminder of the missing stroke. To some artists trained in Western or Chinese traditions, the Tibetan iconometrics may seem rigid or constraining. But even contemporary artist Gonkar Gyatso, who does not make thangka paintings, frequently incorporates proportional grids in his conceptual artworks because the lines and cultural vocabulary embedded in them have significant weight in defining his "Tibetanness" (C. Harris 2012, 247; Reilly 2012, 12). To painters like Tsering Gyal, the grids are their identity too. It is the knowledge transmitted only from *ge gen* to *ge truk* of how, using Webb Keane's words, the invisible world can be made into "a presupposable ground for what practitioners perceive" (2013, 4). With this responsibility, the antecessor of Tsering Gyal might have had the privilege to accept a paintbrush from the bodhisattvas of wisdom.

Yet Rebgong *lha zo* today increasingly encounter challenges and questions for which they cannot find answers from painting manuals, Buddhist scriptures, or their *ge gen*'s instructions written on the margin of sketch papers. In this book I have illustrated a new landscape of art making in Rebgong since the Reform era: the continuous art commissions from Tibetan communities, lay and monastic, for thangkas that are used both in their daily lives and at important moments of their life cycles; the state's agenda of cultural development, including the ICH discourse, which views thangka painting as craft or folk art and emphasizes the economic incentives in art making; the shifting modes of cultural transmission with the establishment of art schools and accelerated training programs; and an intermediate market of non-Tibetans

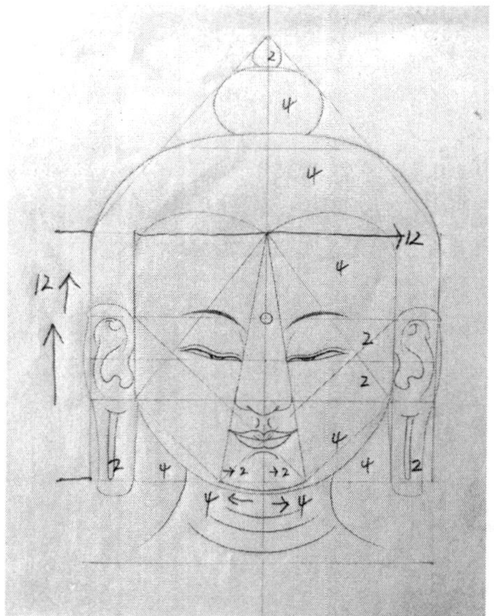

FIGURE 11 The proportional grid of the Buddha's head by Tashi Gyatso's son, who used this sketch for demonstration in the art school. Photo courtesy of the artist, 2022.

who pursue the religious efficacy of Rebgong thangkas without strictly following the conventional protocols of art commission and circulation.

Building on the existing anthropological discussion of the local arts going on global markets, this book reveals how Rebgong *lha zo* define themselves and their artwork in a rapidly changing world. But more importantly, I point out how Rebgong thangka art adds new insights to the anthropology of art: because Rebgong thangka paintings have not changed significantly in form, content, and in many cases, function, Rebgong *lha zo* have met challenges and opportunities many other indigenous/native artists have not faced. One essential problem for Rebgong art makers today is how the religious value of Tibetan thangka is understood, made, and negotiated as painters navigate the various markets. This issue encourages a fluid understanding of Tibetan thangka and directs our attention to the particular context where thangkas are commissioned, produced, circulated, and used. By forging a novel intersection between the material, ontological, and social discourses in anthropology, I not only examine the material and ritual practices that equip the image's potency but also look at how personal relationships and social conditions mediate the making of an efficacious image as well as the plurality of engagements people have with thangka paintings. Ethnographic encounters in Rebgong unravel the process of how *lha zo* accept commissions, work on canvases, and display their thangkas in different places while demonstrating how art making in Rebgong is integrated into various aspect of life in this rapidly modernizing and commercializing society that is still deeply religious. The value of this work, as my *ge gen* Jampa sees it, is to generate realistic and complex knowledge of "traditional" art making in the contemporary world.

The Wish-Granting Gem, the fifteenth-century art making treatise still used by thangka painters today, does not tell contemporary *lha zo* what an appropriate relationship between the patron and the artist looks like if the painter is a woman or if the patron is not a Tibetan Buddhist or if, as in *The Great Thangka*'s case, the idea of the art project comes from the painter instead of from their patrons. The painting manuals do not give instruction to Rebgong *lha zo* on how to adapt their knowledge of Tibetan art to produce ritual images used in other Buddhist traditions. Buddhist scriptures proscribe the selling of religious objects for profit, but what if a thangka painting is purchased by a museum for its collection? What if a high-end client at an art auction sees her bid price for the thangka of Avalokiteshvara as an offering following the guidance of her guru? What if a *lha zo pa* uses the "profit" he made from his affluent non-Tibetan clients to nourish his monastic commissions? From the stories told in this book, we see no smooth or steady line drawn between sacred object and commodity. Painters' responses to these various situations are also not always unified. Rebgong *lha zo* constantly negotiate their identities, expectations, and understandings of art in the new terrain of image making. Although some of their practices deviate from words written in art making treatises, the images they produce do not necessarily lose their aura.

In Tsering Gyal's version of the origin myth, only one monk in the region "barely drew horses and trees."[4] Today there are over twenty thousand people in Rebgong who rely on art making for their living. Hundreds of officially recognized "Arts and Crafts Masters" and "ICH Inheritors" can paint a lively mouse that tricks a hungry cat. The unprecedented level of competition, on one hand, enhances the artistic achievement of Rebgong painters, but on the other hand, it creates conflict and damages trust among local art makers. For instance, appropriating or stealing others' artwork happens from time to time—there is not always a ruler that raps the misbehaving hand. Women *lha zo* shoulder extra pressure because they have entered a market previously dominated by men. Some women painters become scapegoats for local residents who have tasted the bitter fruit of this competition. The still-operable gender and cultural expectations discourage village-based women, to various extents, from becoming professional *lha zo* following the path available to their male counterparts. Lutso is the only exception—opening a thangka studio and training her own apprentices—though she is still expected to return to the village when her parents need her help at home or in the fields and to avoid meeting male clients, which might stir up gossip.

The new markets and competition also send many Rebgong painters to places that are not their normal destinations. Painters like Norbu, Leshe, and Jampa have traveled to China's urban centers; some stayed in these places for an extended period of time, longer than they might have planned. It is their wives, sisters, and mothers in the village who plant seeds in the soil for the family and accumulate merits through their footsteps for the collective fortune of the community. Some families have moved together to Rongwo town, to Xining, or to other cities for art making and thangka business. Without the sight of the mountains, the sound of Guchu River, or the experience of the cycle of the seasons and the circle of lives in the valley, the wandering painters have lost the "grids" that anchor social relationships and moral obligations in the village. How do they know when to participate in the village *cho kor*, when to pray for a sick neighbor, when to send *go re* to the family of a deceased elderly person, when to renovate the family shrine room, and eventually, when it is time to come home?

"Oh, that's easy," said Norbu's apprentice, when he heard Norbu and me, sitting in his home studio, chatting about the changes in family lives and painters' concerns. "We'd go to the diviner," the apprentice continued. "He will tell us what to do."

At the beginning of the new year, some painters bring offerings and gifts to the *mo pa* (Tib. diviner)—either the monk in the monastery or the venerated man in the village who knows about astrology—to ask for his opinion about their travel plans for the coming year. "No," the *mo pa* shakes his head, "It would be best if you stay in the village, minding the house, the fields, and the renovation of the village monastery." This happened to Jampa in 2020, when he asked the diviner if he should go to Shandong to make art in the following months. The outbreak of COVID-19 and the subsequent travel restrictions proved the *mo pa*'s advice valuable. While many families used to and still do visit diviners and religious teachers to have their guidance on the prayers to be chanted during the New Year celebration, the offerings to be made to Buddhist deities and mountain gods, the images to be commissioned to overcome obstacles, more and more people also bring questions from the new markets: is it a good time for me to open my thangka shop? Shall I sign the contract with this gallery? Should I take part in the exhibition in Shandong or prepare for the art competition in town?

The *mo pa* seems to have considerable authority in deciding what the painter should do—some families, for example, did not let their daughters pursue thangka painting because the diviner said no. As painters navigate the new terrain of art making and miss the grids that used to provide them certainty and assurance, advice from the diviner becomes especially helpful. To consult a diviner without following his conclusion, though it does happen, sounds surprising, if not horrifying, to many Rebgong residents, who believe that bad consequences will come to the disobedient. On the other hand, painters do not passively let the calculation determine their destiny. For Jampa the divination only happened after he had negotiated with the hospital and brought Ama's body back to Rebgong immediately to proceed with the funeral rites. Staying in the village and preparing for the art competition might be an auspicious choice for Tsering Gyal, but the divination would not have guaranteed his success if he had not put months of hard work into the thangka painting submitted to the prefecture. With a *mo pa*'s approval, Lutso agreed to sign a contract with an art gallery on the east coast of China. But she was able to reduce the number of paintings commissioned by the gallery annually after a series of discussions with the gallery owner, revising the terms on the contract, since Lutso insisted on giving herself more time for innovative works—deities and stories she had not depicted previously.

While divination illuminates the future, the grids are an important legacy that Rebgong *lha zo* have carried forward from the past. In between, the painter needs to know how to ask the right question—which is not always easy, as Norbu's apprentice expressed. When Namgyal had the idea of accepting female apprentices, he consulted a diviner. Instead of asking whether teaching women art making would be a good decision *for him*, Namgyal asked three questions. Would learning thangka painting be good for this apprentice? Does this apprentice have a good nature? Would the thangkas made by this apprentice be able to help others? This was how Namgyal came to accept Lhamo, Tsomo, and other female students; how Tashi Gyatso and Chodrak agreed to teach Fan thangka painting; and in many other cases, how a *ge gen* welcomed a *ge truk* into his home and passed his knowledge and skills onto the new pair of hands.

Certainly, in the new terrain of art making, with clients from the various markets who commission or purchase Rebgong thangkas for all kinds of reasons, many painters would like to know if art making would be good "for me," hoping that the *mo pa*'s advice could help them advance their individual career and improve their family's life. But there are still many painters who emphasize faith (Tib. *dad pa*) in accepting a commission and doing an artwork, even if their final product would sit with a price tag in a commercial gallery. With the proportional grids "imprinted in the heart," to use Tsering Gyal's words, many *lha zo*, women and men, paint thangkas to authenticate their religious identity, preserve the unique art tradition in Rebgong, and establish their artistic authority in the broader world. They continue inscribing the sacred seed syllables *om ah hum* on the back of thangka paintings, inviting the Buddha and deities to reside in the image and bring protection and blessings to the viewers who venerate them.

I will always remember one afternoon many years ago. I stood at the front yard of Namgyal's art school. The building in front of me was newly constructed—well, not quite, the roof still needed some work, and the pillars awaited more layers of paint. His apprentices stayed in the two studios on the first floor. That summer, in addition to painting thangkas and helping their *ge gen*'s family harvest wheat and barley, the apprentices also participated in the construction of their school building—applying paint on pillars and wood carvings, unloading supplies from trucks, installing lights and furniture, cleaning up trash left behind by construction workers. That afternoon Namgyal closed the door of the studio. All the apprentices began to hop on a truck. They were off to the riverbank to pick up pebbles—to pave the front yard.

As I joined them, I glanced at the studio. The apprentices had left cups of pigments on the floor. Since they would be back soon, there was no need to lock the pigments back into the box. But they covered the artwork in progress with a piece of cloth—to protect the image of deities from flies. The apprentices had seemed happy, chatting and giggling in the back of the truck. It must have been exciting for them to get out of the studio once in a while, like the young Tsering Gyal stepping into the water, napping under trees.

Just a few days earlier, Namgyal had led me to the top floor of the school building. There was a statue of the Buddhist teacher Tsongkhapa, sitting in the center of a shrine. "Do you know why the teaching of Tsongkhapa is still alive today?" asked Namgyal. He made a gesture of offering and continued: "Just like we use one butter lamp to light another, we pass the teaching of

Tsongkhapa from one person to another, then to the next one, and the next one. It has continued for centuries. It will continue in the future."

As I sat in the bed of the truck with the apprentices, all of a sudden it was as if a string flew through my mind, connecting all the scenes in front of my eyes: the unfinished building, the unfinished painting, the unfinished learning, the unfinished teaching (plate 10).

These have not come to an end. They will continue.

NOTES

1. In Wylie transliteration, both *lha bzo* and *lha bris* mean "the depicter of the sacred image." Note that *bris* means "to write" or "to paint"; therefore, *lha bris* is a term exclusively for thangka painters, while *lha bzo* can describe both painters and sculptors. In Rebgong many thangka painters address themselves as *lha bzo* or *lha bzo pa*. In the book I interchangeably use *lha zo* and *lha zo pa* (the THL renderings) except for direct quotations.

2. Inscribing the seed syllables *om* (body), *ah* (speech), and *hum* (mind) on the back of the thangka behind the forehead, throat, and heart of each deity is done to purify and consecrate the thangka, inviting sacred beings to reside in the image as living essences. For more on the inscriptions on the back of a thangka, see Quintman 2013.

3. I adapt this term from Yael Bentor's (1993) research on different markets for Tibetan thangka paintings in the Kathmandu Valley. Bentor writes of an "intermediate audience," a market consisting of non-Tibetan practitioners of Tibetan Buddhism from various regions (e.g., South Asia, Europe, and the United States), that coexists with the "internal audience" and the "external audience" in Nepal. Bentor's term has been used in subsequent studies of tourism and the selling of religious objects in the Tibetan context (e.g., Costa and Ferrone 1995; McGuckin 1996; Harris 2007).

4. This is different from female artisans, who transform locally produced textiles, embroidery, ceramics, and the like—the conventional female domain of art making—into "crafts" for the global market (see, e.g., Babcock 1993; Nash 1993; Stephen 2005).

5. The newly built highway in 2018 reduced the driving distance between Rebgong and Xining to approximately one hundred miles.

6. *Regong* is the Chinese Pinyin rendering of the Tibetan term and also how it appears in UNESCO's official documentation.

7. When I conducted my fieldwork, it was Tongren County (Ch. *tong ren xian*). In 2020 it became Tongren City (Ch. *tong ren shi*), administrating largely the same towns and villages.

8. The published data of the 2020 census only breaks down Han (9.77 percent) and non-Han minority groups (90.23 percent) (accessed April 2, 2022, http://

www.hntongren.gov.cn/html/5701/417113.html). According to the official
description of Tongren City published on June 27, 2024, Tibetans make up
about 74.3 percent of the population (accessed March 24, 2025, http://www
.hntongren.gov.cn/html/5793/426920.html).

9. *The Political and Religious History of Amdo* was authored by Tenpa Rapgye (Tib.
bstan pa rab rgyas) in the nineteenth century. I consult both the Tibetan version
(*mdo smad chos 'byung*) published in 1982 and the Chinese version (*an duo zheng
jiao shi*) published in 1989.

10. Although the Geluk has a stronghold in Rebgong, there are also communities
of Nyingma and Sakya tantric practitioners as well as Bon tradition followers
(Dhondup 2011, 35).

11. For Tibetan Buddhism in Qing China, see Berger 2003; and Tuttle 2005.

12. The art making villages include Nyantok (Tib. *gnyan thog*, Ch. *nian du hu*),
Upper Sengeshong (Tib. *seng ge gshong ya mgo*, Ch. *wu tun shang zhuang*),
Lower Sengeshong (Tib. *seng ge gshong ma mgo*, Ch. *wu tun xia zhuang*), Gomar
(Tib. *sgo dmar*, Ch. *guo ma ri*), Gasar (Tib. *rka gsar* or *ska sar*, Ch. *ga sha ri*), and
Thokya (Tib. *tho rgya*, Ch. *bao an*).

13. Iconography describes what the Buddha or deities look like (e.g., their gestures,
apparels, the colors of skin), while iconometry gives the measurements and
proportions of the subject depicted.

14. These references were communicated through personal communication with
Chamba, January 5, May 22, and October 8, 2022; Tsewang Tashi, June 4 and
June 6, 2022; and Tashi Gyatso, August 16, 2019, and October 4, 2022. For other
art making treatises, see Jackson and Jackson 1988, 50.

    For the Buddhist texts that painters consult, see, for example, *sku gzugs kyi
mtshan nyid* and *rdzogs pa'i sangs rgyas kyis gsungs pa'i sku gzugs kyi mtshan nyid
kyi rnam 'grel* in the section of "Technology and Arts" (Tib. *bzo rig pa*) in *Tengyur*.

    The full name of Menla Dondrub's treatise is *The Wish-Granting Gem: A Trea-
tise on the Iconography and Proportions of the Buddha* (Tib. *bde bar gshegs pa'i sku
gzugs kyi tshad kyi rab tu byed pa yid bzhin nor bu*, Ch. *zao xiang liang du ru yi bao*).

    The Buddha's Teaching on the Iconometry in Image Making (Ch. *fo shuo zao
xiang liang du jing*) was compiled and translated by Gonpo Kyap (Tib. *mgon po
skyabs*) in 1742 (Chamba 2019, 44).

15. Rebgong apprentices today also use a printed "manual" containing templates
of Buddhas and deities with their measurements, proportions, and characteristics. This manual can be found in many shops selling religious paraphernalia
in town. According to Tashi Gyatso (personal communication, June 2, 2022),
the images in the book were assembled by an artist from Kumbum Monastery
and are widely circulated in the Amdo region. Such a manual is designed for
beginners. More sophisticated painters will consult the Buddhist scripture or
seek advice from monks to arrange the composition of the painting.

16. The practice of sketching continues during the entire learning process. Many
accomplished painters draw or sketch new compositions on paper in their

leisure time. The *ge gen*'s corrections and notes on an apprentice's drawing are also an important reference for learning.

17. David and Janice Jackson's book *Tibetan Thangka Painting: Methods and Materials* (1988), abundantly documents the material and procedure of thangka painting, focusing on the Menri style.

18. In thangka painting, "opening the eyes" (Tib. *spyan 'byed*) means to paint or dot the eyes for all deities depicted on a thangka. This is not to be confused with the consecration ritual (Tib. *rab gnas*, Ch. *kai guang*) carried out by monks. In Rebgong thangka painters often dot the eyes for deities in the workshop and take the painting to a monastery for consecration. For more details about the consecration rituals, see Bentor 1996.

19. Similarly, in the Chinese Buddhist tradition, devotees praying to Buddhist images already knew that the Buddha acted through the painting or that "Guanyin was *present* at the site of the image" (Kieschnick 2003, 57).

20. Tibetan thangkas have always assimilated influence from other art forms, so I do not use *traditional* to suggest something static in time. My aim here is to compare Rebgong thangka with "arts of acculturation," or "transitional, commercial, or airport art," defined by Graburn (1969, 457) as "art production, which differs significantly from traditional expressions in form, content, function, and often medium, which also differs from the various forms of art production indigenous to ever-growing 'civilization.'"

21. For instance, Nelson Graburn has distinguished the symbolically and ritually embedded "traditional art" from "derivative or tourist art" embedded in culturally plural contexts (1999, 343; also see Graburn 1969; 1984). In the same vein, Shelly Errington argues that "cult objects and art objects ought to be regarded as different kinds of things" because "cult objects" are not for exchange, not meant to be portable, and not necessarily durable (1998, 108).

22. For details about the material fabrication and mediums' practices, see Venkatesan 2020; Kendall 2021; and Reich 2024. For people's reaction to efficacious images or their response to the image's unexpected agency, see Morgan 2005; Palmer, Tse, and Colwell 2019; and Kendall and Ariati 2020.

23. For instance, Chibnik (2003; 2011) provides a detailed analysis of how Oaxacan wood carvers factor economic, social, and political conditions into their decisions of art making. Michaels (1994) discusses the sovereignty of cultural knowledge and knowledge production among Australian Aboriginal art makers, especially in "the age of TV." The volume edited by Phillips and Steiner (1999) generates a dynamic and sophisticated understanding of the interaction between art makers, dealers, collectors, and consumers in the global market.

24. Thangka paintings thus can be seen as something that dictates a plurality of ontologies; see Kopytoff 1986; Meyer 2015; and Holbraad and Pedersen 2017.

25. Buddhist teaching and religious practices in Tibet were severely disrupted by various political movements, including the Anti-Rightist Campaign (1957–59), the Great Leap Forward (1958–62), and the Cultural Revolution (1966–76).

Rebgong art making almost came to a halt in the mid-twentieth century (Linrothe 2001; Stevenson 2002; Kalzang Tseden 2011).

26. Charlene Makley translated and cited the article written by Li Xuansheng, the former party secretary of Huangnan TAP, describing his 2006–7 development plans (2018, 237).

27. For more discussion of Rebgong's cultural development/industry, see Makley 2018, 69–70.

28. This famed Chinese artist's name was also spelled as *Chang Dai-chien*.

29. The Reform era (Ch. *gai ge kai fang*) in China began in 1978 with a variety of economic reforms transforming China from a planned economy to a market-oriented economy.

30. See Kossak, Singer, and Bruce-Gardner 1998.

31. Lopez (2018, 140–44) criticizes early works by Giuseppe Tucci (1949), Fokke Sierksma (1966), and Pratapaditya Pal (1969; 1990), who consider Tibetan art as art makers' responses to the harsh natural environment or an unbearable social life. For instance, Tucci's photographer Fosco Maraini characterizes the making of Tibetan art as "the need for horror."

32. In explaining the cover image of the exhibition catalog, *Paramasukha-Chakrasamvara Father-Mother* (Tib. *yab yum*, for images depicting the deity and consort in union), Rhie and Thurman emphasize that this image represents "the deepest archetypes of the unconscious, integrating the powerful, instinctual energies of life into a consciously sublimated and exalted state," and that such spiritual depth is "Tibet's most precious gifts to civilization" (1991, 17). This type of representation leads Clare Harris to allege that by the beginning of the twenty-first century, Tibetan art has been perceived "as a delight for the eyes or a balm for the troubled soul" (2012, 21).

33. For instance, *The Tibetan Buddhist Altar* in the Newark Museum of Art, *The Tibetan Buddhist Shrine Room* in the Rubin Museum of Art and in Smithsonian's Sackler Gallery.

34. His name appears as Jampa Tseten in Harris 1999 and as Amdo Chamba in Harris 2012. For Amdo Jampa's biography, I refer to Tsewang Tashi's (2018, 39) account.

35. Bourdieu uses *pure gaze* to indicate an aesthetic response from people with prolonged exposure to schooling and an aesthetic appreciation, in contrast to the practical or functional reading of an artwork.

36. Although the Tibetan expression the brothers used is translated literally as "true *lha zo*," or "true iconographers," on occasions when Tashi Gyatso and Chodrak expressed this phrase in Chinese, they used *zhen zheng de yi shu jia*, the "true artist."

37. Prominent names of this group include, but are not limited to, Gade (Tib. *dga' bde*, b. 1971), Gonkar Gyatso (Tib. *gong dkar rgya mtsho*, b. 1961), Norbu Tsering (also known as Nortse, Tib. *nor tshe*, b. 1963), and Tsewang Tashi (Tib. *tshed dbang bkra shis*, b. 1963).

38. An exception is Nyantok, a village a few miles north of Rongwo town and well-known for its appliqué thangkas (Kalzang Tseden 2011, 102–3). The production of large-sized appliqué thangkas in Nyantok usually involves multiple families. Experienced male painters make the design and sketch it on an empty canvas, while other female and male family members cut the fabric and glue the pieces onto the canvas, following the sketch.

39. This contrasts to, for instance, Oaxacan wood carving families, in which men are in charge of carving while women do most of the painting. The well-known female artisan María Jiménez of San Martín is famous for her painting design; her male family members provide her the carving (Chibnik 2003, 162–66).

40. For instance, Tsering Drolma (Tsewang Tashi 2018, 236–39) and Monsal Pekar (Schneider 2020).

41. Rajan (2015) also offers critiques on Tibetan women's empowerment activists and points out the contradictions embedded in their discourses.

42. In addition to their native language or dialect and Mandarin, many "non-Tibetan" art makers speak Amdo Tibetan (Makley 2018, 7; Roche 2019, 5) or at least use Tibetan in religious contexts and art making because Buddhist scriptures and painting manuals are written in Tibetan.

43. Anthropologist Ruth Behar (1996, 5) uses the term *oxymoron* to describe the role of participant observer in her autobiographical ethnography. For more discussions on participant observation, see Shah 2017; and McGranahan 2018.

44. Collins (2014), Makley (2018), and Grant (2022) discuss the challenges of doing research and living in rural Tibet as foreigners.

45. For more on languages and dialects in Rebgong, see Dhondup 2011, 51; Roche and Lcag mo tshe ring 2013, 169; and Collins 2014, 11.

1. PAINTING A REGIONAL ART TRADITION

1. See *New York Times*, March 29, 2009, "In 1999, artists in the area [Rebgong] finished the 675-yard-long Great Thangka, which Guinness World Records certified as the biggest thangka in the world"; and the Guinness World Records, "The most people drawing thangkas simultaneously is 1,005 people and was achieved by Tongren County People's Government [China] in Huangnan, Qinghai, China, on 28 July 2019" (accessed on January 11, 2022), https://www .guinnessworldrecords.com/world-records/576381-most-people-drawing -thangkas-simultaneously.

2. The Chinese title of the exhibition was "qing hai sheng wu tun zang zu min jian hui hua cai su yi shu zhan."

3. Tibetan artists such as Rigzin Namgyal (Tib. *rig 'dzin rnam rgyal*), Nyima Tsering (Tib. *nyi ma tshe ring*), Yeshe Tsering (Tib. *ye shes tshe ring*), and Lobzang Jangchu (Tib. *blo bzang byang chub*); Chinese artists such as Mei Dingkai, Chen Bingxi, and Lü Shuming.

4. For the image of this painting, see Harris1999, 152; and Tsewang Tashi 2018, 199.

5. Kalzang Yeshe (Tib. *skal bzang ye shes*) and Lobzang Jangchu (Tib. *blo bzang byang chub*).

6. For instance, see *Gan Zi Zang Hua* (1986), the catalog published in Sichuan, and Tsewang Tashi 2018, 196–200.

7. For the impact of political turbulence on Rebgong painters, also see Stevenson 2002, 206–8.

8. Linrothe estimates about two hundred monasteries in Rebgong and nearby Amdo regions where Rebgong artists might have been invited (2001, 14).

9. Gesso is a mixture of plaster, glue, and water, used as a base paint on wood, canvas, or wall so that other pigments or materials can be applied over it. For more on the treatment of canvas in thangka painting, see Jackson and Jackson 1988, 15–22.

10. According to Kalzang Tseden's interview with Shawo Tsering on January 27, 1994, Zhang and Rebgong painters had used cotton canvas for in situ copying of Dunhuang murals (Kalzang Tseden 2011, 98). This is slightly different from Fraser's account (2011, 122), although Zhang and his team had also used paper soaked in diesel fuel, placing the treated paper on the wall to do direct tracing, as Fraser points out.

11. According to Sarah Fraser, some of the original copies and Zhang's sketch notes are kept in Sichuan, while other copies traveled with Zhang to various places until he settled in Taiwan (2011, 122).

12. See Christie's catalog published with Zhang Daqian's biography (Christie's website, accessed on March 9, 2022, https://www.christies.com/en/stories/10 -things-to-know-about-zhang-daqian-f2b919800c46463e8f5fab5e774e0d1e).

13. The inscription on the back of a painting is called *thang ga'i rgyab yig* in Tibetan, or *tang ka bei wen* in Chinese. The texts can include prayers or wishes (sometimes authored by a venerable tulku) and usually record the name(s) of the patron and the time and place the image was commissioned (Quintman 2013). In some cases, the patron is also depicted as a monk holding offerings on a thangka painting (Linrothe 2001, 30, 32; Chen 2013, 139).

14. Also see Sarah Fraser, "Decolonizing Dunhuang: Tibetan Contributions to a National Site in the 20th Century," Presented at *Then and Now: Collecting Art and Exhibiting Cultures in Asia* conference, Lingnan University, Hong Kong, May 2021.

15. Leading artists in Rebgong included Gyamtso (Tib. *rgya mtsho*, 1915–92), Kunzang (Tib. *kun bzang*, 1919–96), and Chogyal (Tib. *chos rgyal*, 1940–2007); for more on prominent artists in Rebgong, see Stevenson 2002; Kalzang Tseden 2011; and Menchok Dondrub 2016.

16. *The Great Thangka* is now kept and exhibited in the Tibetan Culture Museum in Xining; accessed on January 27, 2022, https://www.tbtmm.com.

17. Recent religious figures on *The Great Thangka* are also included, including the tenth Panchen Lama (1938–89), the seventeenth Karmapa and likely the current Dalai Lama (Linrothe 2001, 58), when the painting was first completed. For an exhausted list of subjects, see Kalzang Tseden 2011, 34–90.

18. According to a retired Tibetan official who used to work for the prefecture (personal communication, February 16, 2012).

19. The book was originally published in Tibetan in 1999 (Tib. *krung go bod kyi rig gnas sgyu rtsal kun 'dus zhal thang chen mo'i rnam bshad mthong grol kun gsal me lung*). The Chinese translation (Ch. *zhong guo zang zu wen hua yi shu cai hui da guan tu shuo ming jing*) was published in 2002.

20. Personal communication with Rinchen, February 12, 2012; and Chamba, January 13, 2022.

21. According to my interview with the retired Tibetan official who participated in exhibiting *The Great Thangka* in Rebgong (personal communication, February 15, 2012).

22. According to the records of Tsondru Rapgye in *The Bright Mirror*, the initial loan from the government was RMB 350,000. Upon the completion of this painting, the loan had increased to over RMB 20 million (2002, 535, 539).

23. UNESCO defines *cultural heritage* beyond monuments and collections of objects by including "traditions or living expressions inherited from our ancestors and passed on to our descendants, such as oral traditions, performing arts, social practices, rituals, festive events, knowledge and practices concerning nature and the universe or the knowledge and skills to produce traditional crafts." Thus, the "intangible cultural heritage" described by UNESCO has the following four attributes: "traditional, contemporary and living at the same time; inclusive; representative; and community-based." See UNESCO Intangible Cultural Heritage official web page, accessed on May 12, 2024, https://ich.unesco.org/en/what-is-intangible-heritage-00003. The definition of *intangible cultural heritage* in China largely follows that of UNESCO. The detailed definition of China's ICH can be found in the "Law on Intangible Cultural Heritage" (2011) (Ch. *fei wu zhi wen hua yi chan fa*) and the official website, accessed on May 12, 2024, https://www.gov.cn/flfg/2011–02/25/content_1857449.htm.

24. Silverman and Blumenfield also point out that the government's enthusiasm about ICH and collaborations with UNESCO are largely motivated by economic returns where the cultural heritage tourism "is the genie let out of the bottle" (2013, 9).

25. According to my interview with the retired Tibetan official who used to work for the prefecture's Cultural Bureau (February 15, 2012) and an official from Tongren County (February 20, 2012).

26. Maags's research on ICH transmitters in Jiangsu and Jiangxi observes similar practices (2018, 130).

27. Ch. *huang nan zhou min jian gong yi shi ji zhou ji fei yi xiang mu dai biao xing chuan cheng ren ping shen ren ding biao zhun he shi shi zhun ze.*

28. See "The Summary of the Preservation Practices of Rebgong Art," published on China's official ICH website in 2019, accessed on November 12, 2021, https://www.ihchina.cn/tenyear_protect_detail/20396.html.

29. Mini-thangkas (Tib. *tsa ka chung chung*, Ch. *xiao tang ka*) are the size of a palm of

the hand and are kept with Tibetan people for religious practices. In today's market, many non-Tibetan clients prefer mini-thangkas to regular-sized ones because mini-thangkas are much cheaper and easier to carry around while traveling.

30. These were the things painters described to me as necessary experience in order to apply for various levels of ICH inheritance.

2. "AURA" IN THE ART MARKET

1. For the iconography and practices associated with Loma Gyonma, see Vargas-O'Bryan 2011.

2. For instance, Miller (2001) argues that the "inalienable" value of an object largely depends on the relationship between people and things. Kalb (1994) reveals the different understandings of tradition among *santeros* in New Mexico and how artisans negotiate value in their works. Steiner (1995), Myers (2004), Morphy (2007), and Phillips (2015) also discuss how local art makers create or negotiate cultural authenticities on global markets, although their arts, unlike Rebgong thangkas, are derived from traditional designs and are not used by local residents in rituals or ceremonies.

3. By highlighting the "object biography," Kopytoff suggests that commodification should be understood as "a process of becoming rather than as an all-or-none state of being" (1986, 73).

4. Some Buddhist scriptures even warn the artist not to accept wages because the act of painting is already "greatly rewarded with merits" (Catanese 2019, 25); see also Jackson and Jackson 1988, 12; and Catanese 2019, 74–77.

5. In Wylie transliteration *yon bdag* describes patrons who commission religious images or donate to the monastery, whereas *sbyin bdag* is a more generic description of people who make donations, such as to a school. Note that *shyin bdag* is also the term used by monks for their Han and foreign "supporters."

6. The gold details include gold linings on things like nimbi, seats, flower leaves, robes, and colored lotuses as well as gold brocade designs and ornaments; see Jackson and Jackson 1988, 130–35.

7. Mark Stevenson points out that the earliest demand for Rebgong thangkas by non-Tibetan clients began around 1991 (2002, 211), while Alex John Catanese suggests that painters opening thangka shops for direct sales to non-Tibetan consumers was a more recent phenomenon in Rebgong and nearby Tibetan communities, occurring only around 2004 (2019, 114).

8. The same narrative is applied to the Tibetan Museum in Lhasa, where Tibetan culture is presented as "a set of beautiful things accompanied by some quaintly archaic 'folk' customs" without any emphasis on the philosophy and practice of Tibetan Buddhism (C. Harris 2012, 187).

9. For instance, Graburn clearly puts "isolated tradition" and "modern pluralism" on two poles of the axis (1984, 396–99, especially figure 1). Errington (1998, 108) makes similar arguments on "cult objects," which she considers not meant to be circulated in the art market. Moreover, Benjamin (1969) follows Weber's (1981)

thesis that the modern urban marketplace is a rationalized and secularized social sphere and considers the production of a commodity for the marketplace as the antithesis of the creation of sacred objects for ritual use.

10. This was before the "Criteria and Rules" was established and came into effect in 2014.

11. The closest Tibetan term is *bla dpon chen mo*, which describes those accomplished artists or leading art teachers.

12. This was before vlog, e-commerce, or social network platforms like WeChat and TikTok became prevalent in China.

13. Yonghe Temple was built in the late seventeenth century and is the largest Tibetan monastery in Beijing. It is now a popular place of worship for both Tibetans and non-Tibetans. It also attracts millions of domestic and foreign tourists annually.

14. The "thangka master" I describe in this chapter is not a singular or extreme example. In my research, painters and local officials were able to identify several "masters" who shared the same experience and practice, especially after Rebgong art was recognized as a national ICH in 2006 and before the "Criteria and Rules" came into effect in 2014.

15. The use of the Tibetan term *sgyu rtsal gling* is possibly adapted from Mandarin, after the emergence of art institutions or schools that publicly accept students and produce thangka paintings beyond the scale of family-owned workshops (Chamba, personal communication, May 13, 2021).

16. In this context Rebgong painters use *borrow* (Tib. *gyar ba*) and *take* (Tib. *'khyer ba*) interchangeably.

17. In Tibetan, *ngas khyod kyi thang ga khyer nas sbyin bdag la bstan te dgos na blus chog gam.*

18. In Namgyal's art school, as well as in some other studios and art schools in Rebgong, the transmission of thangka follows the apprenticeship style of teaching. Apprentices are assigned to different tasks based on their skill level. Helping the *ge gen* with commissions is an important way of learning and improving thangka painting skills. The *ge gen* does not charge tuition and needs to provide apprentices food, lodging, and allowances as the paid apprenticeship. It's the *ge gen's* responsibility to find money to keep the studio or school running.

19. Government-sponsored accelerated training programs were first established in a few ready-built art schools around 2010 and expanded to galleries and family workshops from 2013. The accelerated programs provide a painter enough training to be able to complete one piece of thangka painting independently. Painters may stay in the accelerated program for weeks, months, or a year at most. In 2019 the government offered about RMB 80,000 to an art school if it agreed to provide accelerated training for twenty to twenty-five students in addition to its regular training of apprentices.

20. Other examples of artistic creativity in thangka art include Gendun Chopel (Harris 1999, 115–19) and Amdo Jampa (Tsewang Tashi 2018, 46–47).

21. For more discussions on the representation of ethnic groups in China, see Costello 2002; Oakes and Sutton 2010; Silverman and Blumenfield 2013.

22. Ledderose points out that Chinese art makers "tried to create along the *principles* of nature. These principles included prodigious creation of large numbers of organisms. Variations, mutations, changes here and there add up over time, eventually resulting in entirely new shapes" (2000, 7). Although painters like Namgyal follow the rules of iconography and composition—in a sense, copying or reproducing existing works—their study and conversation with monks about Buddhist scriptures (therefore, understanding of the texts) contribute to the "variations, mutations, [and] changes" that Ledderose sees as causing the art to evolve over time.

3. WOMEN WHO PAINT THANGKAS

1. Schein (2000, 285) uses the term *feminine hinge* to describe the association of women and minorities with a static past, whereas Han and, in many cases, ethnic minority men internalize this characterization while embracing the advancing national modernity. Makley (2007, 167) extends this concept to the Tibetan context and suggests that the "feminine hinge" has produced "very different consequences for the mobility of Tibetan men versus women in the Labrang region" during the post-Mao Reform era.

2. While monks and thangka teachers may each have a list of forbidden subjects for female painters, some local scholars oppose this idea and argue that no Buddhist text articulates this taboo (see Chamba, personal communication, February 25 and December 2, 2021). Nevertheless, women painters usually refrain from painting certain deities. In Namgyal's art school, for instance, male painters stay in a different room if they need to paint the image of Yamantaka.

3. An increasing number of young couples purchase apartments in town. Some use the apartment as their art studio; some simply prefer spending some time alone away from the village. When it comes to schooling, some children attending schools in town live with their grandparents in their apartment, while their parents go back to the village to take care of farmwork and art making. Levine (2021, 91–92) also points out that education and economic opportunities are important factors in families' decisions about where to live in Amdo Tibet.

4. Many rural families still practice father-son inheritance, although an increasing number of families are deciding to distribute farmland and wealth equally among their sons and daughters. Note that a son inherits the religious lineage and protector deity from his father too. A married woman may change her lineage and worship her husband's family protector or worship both. This is why before families agree upon a marriage, they arrange a divination (Tib. *mo* or *mo rtsis*) to see if the woman's protector deity would fight with that of her future husband (also see Wu 2013, 130).

5. Recordkeeping of the exchange of social support and gifts is prevalent in several villages in Rebgong. Families keep their gift registers in private, whereas entries

of *skyes tho* for public events, such as the renovation of the village monastery, are usually recorded and kept by a group of village leaders.

6. In 2019, for instance, tractor drivers from outside of Rebgong, with their harvesters imported from Japan, charged local residents RMB 50 to 100 (about USD 7 to 14) per *mu* (approx. 0.16 acres) of farmland and completed the harvest for each household in a couple of hours. Without a harvester, it takes more than a week for one household to manually do the harvest.

7. De-agriculturalization and rural multifunctionality (Liang et al. 2020; Mölders 2014) have become pervasive ideologies in China; that is, rural areas need to diversify their functions, including farming, industry, tourism, and commerce, including e-commerce, in the planning of land use. Makley describes the state-led market participation and commoditizing of rural land based on her research in Rebgong since the early 2000s (2018, 174–81). From my own observation from around 2013, I can attest that an increasing amount of farmland has been repurposed to build art institutions or facilities that accommodate cultural industry and ethnic tourism projects.

8. The word *grib* is used for both physical pollution (e.g., dirty water poured into the river) and moral or spiritual pollution (e.g., smoking tobacco in front of an image of the Buddha).

9. The average annual income of Huangnan residents in 2018 was RMB 15,249 (about USD 2,180). This number takes into account both rural residents (whose average income falls below RMB 15,249) and those who live in town. See a report of residents' income in 2018 by the Statistics Bureau of Huangnan Tibetan Autonomous Prefecture, http://www.tjcn.org/tjnj/29qh/38086.html, May 14, 2019.

10. The local government makes a great effort to implement the "nine-year compulsory education" (Ch. *jiu nian zhi yi wu jiao yu*) policy in Rebgong's rural areas. Some painting families choose to let their children drop out of school after elementary education to become full-time apprentices of thangka painting.

11. Several female painters in Rebgong, before they started to learn thangka painting, spent a few months each year harvesting caterpillar fungus on the mountains in nearby highland towns (e.g., Lancai County). According to them, when the harvest was good, selling caterpillar fungus added about RMB 30,000 to 40,000 (approx. USD 4,300 to 5,700) additional income to a household every year. In addition, some rural women in Rebgong also sell farm produce—radishes, potatoes, scallions—and home-baked bread, *go re*, on village roads or in town.

12. According to Levine, the fixed land contracts have been implemented since the late 1990s (2021, 88). Pastoralist resettlement occurred in the 2000s in eastern Tibetan regions in China (see, e.g., Gyal 2015; Ptackova 2020).

13. Eighteen women among the twenty-eight female painters I talked to told me that they were sent to art schools and started painting thangkas after this sort of family conversation. Some other families have left their daughters' fate to a

diviner (Tib. *mo pa*)—there are unfortunate cases in which the daughter did not
pursue thangka painting because the diviner disapproved of such a choice.

14. Intervillage marriage is common in Rebgong. A woman who marries into
another village may also introduce her siblings to desirable art teachers in her
husband's village (Chen 2013, 62).

15. A *tso wa* (Tib. *tso wa*) consists of many families (usually from the same village
but not necessarily biologically related) and functions as a mutual aid group. A
tso wa has its own temple, worshipping its protector deity in the village. Many
tso wa in Rebgong rent a piece of land on mountains outside Rebgong during
the caterpillar fungus picking season and only allow members of the same *tso
wa* to harvest on the contracted land.

16. The average time spent on painting is calculated through my surveys with
thirty-four male thangka painters from Sengeshong and Gasar in 2012. This is
also consistent with my observations in Rebgong.

17. Laurel Kendall brought up this comparison to me in planning an exhibition of
Tibetan thangka at the American Museum of Natural History (personal communication, February 26, 2021).

18. The commodification of Tibetanness is not confined to women. Tenzin (translated in Chinese as *ding zhen*), a young Tibetan man from Litang County (Tib.
li thang rdzong) in Sichuan, has been a rising star among Han netizens, who
admire his looks, wildness, and innocent nature, which resonates with their
imagination of Kham Tibetan men. In 2021 Tenzin became the public face for
the Department of Tourism in Sichuan.

19. Although some village women in Rebgong have engaged in selling caterpillar
fungus and farm produce on village roads or in town, running the business
of thangka art is somewhat different. Operating one's own thangka studio
not only requires the artist to train his or her apprentices and meet clients (or
tourists) in the studio but also to travel to places near and far, to socialize with
clients and/or to participate in social events such as gallery openings, cultural
expos, and banquets.

20. A common exclamation, equivalent to "okay" or "sure."

21. *Ja tung* (Tib. *ja 'thung*) means "to drink tea."

22. Rongwo Gonpa (Tib. *rong bo dgon pa*) literally means the Rongwo Monastery.
Jampa used it here as an exclamation, something equivalent to "Oh my god."

23. *Chu dak* (Tib. *chu bdag* or *'grig bdag*, Ch. *nong geng jian hu ren*) are chosen from
each village clan (*tso wa*) to supervise the agricultural cycle and regulate the
use of water and other resources (also see Tshe ring skyid 2015). There are no
female *chu dak* in Gasar village.

24. The protector deity is *tso shi ri lang* in Tibetan or *er lang shen* in Chinese.

25. There are three village temples in Gasar, each belonging to one *tso wa* of the village
and worshipping specific protector deities (Wang 2010; Tshe ring skyid 2015, 263).

26. Wang (2010) documents a similar event and expression, which takes place at the
Lurol festival.

27. It's called "chos skor la sgor mo byin" in Tibetan.

28. The gift and food brought back from a pilgrimage trip are called "mjal sil or skor sbrang" in Tibetan, translated as *bai pin* in Chinese (Chamba, personal communication, December 20, 2021).

29. The two pathways are G213, the one going through Gasar, and S306, the parallel road on the other side of the Guchu River.

30. Makley uses the pseudonyms Langmo and Kharnak for these two villages.

31. I thank an anonymous reviewer for pointing out other factors, including Sengeshong's position on what was originally the only highway between Xining and Rebgong as well as Upper Sengeshong being the home of the famed Rebgong artist Shawo Tsering.

32. For Gasar's orchard projects, see Tshe ring skyid 2015, 255.

33. Some used the Tibetan expression, "sems gting nas dga' byung," while others expressed it in Chinese, "da xin di jue de gao xing."

34. Guanyin is the female form of Avalokiteshvara in East Asian Buddhist traditions, such as in Chinese and Japanese Buddhism (Blofeld 1979; Yü 2001). In Tibetan Buddhism, as in the iconography of Tibetan thangka art, Avalokiteshvara appears as a male.

35. The mantra script is adapted from Dekyi Drolma 2007, which also offers occasions when Tibetan women worship the image of Tara or recite Tara's mantra (221–39).

36. The deity Tara has many manifestations, each with a different name as well as unique attributes and power.

4. THE TRAVELS OF A THANGKA

1. Although there is no standardized title for this painting, Lutso calls it *spyan ras gzigs sems nyid ngal gso* in Tibetan. It can be translated as *Avalokiteshvara Relaxing in the Nature of Mind* or *Avalokiteshvara with Mind at Rest* (Andrew Quintman, personal communication, March 3, 2021). Lutso calls it *ming xiang guan yin* or *guan yin ming xiang xiang* in Chinese when she talks to non-Tibetan audiences.

2. Eveline Washul points out that many Tibetans consider government jobs desirable because they "bring a family socioeconomic status and financial security" (2018, 505). Such jobs usually require bachelor or higher degrees.

3. The story of this divination is recounted from interviews I did with Lutso in 2013 and 2018 and with her father in 2018.

4. For the 2006 data, see "Rebgong Art Is Included in UNESCO's Representative List of the ICH," November 30, 2009, http://news.sina.com.cn/o/2009-11-30 /071316690038s.shtml. The 2022 data is based on a promotional video produced by Tongren City and published on the government's website, "Tongren City 2022 Promotional Video," July 15, 2022, http://www.hntongren.gov.cn /html/5399/420478.html.

5. According to my interviews with Lutso's two female apprentices on August 16, 2019.

6. There is no nunnery in Rongwo Valley. Besides, Lutso has not thought of pursuing a monastic life.

7. "Dying" in the sense that the local people who produce the art or object do not use it anymore. Errington (1998, 129) points out one possibility is that people who used to produce cult objects for their local rituals have converted to a Christianity or Islam (also see Steiner 1994). Although they preserve some of their art skills and traditional designs, they now produce "cult objects" as decorative or folk art only for the global market. Criticisms of AMNH's permanent exhibits include Haraway 1984; and Harding and Martin 2016. Harding and Martin focus on the museum's cultural halls in particular. In addition, C. Harris (2012) offers specific critiques on the problem of representing Tibet in Western museums.

5. ARTISAN OR ARTIST?

1. The promotional material for Rinchen's gallery show was written in Chinese, and he talked to me in Mandarin as well.

2. There is no significant difference between the Chinese term *seng ren* and *seng lü*. The gallery might use *seng lü* as a more formal term or to manage viewers' impressions better.

3. For critiques on the autonomy or originality of the artist, see Marcus and Myers 1995, 22–23; and Wong 2013, 162–71.

4. Kisin and Myers 2019, 318–19. More discussions on the changing value of a religious or indigenous object as it moves across different social spheres, see Clifford 1988; Michaels 1994; Marcus and Myers 1995; Sullivan 2015a; and Tythacott and Bellini 2020.

5. Geismar (2015) shows how ethnographic objects in museums can be contextualized differently, highlighting works of contemporary artists such as Fred Wilson and Lisa Reihana.

6. Mount Wutai is the major cult center of Manjushri located in Shanxi and has a long association with Tibetan Buddhism from the Tang dynasty (Tuttle 2006, 2; Zhang 2019, 155).

7. The quotes capture how Rinchen restated what he had heard from museum audiences and art dealers.

8. Rinchen used the phrase *las dbang* in Tibetan and *ye li* in Chinese to refer to the power of karma.

9. The English exhibition title is translated by the author.

10. One artist who participated in this exhibition (who preferred to be anonymous) told me that these were some questions he received from museum visitors in Beijing (personal communication, July 26, 2018).

11. Quotes from a Chinese-language essay, with tips from "experts" on how to evaluate and collect Tibetan thangka paintings, in Finance.ifeng.com, accessed on July 19, 2016, https://finance.ifeng.com/a/20150106/13408895_0.shtml.

12. See Linrothe 2001, 34; and C. Harris 2012, 6–7. For critiques on the display of Tibetan sacred objects in Western museums, see Clark 2016.

13. The cartoon appeared in the blog *Anthropologizing* on June 20, 2011, https://
    anthropologizing.com/2011/06/20/anthropologists-anthropologists.

14. See Linrothe 2001, 18–19, for a detailed description about the use of color in
    Rebgong thangkas. The color palette Thondup prefers seems closer to the
    karma sgar bris style.

15. Fred Myers uses the word *efficacy* in his various works (e.g., 2002, 5; 2019, 322) in
    the sense of artists fostering conversations about indigenous rights, sovereignty,
    and identity with art viewers. This is different from the Buddhist understand-
    ing of efficacy. It is necessary to point this out because I cite Myers's work in
    this book where religious efficacy is also discussed.

16. The dharma assembly is the gathering of religious teachers, monks, and lay
    practitioners, usually in the course of a few days, to study and practice Buddhist
    teachings.

17. Unless otherwise noted, I adapt Phillip Bloom's (2013) translation of religious
    and artistic terms associated with the Water and Land Ritual.

18. We should note that many figures from Confucianism, ghosts from folklore,
    and secular people are not depicted as beings to be venerated at the Water
    and Land Retreat but are "wandering spirits that have been called to assemble
    at a ritual site so that they might attain a better rebirth" (Bloom 2013, 39; Dai
    2009).

19. For instance, a set of 136 *Water and Land Ritual* paintings from the Ming
    dynasty (1368–1644) from Baoning Monastery is now in the collection of the
    Shanxi Provincial Museum. This set of images is also widely circulated on
    Chinese-language websites and publications, likely giving the first impression
    of *Water and Land Ritual* paintings.

20. The variation is exemplified in art historian Phillip Bloom's 2013 work, whose
    dissertation demonstrates an abundant collection of *Water and Land* images
    from temples, caves, and museums in China, Japan, France, the United States,
    and other places.

21. For Tibetan iconometric theory, see Jackson and Jackson 1988, 50–55. Note
    that the Buddha, bodhisattvas, goddesses, and deities use slightly different
    measurements.

22. I adapt John Kieschnick's translation of *zhuang yan* as "splendor" (2003, 10).

23. The original texts in the *Protocols* read: "說曰。此席原畫。但寫牌位。別無繪
    像。似覺缺憾。余惟水陸佛事。動地驚天之大法。必藉壇儀。方成嚴衞。故
    囑畫師。将本寺殿閣堂宇。繪爲三幅題名。何處设大壇。何處设内壇等。其
    中法師。香燈。及經筵懺席諸師。並陳列繪上。用作瞻觀。俾齋家生敬信。
    如別寺所繪。隨各寺殿堂。善巧布置畫之可也。" The English version is not
    a direct translation but an interpretation of the scripture. My interpretation
    was generated in consultation with Tashi Gyatso and Fan to reveal how the
    artists understood the scripture and how they visualized the texts in paintings.
    According to Fan, they also asked religious specialists and art historians to
    interpret the scripture for them in modern Chinese and to help them check the

coordination between the sketches and the scripture before they finalized the design and proceeded to coloring.

24. While its earliest roots could be traced back to Emperor Wu of the Liang dynasty (464–549), the practice of the Water and Land Retreat has been passed on but constantly modified, especially during the Song dynasty (Bloom 2013, 45).

25. *Wan fa gui yi tu*, ink and color on silk, 1771 (Qianlong reign, thirty-sixth year), collection of the Palace Museum in Beijing.

26. *Qing ming shang he tu*, ink and color on silk, Northern Song dynasty, collection of the Palace Museum in Beijing. *Qing Sun Wen hui quan ben hong lou meng tu*, ink and color on silk, Qing dynasty, collection of Lüshun Museum in Dalian, China.

27. For other examples, see a nineteenth-century Indian painting from Punjab Hills in Kangra, *Radha and Krishna*, in the collection of the Victoria and Albert Museum in London; and a second-century stone medallion carved with "Chaddanta *jataka*" (Dehejia 1990, 384).

28. For this painting he referenced the "Great Praise of the Ten Acts of the Buddha" (Tib. *thub pa'i bstod pa thabs mkhas thugs rje ma*) kept in Lower Wutun Monastery (Tib. *seng ge gshong ma mgo dgon pa*).

29. Also see Wu Hung's explanation of the spatial logic of the wall painting in Cave 196 in Dunhuang (Wu 2022a, 269–77).

6. THE LIFE OF A PAINTING

1. Pema Tseden (Tib. *pad ma tshe brtan*, Ch. *wan ma cai dan*, 1969–2023) is a Tibetan filmmaker and writer. This short story by Pema Tseden was first published in Chinese in 2014 and later translated into Tibetan by students and scholars at Minzu University of China in 2019. The English excerpt is translated by Xue Ming. For more about Pema Tseden's biography and works, see Berry 2024. The original excerpt reads, "第二天，活佛从附近寺院请来七个喇嘛，大张旗鼓地念了七天七夜的经。之后，刻石老人再也没有到过洛桑的梦里。有时候在月亮很大很圆很亮的夜晚，洛桑喝醉酒一个人回家时，偶尔还能听到远处有人敲嘛呢石的声音，静静的像一首无字的歌谣。"

2. In Wylie transliteration, *skyes* means "birth" or "be born." Rebgong painters call it "*skyes sgo* thangka," while Lo Bue (2017, 9) describes it as *skyes rtags* ("signs for rebirth," which include both paintings and statues). Families can make either a *kye go* thangka or *kye go* statue for the deceased and use the image for funeral rites and subsequent veneration.

3. Only a few studies briefly describe the use of *kye go* images and the divination associated with them; see, e.g., Jackson and Jackson 1988; Bentor 1993; and Lo Bue 2017.

4. In Rebgong most residents do cremation (Tib. *pur sbyong*) instead of sky burials (Tib. *bya gtor*) for the deceased. *Dgongs rdzogs*, literally meaning "to fulfill the intentions," is also labeled *yuan man* or *qian gong fa hui* in Mandarin, during which commemoration offerings (e.g., butter lamps, purified water, *tor ma*, or flowers) are made for the deceased to complete the funeral and mourning.

5. For a slightly different version, see Lopez 2018, 68.

6. There are three *bar do* during the forty-nine-day interim between death and rebirth: the moment of death (*'chi kha'i bar do*), the *bar do* of reality (*chos nyid bar do*), and the *bar do* of mundane existence (*srid pa'i bar do*), during which the deceased is either liberated from rebirth or is reborn into one of the six modes of existence (Lopez 2018, 49).

7. For more on the dynamics between monastic and lay communities, see Gernet 1995; and Caple 2019.

8. For more on haunting and social changes in China, see Mueggler 2001; van der Veer 2015; Wu 2015; Kipnis 2021; and Weller and Wu 2021.

9. Mani stones are stone plates, rocks, or pebbles inscribed with the sacred mantra, Buddhist signs, or images of Buddhist deities. Many Tibetans commission and make mani stones carved with the six-syllabled mantra of Avalokiteshvara (*om ma ni pad me hung*) as a form of merit making.

10. For more on the Tibetan philosophy in facing death, see Lopez 2007.

11. Dharma ending age, also known as the "age of the final dharma," indicates a time when Buddhist practitioners are scarce, Buddhist teachings cannot be transmitted appropriately, and very few people can reach enlightenment. For more discussion, see Batchelor 2012.

12. Makley (2007), Fischer (2011), and Washul (2018) write about the increasing mobility in Tibetan communities brought by tourism, development, and urbanization. For more on the changing political, ecological, and religious landscape in Tibet, see Barnett 2012; Yeh 2013; Yeh and Coggins 2014; Gyal 2015; and Makley 2018.

13. Although I did not extensively survey whether or when painters in Rebgong decided to teach their children thangka painting, most protagonists in this book have sent their children to public schools or let their children stay in school at the age when they themselves had started thangka painting.

14. The "project economy" (*xiang mu jing ji*) refers to the state-led development projects that aim to modernize Tibetans' livelihood and lifestyle. While some local Tibetans understand *xiang mu* to mean "doing business," the participants and economic benefits often vary. For more details, see Gyal 2015, 253; and Makley 2018.

15. When Laurel Kendall began her fieldwork with Korean shamans in the 1970s, people already spoke of "the old days" and lamented about changes in their time. She points out that "tradition dies multiple deaths and its mourning accompanies each stratigraphic layer of lived modernity" and advises us not to focus only on the "loss" but also on how agents (in her case, shamans and their clients) "have absorbed the profound changes" (Kendall 2009, xxvi, xix).

16. This is a common belief in many places, including other parts of China and Korea (Laurel Kendall, personal communication, June 16, 2022), so some hospitals have developed funeral parlors and involved funeral specialists to accommodate this special situation (also see Kipnis 2021).

17. Giving a "red packet" (an envelope containing cash) to doctors is a common practice in China, the patient and the family believing it may lead the doctor to be more favorable to the patient (Yang 2013). In Jampa's case, however, he gave the red packet to the doctor more as appreciation than "bribery," since the doctor helped him obtain the permission to take Ama's body out of the hospital before going through the time-consuming paperwork.

18. Except in some rare cases, once a *kye go* thangka is hung in the monastic hall, it will not be removed or replaced.

19. According to a few monks in local monasteries, the stealing of monastery possessions—including religious objects, offerings, and artworks—did happen from time to time, even after security cameras had been installed in recent years.

20. I focus on Western exhibition practices because there is hardly any public exhibit of a Tibetan shrine room in China.

21. The Rubin Museum of Art closed its physical space in October 2024. The Tibetan shrine room exhibit has been moved to the Brooklyn Museum in 2025.

22. See visitors' quotes on the Rubin Museum's Tibetan Buddhist Shrine Room exhibit home page, accessed on May 19, 2022, https://rubinmuseum.org/events /exhibitions/the-tibetan-buddhist-shrine-room.

23. In 2010 the Rubin Museum held an exhibition, *Bardo: Tibetan Art of the Afterlife*, which displayed images associated with the "bardo experiences that confront one upon death." Yet this was a separate exhibition from the Shrine Room exhibit (exhibition catalog accessed on May 8, 2022, https://rubinmuseum.org /events/exhibitions/bardo).

24. In Tibetan *kun dga'* means "joy" or "pleasure," while *ra ba* means "enclosure." Literally, *kun dga' ra ba* is translated as the "pleasure grove," or *xin sheng huan xi zhi di* in Mandarin.

25. *Man dal*, also known as the "universal mandala" or "grain mandala set," consists of embossed silver plates stacked together with valued particles, such as rice, barley, powdered medical herbs, and gemstones.

26. This type of thangka is named *rang gi lha skal* in Tibetan. *Rang gi* means "one's own," *lha* means "god" or "deity," and *skal* means "share." This term effectively means to put everyone's deity on a shared painting. Although the birth deity on a *rang gi lha skal* is usually the same as that on a *kye go* thangka, people do not use *kye go* thangka to describe the painting depicting the birth deity of a living person.

27. There are stories of young children who are believed to be incarnations of deceased village fellows, remembering the past lives and being treated warmly by their "relatives in the past life" (Chen 2013, 219–20).

28. Although I have never seen any family put photos of household members in the shrine room, many residents put photographs or prints of prominent religious teachers, such as the tenth Panchen Lama and the eighth Shartshang Lama, on the wall or next to the *kun dga' ra ba* (cabinet) in their domestic shrine rooms.

29. This is different from the genealogy books (Ch. *jia pu* or *zu pu*) kept in many Han families, which record the generational relationship, a family tree, of both

living and deceased family members. The Tibetan *bsngo yig* records names of
the deceased family members, chronologically arranged by time of death.

30. The architectural painting skills include *tshon ris* (decorative coloring), *khra ris*
(multicolored or patterned design), *dkar bcad nag bcad* (white and black outlin-
ing), *'brug ris* (dragon design), and *gser sbyar ba* (gold decoration), among others
(Chodrak, personal communication, May 22, 2022).

31. Bruce Sullivan (2015b, 35–41) examines various types of yoga classes offered in
Western museums and programed as public events. Not all of them are necessarily associated with religious practice.

32. In a report in *Buddhist Art News*, art historian Melissa Kerin describes Tibetan
Buddhist shrines as "incredibly layered" with religious objects and offerings, not
only because the shrine room houses an abundance of material objects but also
because images painted or hung on walls are layered one over another across a
long period of time, preserving both personal and communal memories (interview accessed on May 16, 2022, https://buddhistartnews.wordpress.com
/2013/05/20/kerin-awarded-mednick-grant-to-study-tibetan-buddhist-shrines;
also see Kerin 2015).

33. *Sman bla'i mdo chog bzhugs so*, "The liturgical method for the worship of the
Medicine Buddha," or *yao shi fo xiu xin yi gui* in Mandarin.

EPILOGUE

1. Skal ldan rgya mtsho (1607–77) was recognized as the first Shartshang Lama.

2. Yellow Jambhala holds a mongoose (Tib. *ne'u le*) in his left hand that spews forth
gems from its mouth. On Rebgong thangka paintings, it is usually depicted as a
mouselike creature, with a long and slim tail. It is call *tu bao shu* in Chinese.

3. The finger-width, or *sor in Tibetan* (Ch. *zhi*), is a measurement unit in Buddhist
iconometry (also see Jackson and Jackson 1988, 50). It does not have an absolute
value and is only used to indicate the proportional measure of each body
part within one deity. The numbers given here are measurements of a seated
Buddha.

4. For other versions, see Kalzang Tseden 2011, 196; and Menchok Dondrub's
(2016) oral history accounts of Rebgong painters.

REFERENCES

Abu-Lughod, Lila. 2008. *Writing Women's Worlds: Bedouin Stories.* Berkeley: University of California Press.

Agarwal, Bina. 1997. "'Bargaining' and Gender Relations: Within and beyond the Household." *Feminist Economics* 3, no. 1: 1–51.

Appadurai, Arjun, ed. 1986. *The Social Life of Things: Commodities in Cultural Perspective.* Cambridge: Cambridge University Press.

Ashworth, Gregory. 2014. "Heritage and Economic Development: Selling the Unsellable." *Heritage and Society* 7, no. 1: 3–17.

Babcock, Barbara A. 1993. "At Home, No Womens Are Storytellers: Ceramic Creativity and the Politics of Discourse in Cochiti Pueblo." In *Creativity/Anthropology*, edited by Smadar Lavie, Kirin Narayan, and Renato Rosaldo, 71–99. Ithaca: Cornell University Press.

Barnett, Robert. 2006. *Lhasa: Street with Memories.* New York: Columbia University Press.

Barnett, Robert. 2012. "Restrictions and Their Anomalies: The Third Forum and the Regulation of Religion in Tibet." *Journal of Current Chinese Affairs* 41, no. 4: 45–107.

Batchelor, Stephen. 2012. "A Secular Buddhism." *Journal of Global Buddhism* 13:87–107.

Bauer, Kenneth. 2006. "Common Property and Power: Insights from a Spatial Analysis of Historical and Contemporary Pasture Boundaries among Pastoralists in Central Tibet." *Journal of Political Ecology* 13, no. 1: 24–47.

Behar, Ruth. 1995. "Introduction: Out of Exile." In *Women Writing Culture*, edited by Ruth Behar and Deborah Gordon, 1–29. Berkeley: University of California Press.

Behar, Ruth. 1996. *The Vulnerable Observer: Anthropology That Breaks Your Heart.* Boston: Beacon Press.

Belting, Hans. 2014. *An Anthropology of Images: Picture, Medium, Body.* Princeton: Princeton University Press.

Benjamin, Walter. 1969. "The Work of Art in the Age of Mechanical Reproduction." In *Illuminations*, edited by Hannah Arendt, translated by Harry Zohn, 217–52. New York: Schocken Books. First published 1935.

Bentor, Yael. 1993. "Tibetan Tourist Thangkas in the Kathmandu Valley." *Annals of Tourism Research* 20:107–37.

Bentor, Yael. 1996. *Consecration of Images and Stupas in Indo-Tibetan Tantric Buddhism*. Leiden: Brill.

Berger, Patricia. 2003. *Empire of Emptiness: Buddhist Art and Political Authority in Qing China*. Honolulu: University of Hawaii Press.

Berry, Chris. 2024. "Pema Tseden (1969–2023): A Tribute." *Film Quarterly* 77, no. 3: 22–30.

Beyer, Stephan. 1988. *Magic and Ritual in Tibet*. New Delhi: Motilal Banarsidass Publishing House.

Bian, Yanjie. 2018. "The Prevalence and the Increasing Significance of *Guanxi*." *China Quarterly* 235, no. 3: 597–621.

Blofeld, John. 1979. "Kuan Yin and Tara: Embodiments of Wisdom-Compassion Void." *Tibet Journal* 4, no. 3: 28–63.

Bloom, Phillip. 2013. "Descent of the Deities: The Water-Land Retreat and the Transformation of the Visual Culture of Song Dynasty (960–1279) Buddhism." PhD diss., Harvard University.

Blumenfield, Tami. 2018. "Recognition and Misrecognition: The Politics of Intangible Cultural Heritage in Southwest China." In *Chinese Heritage in the Making: Experiences, Negotiations, and Contestations*, edited by Christina Maags and Marina Svensson, 169–94. Amsterdam: Amsterdam University Press.

Bourdieu, Pierre. 1984. *Distinction: A Social Critique of the Judgment of Taste*. London: Routledge. First published 1979.

Bourdieu, Pierre. 1993. *The Field of Cultural Production: Essays on Art and Literature*. New York: Columbia University Press.

Brox, Trine. 2019. "The Aura of Buddhist Material Objects in the Age of Mass-Production." *Journal of Global Buddhism* 20:105–25.

Brox, Trine, and Elizabeth Williams-Oerberg. 2017. "Buddhism, Business, and Economics." In *The Oxford Handbook of Contemporary Buddhism*, edited by Michael Jerryson, 504–17. New York: Oxford University Press.

Bundgaard, Helle. 1999. "Contending Indian Art Worlds." *Journal of Material Culture* 4, no. 3: 321–37.

Caple, Jane. 2019. *Morality and Monastic Revival in Post-Mao Tibet*. Honolulu: University of Hawaii Press.

Caple, Jane. 2020. "Rethinking Tibetan Buddhism in Post-Mao China, 1980–2015." *Review of Religion and Chinese Society* 7, no. 1: 62–91.

Catanese, Alex John. 2019. *Buddha in the Marketplace: The Commodification of Buddhist Objects in Tibet*. Charlottesville: University of Virginia Press.

Cave, Roderick. 1998. *Chinese Paper Offerings*. Oxford: Oxford University Press.

Chamba (byams pa). 2019. "On the Academic Background and Intellectual Exchanges of *Gung gön po kyap*, the General Director of the School of Foreigners during the Qing Dynasty." *Journal of Tibet University* 140, no. 4: 40–47.

Chao, Emily. 2012. *Lijiang Stories: Shamans, Taxi Drivers, and Runaway Brides in Reform-Era China*. Seattle: University of Washington Press.

Chen, Naihua. 2013. *Wuming de Zaoshenzhe: Regong Tangka Yiren Yanjiu* (Anonymous Depicters of the Buddha: A Study of Rebgong Thangka Painters). Beijing: Shijie Tushu Chubangongsi.

Chibnik, Michael. 2003. *Crafting Tradition: The Making and Marketing of Oaxacan Wood Carvings.* Austin: University of Texas Press.

Chibnik, Michael. 2011. *Anthropology, Economics, and Choices.* Austin: University of Texas Press.

Chio, Jenny. 2014. *A Landscape of Travel: The Work of Tourism in Rural Ethnic China.* Seattle: University of Washington Press.

Clark, Imogen. 2016. "Exhibiting the Exotic, Stimulating the Sacred: Tibetan Shrines at British and American Museums." *Ateliers d'anthropologie. Revue éditée par le Laboratoire d'Ethnologie et de Sociologie Comparative* 43. Posted online on October 5, 2016, https://doi.org/10.4000/ateliers.10300.

Clarke, John. 2015. "Planning the Robert H. N. Ho Family Foundation Gallery of Buddhist Sculpture, 2009–2014." In *Sacred Objects in Secular Spaces: Exhibiting Asian Religions in Museums,* edited by Bruce Sullivan, 67–79. London: Bloomsbury.

Clifford, James. 1988. *The Predicament of Culture.* Cambridge: Harvard University Press.

Collins, Dawn. 2014. "Presence in Tibetan Landscapes: Spirited Agency and Ritual Healing in Rebgong." PhD diss., Cardiff University.

Costa, Jorge, and Livio Ferrone. 1995. "Sociocultural Perspectives on Tourism Planning and Development." *International Journal of Contemporary Hospitality Management* 7, no. 7: 27–35.

Costello, Susan. 2002. "The Economics of Cultural Production in Contemporary Amdo." In *Amdo Tibetans in Transition: Society and Culture in the Post-Mao Era,* edited by Toni Huber, 221–40. Kathmandu: Vajra Publications.

Craig, Sienna. 2020. *The Ends of Kinship: Connecting Himalayan Lives between Nepal and New York.* Seattle: University of Washington Press.

Dai, Xiaoyun. 2009. *Fo jiao shui lu hua yan jiu* [Research on the Buddhist water and land ritual paintings]. Beijing: Zhongguo Shehui Kexue Chubanshe.

Dehejia, Vidya. 1990. "On Modes of Visual Narration in Early Buddhist Art." *Art Bulletin* 72, no. 3: 374–92.

Dekyi Drolma (bde skyid sgrol ma). 2007. *Sheng dian zhong de lian hua: Du mu xin yang jie xi* [The lotus in the sacred palace: An analysis of the belief of Tara]. Beijing: Zhongguo Zangxue Chubanshe.

Demick, Barbara. 2020. *Eat the Buddha: Life and Death in a Tibetan Town.* New York: Random House.

Denton, Kirk. 2005. "Museums, Memorial Sites, and Exhibitionary Culture in the People's Republic of China." *China Quarterly* 183, no. 3: 565–86.

Dhondup, Yangdon. 2011. "Reb kong: Religion, History and Identity of a Sino-Tibetan Borderland Town." *Revue d'Etudes Tibétaines* 20:33–59.

Errington, Shelly. 1998. *The Death of Authentic Primitive Art and Other Tales of Progress.* Berkeley: University of California Press.

Fischer, Andrew. 2011. "The Great Transformation of Tibet? Rapid Labor Transitions in Times of Rapid Growth in the Tibet Autonomous Region." *Himalaya* 30, no. 1: 63–77.

Fischer, Andrew. 2013. *The Disempowered Development of Tibet in China: A Study in the Economics of Marginalization.* Lanham, MD: Rowman & Littlefield.

Fjeld, Heidi. 2021. "Relations as Potential: Pragmatism and Flexibility in Tibetan Kinship." *Inner Asia* 23, no. 1: 103–30.

Fraser, Sarah. 2011. "Sha bo tshe ring, Zhang Daqian and Sino-Tibetan Cultural Exchange, 1941–1943: Defining Research Methods for Amdo Regional Painting Workshops in the Medieval and Modern Periods." In *Art in Tibet: Issues in Traditional Tibetan Art from the 7th to the 12th Century*, edited by Erberto Lo Bue, 115–36. Leiden: Brill.

Gaetano, Arianne, and Tamara Jacka, eds. 2004. *On the Move: Women and Rural-to-Urban Migration in Contemporary China.* New York: Columbia University Press.

Ganzi Zang Hua. 1986. *Gan Zi Zang Hua* [The new Tibetan painting in Garze]. Chengdu: Sichuan Minzu Chubanshe.

Gayley, Holly. 2016. *Love Letters from Golok: A Tantric Couple in Modern Tibet.* New York: Columbia University Press.

Geertz, Hildred. 2004. *The Life of a Balinese Temple: Artistry, Imagination, and History in a Peasant Village.* Honolulu: University of Hawaii Press.

Geismar, Haidy. 2015. "The Art of Anthropology: Questioning Contemporary Art in Ethnographic Display." In *The International Handbooks of Museum Studies: Museum Theory*, edited by Andrea Witcomb and Kylie Message, 183–210. Hoboken, NJ: John Wiley & Sons.

Gell, Alfred. 1998. *Art and Agency: An Anthropological Theory.* Oxford: Clarendon Press.

Germano, David. 2007. "Dying, Death, and Other Opportunities." In *Religions of Tibet in Practice*, edited by Donald S. Lopez Jr., 336–71. Abridged ed. Princeton: Princeton University Press.

Gernet, Jacques. 1995. *Buddhism in Chinese Society: An Economic History from the Fifth to the Tenth Centuries.* Translated by Franciscus Verellen. New York: Columbia University Press.

Goldstein, Melvyn. 1997. *The Snow Lion and the Dragon: China, Tibet, and the Dalai Lama.* Berkeley: University of California Press.

Gong que hu dan ba rao ji. 1989. *An duo zheng jiao shi* [The political and religious history of Amdo]. Lanzhou: Gansu Minzu Chubanshe.

Goodman, David, and Richard Edmonds, eds. 2004. *China's Campaign to "Open Up the West": National, Provincial and Local Perspectives.* Cambridge: Cambridge University Press.

Gopnik, Blake. 2010. "The Tibetan Shrine Puts Relics in Original Light." *Washington Post*, March 21, 2010.

Graburn, Nelson. 1969. "Art and Acculturative Processes." *International Social Science Journal* (UNESCO, Paris) 21, no. 3: 457–68.

Graburn, Nelson, ed. 1976. *Ethnic and Tourist Arts: Cultural Expressions from the Fourth World.* Berkeley: University of California Press.

Graburn, Nelson. 1984. "The Evolution of Tourist Arts." *Annals of Tourism Research* 11:393–419.

Graburn, Nelson. 1999. "Epilogue: Ethnic and Tourist Arts Revisited." In *Unpacking Culture: Art and Commodity in Colonial and Postcolonial Worlds,* edited by Ruth Phillips and Christopher Steiner, 335–54. Berkeley: University of California Press.

Grant, Andrew. 2022. *The Concrete Plateau: Urban Tibetans and the Chinese Civilizing Machine.* Ithaca: Cornell University Press.

Gyal, Huatse. 2015. "The Politics of Standardising and Subordinating Subjects: The Nomadic Settlement Project in Tibetan Areas of Amdo." *Nomadic Peoples* 19, no. 2: 241–60.

Gyal, Huatse. 2019. "'I Am Concerned with the Future of My Children': The Project Economy and Shifting Views of Education in a Tibetan Pastoral Community." *Critical Asian Studies* 51, no. 1: 12–30.

Gyatso, Gonkar. 2003. "No Man's Land: Real and Imaginary Tibet: The Experience of an Exiled Tibetan Artist." *Tibet Journal* 28, nos. 1–2: 147–60.

Gyatso, Janet, and Hanna Havnevik, eds. 2005. *Women in Tibet.* New York: Columbia University Press.

Haraway, Donna. 1984. "Teddy Bear Patriarchy: Taxidermy in the Garden of Eden, New York City, 1908–1936." *Social Text* 11, no. 3: 20–64.

Harding, Susan, and Emily Martin. 2016. "Anthropology Now and Then in the American Museum of Natural History." *Anthropology Now* 8, no. 3: 1–13.

Harrell, Stevan. 2001. "The Anthropology of Reform and the Reform of Anthropology: Anthropological Narratives of Recovery and Progress in China." *Annual Review of Anthropology* 30, no. 1: 139–61.

Harrell, Stevan. 2013. *Ways of Being Ethnic in Southwest China.* Seattle: University of Washington Press.

Harris, Christina. 2007. "Mediators in the Transnational Marketplace: Wholesalers of Tibetan Ceremonial Scarves and the Marketing of Meaning." In *Traders and Trade Routes of Central and Inner Asia: The "Silk Road" Then and Now,* edited by Michael Gervers, Uradyn Bulag and Gillian Long, 189–206. Toronto: University of Toronto.

Harris, Clare. 1999. *In the Image of Tibet: Tibetan Paintings after 1959.* London: Reaktion.

Harris, Clare. 2012. *The Museum on the Roof of the World: Art, Politics, and the Representation of Tibet.* Chicago: University of Chicago Press.

Harris, Tina. 2012. "From Loom to Machine: Tibetan Aprons and the Configuration of Place." *Environment and Planning D: Society and Space* 30, no. 5: 877–95.

Höfer, Regina. 2011. "Making Emptiness Visible: Sonam Dolma and Contemporary Tibetan Abstraction." *Modern Art Asia* 8 (November).

Holbraad, Martin, and Morten Axel Pedersen. 2017. *The Ontological Turn: An Anthropological Exposition.* Cambridge: Cambridge University Press.

Huber, Toni. 1999. *The Cult of Pure Crystal Mountain: Popular Pilgrimage and Visionary Landscape in Southeast Tibet.* Oxford: Oxford University Press.

Jackson, David, and Janice Jackson. 1988. *Tibetan Thangka Painting: Methods and Materials.* Boston: Snow Lion Publications.

Kalb, Laurie. 1994. *Crafting Devotions: Tradition in Contemporary New Mexico Santos.* Albuquerque: University of New Mexico Press.

Kalzang Tseden (bskal bzang tshe brtan). 2011. *Re gong tang ka* (Rebgong Thangka). Xining: Qinghai People's Press.

Kang, Dongjing, and Zhou Li. 2021. "Home-in-Language: Examining Tibetan Migrants' Narratives of Homeplace amid China's Urbanization." *Language and Intercultural Communication* 21, no. 2: 174–89.

Kant, Immanuel. 2000. *Critique of the Power of Judgment.* Translated by Paul Guyer and Eric Matthews. Cambridge: Cambridge University Press. First published 1790.

Keane, Webb. 2013. "On Spirit Writing: Materialities of Language and the Religious Work of Transduction." *Journal of the Royal Anthropological Institute* 19, no. 1: 1–17.

Kendall, Laurel. 2008. "Of Hungry Ghosts and Other Matters of Consumption in the Republic of Korea: The Commodity Becomes a Ritual Prop." *American Ethnologist* 35, no. 1: 154–70.

Kendall, Laurel. 2009. *Shamans, Nostalgias, and the IMF: South Korean Popular Religion in Motion.* Honolulu: University of Hawaii Press.

Kendall, Laurel. 2015. "Can Commodities Be Sacred? Material Religion in Seoul and Hanoi." In *Handbook of Religion and the Asian City: Aspiration and Urbanization in the Twenty-First Century,* edited by Peter van der Veer, 367–84. Oakland: University of California Press.

Kendall, Laurel. 2021. *Mediums and Magical Things: Statues, Paintings, and Masks in Asian Places.* Oakland: University of California Press.

Kendall, Laurel, and Ni Wayan Pasek Ariati. 2020. "Scary Mask / Local Protector: The Curious History of Jero Amerika." *Anthropology and Humanism* 45, no. 2: 279–300.

Kendall, Laurel, Jongsung Yang, and Yul Soo Yoon. 2015. *God Pictures in Korean Contexts: The Ownership and Meaning of Shaman Paintings.* Honolulu: University of Hawaii Press.

Kendall, Laurel, Vu Thi Ha, Vu Thi Thanh Tam, Nguyen Van Huy, and Nguyen Thi Hien. 2013. "Is It a Sin to Sell a Statue? Catholic Statues and the Traffic in Antiquities in Vietnam." *Museum Anthropology* 36, no. 1: 66–82.

Kerin, Melissa. 2015. *Art and Devotion at a Buddhist Temple in the Indian Himalaya.* Bloomington: Indiana University Press.

Kieschnick, John. 2003. *The Impact of Buddhism on Chinese Material Culture.* Princeton: Princeton University Press.

Kipnis, Andrew. 2021. *The Funeral of Mr. Wang: Life, Death, and Ghosts in Urbanizing China.* Oakland: University of California Press.

Kisin, Eugenia, and Fred Myers. 2019. "The Anthropology of Art, after the End of Art: Contesting the Art-Culture System." *Annual Review of Anthropology* 48, no. 1: 317–34.

Kopytoff, Igor. 1986. "The Cultural Biography of Things: Commoditization as Process." In *The Social Life of Things: Commodities in Cultural Perspective*, edited by Arjun Appadurai, 64–91. Cambridge: Cambridge University Press.

Kossak, Steven, Jane Casey Singer, and Robert Bruce-Gardner. 1998. *Sacred Visions: Early Paintings from Central Tibet*. New York: Metropolitan Museum of Art, distributed by Harry N. Abrams. https://www.metmuseum.org/met-publications/sacred-visions-early-paintings-from-central-tibet.

Ledderose, Lothar. 2000. *Ten Thousand Things: Module and Mass Production in Chinese Art*. Princeton: Princeton University Press.

Levine, Nancy. 2021. "Practical Kinship: The Centrality of Siblings in Pastoralist Life." *Inner Asia* 23, no. 1: 79–102.

Li, Yuhang. 2020. *Becoming Guanyin: Artistic Devotion of Buddhist Women in Late Imperial China*. New York: Columbia University Press.

Liang, Xinyuan, Xiaobin Jin, Jie Ren, Zhengming Gu, and Yinkang Zhou. 2020. "A Research Framework of Land Use Transition in Suzhou City Coupled with Land Use Structure and Landscape Multifunctionality." *Science of the Total Environment* 737:1–13.

Linrothe, Robert. 2001. "Creativity, Freedom, and Control in the Contemporary Renaissance of Rebgong Painting." *Tibet Journal* 26, no. 3: 5–90.

Linrothe, Robert. 2004. *Paradise and Plumage: Chinese Connections in Tibetan Arhat Painting*. New York: Rubin Museum of Art.

Linrothe, Robert. 2015. "A Group of Mural Paintings from the 1930s in A mdo reb gong." *Asian Highlands Perspectives* 37:279–95.

Lo Bue, Erberto. 2017. "Tshe ring dngos grub, a Ladaki Painter and Astrologer." *Tibet Journal* 42, no. 1: 3–12.

Lopez, Donald S., Jr., ed. 2004. *Buddhist Scriptures*. London: Penguin.

Lopez, Donald S., Jr. 2007. "Mindfulness of Death." In *Religions of Tibet in Practice*, edited by Donald S. Lopez Jr., 315–35. Abridged ed. Princeton: Princeton University Press.

Lopez, Donald S., Jr. 2018. *Prisoners of Shangri-La: Tibetan Buddhism and the West*. Chicago: University of Chicago Press. First published 1998.

Luo, Yu, and Tim Oakes, and Louisa Schein. 2019. "Resourcing Remoteness and the 'Post-Alteric' Imaginary in China." *Social Anthropology* 27, no. 2: 270–85.

Maags, Christina. 2018. "Hierarchies and Competition within the Chinese ICH Transmitters System." In *Chinese Heritage in the Making: Experiences, Negotiations, and Contestations*, edited by Christina Maags and Marina Svensson, 121–44. Amsterdam: Amsterdam University Press.

Maags, Christina, and Marina Svensson, eds. 2018. *Chinese Heritage in the Making: Experiences, Negotiations and Contestations*. Amsterdam: Amsterdam University Press.

Makley, Charlene. 1994. "Gendered Practices and the Inner Sanctum: The Reconstruction of Tibetan Sacred Space in China's Tibet." *Tibet Journal* 19, no. 2: 61–94.

Makley, Charlene. 1997. "The Meaning of Liberation: Representations of Tibetan Women." *Tibet Journal* 22, no. 2: 4–29.

Makley, Charlene. 2003. "Gendered Boundaries in Motion: Space and Identity on the Sino-Tibetan Frontier." *American Ethnologist* 30, no. 4: 597–619.

Makley, Charlene. 2007. *The Violence of Liberation: Gender and Tibetan Buddhist Revival in Post-Mao China.* Berkeley: University of California Press.

Makley, Charlene. 2015. "The Sociopolitical Lives of Dead Bodies: Tibetan Self-Immolation Protest as Mass Media." *Cultural Anthropology* 30, no. 3: 448–76.

Makley, Charlene. 2018. *The Battle for Fortune: State-Led Development, Personhood, and Power among Tibetans in China.* Ithaca: Cornell University Press.

Makley, Charlene. 2020. "The Afterlives of the Tenth Panchen Lama in China's Tibet." LRCCS Occasional Lecture Series, October 16, 2020. Asian Languages and Cultures, University of Michigan.

Marcus, George, and Fred Myers. 1995. *The Traffic in Culture: Refiguring Anthropology and Art.* Berkeley: University of California Press.

Martin, Dan. 2005. "The Woman Illusion? Research into the Lives of Spiritually Accomplished Women Leaders of the 11th and 12th Centuries." In *Women in Tibet*, edited by Janet Gyatso and Hanna Havnevik, 49–82. New York: Columbia University Press.

Mauss, Marcel. 2002. *The Gift: The Form and Reason for Exchange in Archaic Societies.* Translated by W. D. Halls. Abingdon, Oxfordshire: Routledge Classics. First published 1925.

McGranahan, Carole. 2016. "Theorizing Refusal: An Introduction." *Cultural Anthropology* 31, no. 3: 319–25.

McGranahan, Carole. 2018. "Ethnography beyond Method: The Importance of an Ethnographic Sensibility." *Sites: A Journal of Social Anthropology and Cultural Studies* 15, no. 1: https://doi.org/10.11157/sites-id373.

McGuckin, Eric. 1996. "Thangkas and Tourism in Dharamsala: Preservation through Change." *Tibet Journal* 21, no. 2: 31–52.

Menchok Dondrub (sman mchog don grub). 2016. *Tu xiang zhong yin cang de li shi: Re gong tang ka ji yi ren kou shu kao cha* [The hidden history in the image: Rebgong thangka and the oral history of thangka painters]. Shanghai: Shanghai University Press.

Meyer, Birgit. 2015. "How Pictures Matter: Religious Objects and the Imagination in Ghana." In *Objects and Imaginations: Perspectives on Materialization and Meaning*, edited by Øivind Fuglerud and Leon Wainwright, 160–83. New York: Berghahn Books.

Michaels, Eric. 1994. *Bad Aboriginal Art: Tradition, Media, and Technological Horizons.* Minneapolis: University of Minnesota Press.

Miller, Daniel. 2001. "Alienable Gifts and Inalienable Commodities." In *The Empire of Things: Regimes of Value and Material Culture*, edited by Fred Myers, 91–115. Santa Fe: School of American Research Press.

Mölders, Tanja. 2014. "Multifunctional Agricultural Policies: Pathways towards Sustainable Rural Development?" *International Journal of Sociology of Agriculture and Food* 21, no. 1: 97–114.

Morgan, David. 2005. *The Sacred Gaze: Religious Visual Culture in Theory and Practice.* Berkeley: University of California Press.

Morphy, Howard. 2007. *Becoming Art: Exploring Cross-Cultural Categories.* London: Routledge.

Morphy, Howard, and Morgan Perkins, eds. 2006. *The Anthropology of Art: A Reader.* Oxford: Blackwell.

Mueggler, Erik. 2001. *The Age of Wild Ghosts: Memory, Violence, and Place in Southwest China.* Berkeley: University of California Press.

Myers, Fred, ed. 2001. *The Empire of Things: Regimes of Value and Material Culture.* Santa Fe: School of American Research Press.

Myers, Fred. 2002. *Painting Culture: The Making of an Aboriginal High Art.* Durham, NC: Duke University Press.

Myers, Fred. 2004. "Ontologies of the Image and Economies of Exchange." *American Ethnologist* 31, no. 1: 1–16.

Nash, June, ed. 1993. *Crafts in the World Market: The Impact of Global Exchange on Middle American Artisans.* Albany: SUNY Press.

Ngai, Pun. 2005. *Made in China: Women Factory Workers in a Global Workplace.* Durham, NC: Duke University Press.

Niessen, Sandra. 1999. "Threads of Tradition, Threads of Invention: Unraveling Toba Batak Women's Expressions of Social Change." In *Unpacking Culture: Art and Commodity in Colonial and Postcolonial Worlds*, edited by Ruth Phillips and Christopher Steiner, 162–77. Berkeley: University of California Press.

Niessen, Sandra. 2009. *Legacy in Cloth: Batak Textiles of Indonesia.* Leiden: Brill Academic Publication.

Oakes, Tim. 2016. "Ethnic Tourism in China." In *Handbook on Ethnic Minorities in China*, edited by Xiaowei Zang, 291–315. Cheltenham, UK: Edward Elgar.

Oakes, Tim, and Donald Sutton, eds. 2010. *Faiths on Display: Religion, Tourism, and the Chinese State.* New York: Routledge.

Osburg, John. 2013. *Anxious Wealth: Money and Morality among China's New Rich.* Stanford: Stanford University Press.

Osburg, John. 2020. "Consuming Belief: Luxury, Authenticity, and Chinese Patronage of Tibetan Buddhism in Contemporary China." *HAU: Journal of Ethnographic Theory* 10, no. 1: 69–84.

Paine, Crispin. 2013. *Religious Objects in Museums: Private Lives and Public Duties.* London: Bloomsbury.

Pal, Pratapaditya. 1969. *The Art of Tibet.* New York: Asian Society.

Palmer, David, Martin Tse, and Chip Colwell. 2019. "Guanyin's Limbo: Icons as Demi-Persons and Dividuating Objects." *American Anthropologist* 121, no. 4: 897–910.

Parezo, Nancy. 1983. *Navajo Sandpainting: From Religious Act to Commercial Art.* Tucson: University of Arizona Press.

Pema Tseden (pad ma tshe brtan). 2014. *Ma ni shi, jing jing di qiao* [The silent mani stone]. Beijing: Zhongguo minzu shying yishu chubanshe.

Pema Tseden (pad ma tshe brtan), dir. 2011. *Old Dog*. Color, 88 min. Brooklyn, NY: Icarus Films.

Phillips, Ruth. 2015. "Aesthetic Primitivism Revisited: The Global Diaspora of 'Primitive Art' and the Rise of Indigenous Modernisms." *Journal of Art Historiography* 12:1–25.

Phillips, Ruth. 2022. "The Issue Is Moot: Decolonizing Art/Artifact." *Journal of Material Culture* 27, no. 1: 48–70.

Phillips, Ruth, and Christopher Steiner. 1999. *Unpacking Culture: Art and Commodity in Colonial and Postcolonial Worlds*. Berkeley: University of California Press.

Potter, Pitman. 2003. "Belief in Control: Regulation of Religion in China." *China Quarterly* 174, no. 2: 317–37.

Price, Sally. 1989. *Primitive Art in Civilized Places*. Chicago: University of Chicago Press.

Price, Sally. 2007. "Into the Mainstream: Shifting Authenticities in Art." *American Ethnologist* 34, no. 4: 603–20.

Ptáčková, Jarmila. 2020. *Exile from the Grasslands: Tibetan Herders and Chinese Development Projects*. Seattle: University of Washington Press.

Quintman, Andrew. 2013. "Life Writing as Literary Relic: Image, Inscription, and Consecration in Tibetan Biography." *Material Religion* 9, no. 4: 468–505.

Rajan, Hamsa. 2014. "The Impact of Household Form and Marital Residence on the Economic Dimensions of Women's Vulnerability to Domestic Violence: The Case of Tibetan Communities." *Genus* 70, nos. 2–3: 139–62.

Rajan, Hamsa. 2015. "The Discourse of Tibetan Women's Empowerment Activists." *Revue d'Etudes Tibétaines* 33:127–53.

Reader, Ian, and George Tanabe. 1998. *Practically Religious: Worldly Benefits and the Common Religion*. Honolulu: University of Hawaii Press.

Reich, Aaron. 2024. "Conceptions of Divinity: Statue Making in Contemporary Taiwan and the Ritual of Embedding the Spirit (*rushen*)." *Material Religion* 20, nos. 3–4: 205–32.

Reilly, Maura. 2012. "Gonkar Gyatso: A Product of Occupied Tibet." In *Gonkar Gyatso: Three Realms*, edited by Griffith University Art Gallery and University of Queensland Art Museum, 10–25. Brisbane: Institute of Modern Art.

Reynolds, Elizabeth. 2011. "Social Networks and the Commercialization of Rebgong Tibetan Thangkas." *Columbia East Asia Review* 4, no. 1: 89–105.

Reynolds, Valrae. 1991. *Tibetan Buddhist Altar*. Newark, NJ: Newark Museum.

Rhie, Marilyn, and Robert Thurman. 1991. *Wisdom and Compassion: The Sacred Art of Tibet*. New York: Harry N. Abrams.

Robertson, Iain J. M. 2012. *Heritage from Below*. Farnham, Surrey: Ashgate.

Roche, Gerald. 2019. "Does Ideological Clarification Help Language Maintenance? Exploring the Revitalization Paradox through the Case of Manegacha, a Tibetan Minority Language." *Anthropological Linguistics* 61, no. 1: 1–21.

Roche, Gerald, and Lcag mo tshe ring. 2013. "Notes on the Maintenance of Diversity in Amdo: Language Use in Gnyan Thog Village Annual Rituals." In *Ex Ori-*

ente Lumina: Historiae variae multiethnicae, edited by Tiina Hyytiäinen, Lotta Jalava, Janne Saarikivi, and Erika Sandman, 165–80. Helsinki: Finnish Oriental Society.

Saxer, Martin. 2012. "The Moral Economy of Cultural Identity: Tibet, Cultural Survival, and the Safeguarding of Cultural Heritage." *Civilisations* 61, no. 1: 65–81.

Schein, Louisa. 1997. "Gender and Internal Orientalism in China." *Modern China* 23, no. 1: 69–98.

Schein, Louisa. 2000. *Minority Rules: The Miao and the Feminine in China's Cultural Politics*. Durham, NC: Duke University Press.

Schneider, Nicolas. 2020. "The Female in Contemporary Tibetan Art: The Artist Monsal Pekar (b. 1964)." Asianart.com, https://asianart.com/articles/pekar/index.html.

Shah, Alpa. 2017. "Ethnography? Participant Observation, a Potentially Revolutionary Praxis." *HAU: Journal of Ethnographic Theory* 7, no. 1: 45–59.

Shakya, Tsering. 1999. *The Dragon in the Land of Snows: A History of Modern Tibet since 1947*. New York: Columbia University Press.

Shepherd, Robert. 2009. "Cultural Heritage, UNESCO, and the Chinese State: Whose Heritage and for Whom?" *Heritage Management* 2, no. 1: 55–79.

Shepherd, Robert, and Larry Yu. 2013. *Heritage Management, Tourism, and Governance in China*. New York: Springer.

Sierksma, Fokke. 1966. *Tibet's Terrifying Deities: Sex and Aggression in Religious Acculturation*. The Hague: Mouton.

Silverman, Eric. 1999. "Tourist Art as the Crafting of Identity in the Sepik River (Papua New Guinea)." In *Unpacking Culture: Art and Commodity in Colonial and Postcolonial Worlds*, edited by Ruth Phillips and Christopher Steiner, 51–66. Berkeley: University of California Press.

Silverman, Helaine, and Tami Blumenfield. 2013. "Cultural Heritage Politics in China: An Introduction." In *Cultural Heritage Politics in China*, edited by Tami Blumenfield and Helaine Silverman, 3–22. New York: Springer.

Slattum, Judy, and Paul Schraub. 2003. *Balinese Masks: Spirits of An Ancient Drama*. Singapore: Periplus.

Slobodník, Martin. 2007. "Destruction and Revival: The Fate of the Tibetan Buddhist Monastery Labrang in the People's Republic of China." *Religion, State, and Society* 32, no. 1: 7–19.

Smith, Laurajane. 2006. *Uses of Heritage*. London: Routledge.

Steiner, Christopher. 1994. *African Art in Transit*. Cambridge: Cambridge University Press.

Steiner, Christopher. 1995. "The Art of the Trade: On the Creation of Value and Authenticity in the African Art Market." In *The Traffic in Culture: Refiguring Art and Anthropology*, edited by George Marcus and Fred Myers, 151–65. Berkeley: University of California Press.

Stephen, Lynn. 2005. *Zapotec Women: Gender, Class, and Ethnicity in Globalized Oaxaca*. Durham, NC: Duke University Press.

Stevenson, Mark. 2002. "Art and Life in Amdo Rebgong since 1978." In *Amdo Tibetans in Transition: Society and Culture in the Post-Mao Era*, edited by Toni Huber, 197–219. Kathmandu: Vajra Publications.

Stewart, Michelle Olsgard. 2014. "Caterpillar Fungus Governance in Developing Yunnan." In *Mapping Shangrila: Contested Landscapes in the Sino-Tibetan Borderlands*, edited by Emily Yeh and Chris Coggins, 175–98. Seattle: University of Washington Press.

Su, Junjie. 2020. "Managing Intangible Cultural Heritage in the Context of Tourism: Chinese Officials' Perspectives." *Journal of Tourism and Cultural Change* 18, no. 2: 164–86.

Sullivan, Bruce, ed. 2015a. *Sacred Objects in Secular Spaces: Exhibiting Asian Religions in Museums*. London: Bloomsbury.

Sullivan, Bruce. 2015b. "Reconsecrating the Icons: The New Phenomenon of Yoga in Museums." In *Sacred Objects in Secular Spaces: Exhibiting Asian Religions in Museums*, edited by Bruce Sullivan, 67–79. London: Bloomsbury.

Swergold, Leopold, and Eileen Hsiang-ling Hsu, Stanley Abe, Leigh Adamek, Dorothy Wong, and Qing Chang. 2008. *Treasures Rediscovered: Chinese Stone Sculpture from the Sackler Collections at Columbia University*. New York: Miriam and Ira D. Wallach Art Gallery, Columbia University.

Tang, Zhongshan. 2009. *Re gong yi shu* [Rebgong art]. Xining: Qinghai Renmin Chubanshe.

Tashi, Tsewang (tshe dbang bkra shis). 2018. *20 shi ji xi zang mei shu shi* [A history of art in twentieth-century Tibet]. Beijing: Zhongguo Zangxue Chubanshe.

Tenpa Rabgye (bstan pa rab rgyas). 1982. *Mdo smad chos 'byung* [The political and religious history of Amdo]. Lanzhou: Kan su'u mi rigs dpe skrun khang.

Tenzin, Jinba. 2014. *In the Land of the Eastern Queendom: The Politics of Gender and Ethnicity*. Seattle: University of Washington Press.

Tshe ring skyid. 2015. "Rka gsar, a Monguor Village in Reb gong: Communal Rituals and Everyday Life." *Asian Highlands Perspectives* 36:251–75.

Tsomo, Karma Lekshe, ed. 2019. *Buddhist Feminisms and Femininities*. Albany: State University of New York Press.

Tsondru Rapgye, comp. 2002. *Zhong guo zang zu wen hua yi shu cai hui da guan tu shuo ming jing* [The bright mirror illuminating the meaning of the great thangka of Tibetan art and culture in China]. Beijing: Minzu Chubanshe.

Tucci, Giuseppe. 1949. *Tibetan Painted Scrolls*. Rome: La Libreria dello Stato.

Tuttle, Gray. 2005. *Tibetan Buddhism in the Making of Modern China*. New York: Columbia University Press.

Tuttle, Gray. 2006. "Tibetan Buddhism at Ri bo rtse lnga / Wu tai shan in Modern Times." *Journal of the International Association of Tibetan Studies* 2:1–35.

Tythacott, Louise. 2017. "Curating the Sacred: Exhibiting Buddhism at World Museum Liverpool." *Buddhist Studies Review* 34, no. 1: 115–33.

Tythacott, Louise, and Chiara Bellini. 2020. "Deity and Display: Meanings, Transformations, and Exhibitions of Tibetan Buddhist Objects." *Religions* 11, no. 3: 1–25.

Van der Veer, Peter, ed. 2015. *Handbook of Religion and the Asian City*. Berkeley: University of California Press.

Vargas-O'Bryan, Ivette. 2011. "Disease, the Demons and the Buddhas: A Study of Tibetan Conceptions of Disease and Religious Practice." In *Health and Religious Rituals in South Asia: Disease, Possession and Healing*, edited by Fabrizio Ferrari, 81–99. New York: Routledge.

Venkatesan, Soumhya. 2020. "Object, Subject, Thing: Tamil Hindu Priests' Material Practices and Practical Theories of Animation and Accommodation." *American Ethnologist* 47, no. 4: 447–60.

Wang, Kangkang. 2010. "Re gong liu yue hui yi shi de she hui gong neng yan jiu: Yi Ga sha ri cun wei li" [Rebgong Lurol festival: Rituals and social functions in Rka gsar village]. Master's thesis, Minzu University of China.

Washul, Eveline. 2018. "Tibetan Translocalities: Navigating Urban Opportunities and New Ways of Belonging in Tibetan Pastoral Communities in China." *Critical Asian Studies* 50, no. 4: 493–517.

Weber, Max. 1981. *General Economic History*. New Brunswick, NJ: Transaction Publishers. First published in 1923.

Weiner, Annette. 1992. *Inalienable Possessions: The Paradox of Keeping-while-Giving*. Berkeley: University of California Press.

Weller, Robert, and Keping Wu. 2021. "Overnight Urbanization and Changing Spirits: Disturbed Ecosystems in Southern Jiangsu." *Current Anthropology* 62, no. 5: 602–30.

Wong, Winnie. 2013. *Van Gogh on Demand: China and the Readymade*. Chicago: University of Chicago Press.

Wu, Hung. 2022a. *Kong jian de dun huang: Zou jin mo gao ku (Spatial Dunhuang: Experiencing the Mogao Caves)*. Beijing: SDX Joint Publishing Company.

Wu, Hung. 2022b. *Spatial Dunhuang: Experiencing the Mogao Caves*. Seattle: University of Washington Press.

Wu, Keping. 2015. "'Ghost City': Religion, Urbanization and Spatial Anxieties in Contemporary China." *Geoforum* 65:243–45.

Wu, Qi. 2013. "Tradition and Modernity: Cultural Continuum and Transition among Tibetans in Amdo." PhD diss., University of Helsinki.

Xue Ming. 2013. "Altruism and Reciprocity among Friends and Kin in a Tibetan Village." *Evolution and Human Behavior* 34, no. 5: 323–29.

Xue Ming. 2017. "Gift Giving and Recordkeeping across Cultures." In *Advances in Sociology Research*, edited by Jared Jaworski, 45–74. New York: NOVA.

Yang, Jingqing. 2013. "The Impact of Informal Payments on Quality and Equality in the Chinese Health Care System: A Study from the Perspective of Doctors." *Health Sociology Review* 22, no. 3: 268–81.

Yeh, Emily. 2013. *Taming Tibet: Landscape Transformation and the Gift of Chinese Development*. Ithaca: Cornell University Press.

Yeh, Emily, and Chris Coggins. 2014. *Mapping Shangrila: Contested Landscapes in the Sino-Tibetan Borderlands*. Seattle: University of Washington Press.

Yeh, Emily, and Kunga Lama. 2013. "Following the Caterpillar Fungus: Nature, Commodity Chains, and the Place of Tibet in China's Uneven Geographies." *Social & Cultural Geography* 14, no. 3: 318–40.

Yü, Chün-fang. 2001. *Kuan-yin: The Chinese Transformation of Avalokiteshvara*. New York: Columbia University Press.

Yü, Dan Smyer. 2012. *The Spread of Tibetan Buddhism in China: Charisma, Money, and Enlightenment*. New York: Routledge.

Yü, Dan Smyer. 2014. "Pema Tseden's Transnational Cinema: Screening a Buddhist Landscape of Tibet." *Contemporary Buddhism* 15, no. 1: 125–44.

Zhang, Fan. 2019. "Transcendent Space, Mandala and Our Holy Empire: Multiple Spatial Imaginations of Mount Wutai and Multiple Identifications in the 18th Century." *Chinese Journal of Sociology* 39, no. 6: 149–86.

Zhang, Tracy. 2013. "Factory 'Nuns': The Ethnicization of Migrant Labor in the Making of Tibetan Carpets." *Gender, Place and Culture* 20, no. 6: 754–72.

Zhang, Yinong. 2012. "Between Nation and Religion: The Sino-Tibetan Buddhist Network in Post-Reform China." *Chinese Sociological Review* 45, no. 1: 55–69.

Zheng, Tiantian. 2006. "Cool Masculinity: Male Clients' Sex Consumption and Business Alliance in Urban China's Sex Industry." *Journal of Contemporary China* 15, no. 46: 161–82.

INDEX

iconometry, 8, 128, 135, 161, 170n13,
    183n21, 187n3
identity, 3, 35, 44, 112, 124, 146; artistic,
    36, 107, 161; ethnic, 18, 51, 62, 100;
    religious, 4, 17, 48, 61–62, 90, 95, 108,
    110, 166
income, 59, 69, 71, 88, 132, 146, 156,
    179n9, 179n11; low-, 78; source of,
    66, 69
ink painting, 21, 28
innovation, 4, 13–16, 31, 34–35, 113, 125,
    135–36. *See also* creativity; originality
inscription, 169n2, 174n13
intention, 3, 11, 52, 56, 60, 61, 90, 138, 157,
    184n4
"intercultural fields" (Myers), 11, 60

Japan, 47, 179n6, 181n34, 183n20
Jigme Chokyong (*'jigs med chos skyong*),
    132, 146
Jokhang Temple (*jo khang*), 33, 58
juniper branches (*shug pa*), 19

karma, 53, 88, 90, 114, 133–34, 140, 142,
    182n8; consequences of, 10, 49, 139,
    157
Karma Gadri (*karma sgar bris*), 25, 183n14
Kendall, Laurel, 3, 98, 180n17,
    185nn15–16
khenpo (*mkhan po*), 31
Kumbum Monastery (*sku 'bum byams pa
    gling*), 27, 28, 58, 60, 63, 113, 170n15
Kunzang (*kun bzang*), 27, 31, 84
kye go (*skyes sgo*), 14, 16, 137–43, 148–59,
    184nn2–3, 186n18, 186n26

Labrang Monastery (*bla brang bka shis
    khyil*), 27, 58, 86, 178n1
lama (*bla ma*): reincarnated, 55, 139. *See
    also* Dalai Lama; Panchen Lama;
    Shartshang
Ledderose, Lothar, 63, 178n22
Lhasa, 27, 32, 33, 55, 82, 145, 147, 159;
    museum in, 160, 176n8
Linrothe, Rob, 16, 26, 174n8
loan, 32, 34, 49, 54, 59, 70, 175n22

Loma Gyonma (*lo ma gyon ma*), 46, 51,
    59, 63, 64, 176n1
Lopez, Donald, 14, 172n31
Lower Wutun Monastery (*seng ge
    gshong ma mgo dgon pa*), 26, 50
Lurol festival (*klu rol*), 75, 92, 145
Lutso (*klu mtsho*), 2, 18, 38–44, 73, 93–110,
    164, 165, 181n1

Makley, Charlene, 84, 86, 114, 141,
    172n26, 179n7
mandala, 2, 118, 121, 152, 156, 186n25
Mandarin, 20, 54–55, 66, 74–76, 82,
    173n42
manifestation, 69, 88, 90, 103, 106, 181n6
Manjushri (*'jam dpal dbyangs*), 21, 54, 93,
    160, 182n6
manual (for painting), 8, 119, 161, 163,
    170n15, 173n42, 179n6. *See also*
    treatise
mantras, 103, 141, 147, 164, 174n13
Mao, Chairman, 15, 25, 87, 178n1
market, 3, 60; external, 11, 50, 51, 75, 137;
    intermediate, 15, 51, 58, 62, 75, 118,
    148, 161; internal, 11, 48, 52, 60, 64,
    157, 169n3
marketplace, 10, 63, 86, 116, 177n9
marriage, 72, 73, 76, 94, 96, 98, 178n4,
    180n14
married women, 17, 20, 68, 73–76, 178n4
master: as accreditation, 29, 38–40, 44,
    115, 163; of art, 66; *da shi*, 52–53, 56–63,
    177n14; ritual, 11
material religion, 10–12, 47
Medicine Buddha, 139, 156, 187n33
medium (material), 11, 17, 21, 64, 132,
    171n20
medium (person), 10, 48, 90, 103, 171n22
Menla Dondrub (*sman bla don grub*), 9,
    170n14
Menri style, 9, 171n17
merit (*bsod nams*), 49, 81, 87, 115, 122, 132,
    141, 176n4; accumulation or making,
    2, 11, 22, 33, 88–89, 103, 126, 144, 156,
    164, 185n9; religious, 3, 10, 17, 67, 91,
    108–9. *See also* virtue

meritorious act (*dge las* or *dge ba*), 10, 11, 17, 48, 59, 81, 88, 90, 103

Metropolitan Museum of Art (MoMA), 13, 111

migrant worker, 66, 71, 72, 74, 78, 81, 95, 107

mini-thangka (*tsa ka chung chung*), 43, 92, 97, 99, 107, 175n29

mobility, 17, 74, 83, 89, 143, 178n1, 185n12; versus immobility, 67, 108. *See also* translocality

modernity, 76, 117, 178n1, 185n15

modernization, 24, 66, 118

Mongolian (*meng gu zu*), 29, 32, 63, 123

Monguor (*tu zu*), 5, 18

moral economy, 64

mother, 66, 67, 73, 74, 91, 164; author's, 119–21; Jampa's, 138–50; Lutso's, 96–107; Shakyamuni's, 131–32. See also *a ma*

motif, 10, 25, 43, 104, 116

motorcycle, 19, 79, 83, 147

Mount Wutai (*ri bo rtse lnga*), 15, 113, 125, 126, 132, 155, 182n6

mourning, 14, 137, 143, 150, 157

mtshal thang (red thangka), 93

mural, 13, 28, 32, 147, 155, 160; Dunhuang, 24, 174n10

New Tibetan Painting, 13, 23, 25, 26, 32, 34, 136

New Year: celebration, 54, 74, 91, 96, 154, 164; prints, 13, 25, 122

next life, 89, 140

nirvana (*mya ngan las 'das pa*), 140

Nyantok (*gnyan thog*), 20, 21, 170n12, 173n38

Nyingma, 170n10

Oaxacan wood carving, 60, 68, 72, 173n39

offering, 48, 92, 118, 140, 143, 152–59, 163–66, 184n4

open the eyes (*spyan 'byed*), 9, 69, 104, 171n18

orchard, 80, 84, 85, 86, 181n32

originality, 15, 47, 57, 94, 112, 182n3. *See also* creativity; innovation

paintbrush, 8, 30, 41, 69, 73, 116, 148, 160–61

Palden Lhamo (*dpal ldan lha mo*), 68, 106

Panchen Lama, 174n17, 186n28

paraphernalia, 19, 116, 170n15

pastoralists, 17, 70, 72, 152, 179n12

pear, 80, 84–86

Pema Tseden, 137, 138, 143–49, 157, 159, 184n1

perspective (painting technique), 131

perspective (viewpoint), 4, 14, 15, 29, 88, 128, 151, 158

pigment: as painting material, 8, 9, 19, 49, 69, 93, 106, 128, 143, 174n9; as selling point, 1, 28, 33, 50, 114–16

pilgrimage, 82, 86, 92, 145, 147, 159, 181n28

"politics of presence" (Makley), 61, 63, 159

pollution (*grib*), 70, 118, 179n8

posture, 60, 93, 96, 107

Potala Palace, 8

power: bargaining, 72; political, 25, 36, 87, 152; spiritual or ritual, 46, 132, 138, 157, 181, 182

prayer wheel, 98, 139, 143, 154

proportion, 8, 128, 135, 161, 170n13, 183n21, 187n3

protection: cultural, 37; religious or ritual, 33, 89–90, 103, 110, 123, 141

Protection Zone, 36, 84, 147

protector deity (*lha pa*), 80, 86, 178n4, 180n15, 180nn24–25

protest, 114, 119

protocol: art-making procedure and rule, 3, 112, 135, 162; ritual procedure and rule, 16, 17, 57, 89, 125, 134

Protocols, 127–31, 183n23

"pure gaze" (Bourdieu), 15, 113, 172n35

purification, 139, 141, 143

Qinghai, 2, 5, 20, 40, 99, 115, 145, 173n1; administration, 27, 36, 114

Qinghai Art Association, 27

Qinghai Lake, 113
Qinghainese, 20

ready-made, 2, 47, 51, 57
Rebgong Art Research Institute (group),
    27, 29–31
rebirth ('khor ba), 2, 14, 88, 139–41, 150,
    157, 183n18, 185n6
Reform era (gai ge kai fang), 13, 24, 25, 48,
    172n29, 178n1
Refuge, The, 156
religious text, 63, 112, 126, 132, 135. *See
    also* scripture
"renaissance" (Linrothe), 13, 26, 27, 35, 136,
    146
reproduction, 47, 90, 94, 117
Rongwo: monastery (*rong bo dgon chen
    chos 'khor gling*), 1, 5, 8, 92, 139, 146,
    180n22; town of, 1, 33, 44, 164, 173n38
Rubin Museum of Art, 151, 172n33,
    186nn21–23
rumor, 76, 100

sacred object (art), 12, 63, 112, 177n9,
    182n12; versus commodity, 45–48, 51,
    64, 112, 163
sacred receptacles (*sku rten*), 10, 152, 157
sacred seed syllables (*om ah hum*), 3, 166,
    169n2
Sakya, 5, 170n10
Samten Rinchen (*bsam gtan rin chen*), 5
scapegoat, 77, 164
scripture: for art making, 10, 113, 122,
    128–35, 161, 183n23; as Buddhist text,
    15–16, 55, 60, 106, 127, 156, 163, 176n4;
    for chanting or praying, 119, 137–43,
    154, 156; for *cho kor*, 80–89, 138, *158*,
    159; for divination, 95–96. *See also*
    religious text
sculptor, 11, 49, 119, 169n1
secularization, 23, 49, 136. *See also*
    commodification
Sengeshong (*seng ge gshong*), 28, 41, *50*,
    70, 84, 160, 170n12, 181n13
sexuality, 77
shading, 9, 69, 71, 130

Shanghai, 27, 56, 119–24, 134, 148
Shanxi, 15, 53, 111, 113, 182n6, 183n19
Shartshang: the eighth, 33, 92, 139, 150,
    186n28; the first, 160, 187n1. *See also*
    lama (*bla ma*)
Shawo Tsering (*sha bo tshe ring*), 12–15,
    24, 27–30, 45, 135, 174n10
shopkeeper, 38, 41, 47, 116, 125
shrine room (*mchod khang*): cabinet
    (*kun dga' ra ba*), 152, 153, 155, 159,
    186n28; museum exhibit, 14, 151–52,
    172n33, 186n21, 186n23; for ritual,
    19, 138, 151–57, 164, 186n20, 186n28,
    187n32. See also *cho khang*
Sichuan, 5, 25, 77, 147, 174n11, 180n18
six-syllable mantra (*om ma ni pad me
    hung*), 89, 185n9
sketch: pad, 96; paper, 21, 22, 43, 104,
    161; as work of art, 8, 9, 28, 58, *129*, 133,
    162, 174n11, *plate 5*
Smithsonian, 151, 172n33
social media, 20, 59, 116
Socialist Realism, 15, 24; styles, 25
South Korea, 31, 47, 153, 185n16; Korean
    shaman in, 154, 185n15
souvenir, 53, 107, 113, 123, 134
sovereignty, 86, 171n23, 183n15
spirituality, 52, 112–13, 115, 119, 135
statue: Buddhist, 10, 27, 141–42, 151–53,
    166, 184n2; Catholic, 112; for sale, 47
Stevenson, Mark, 26, 31, 176n7
stone, 5, 36, 85, 86, 93, 107, 184n27,
    186n25; mani, 137, 138, 143–46, 149,
    159, 185n9; used to prepare canvas
    (*dbur rdo*), 28
stretcher, 8, 28, 41, 101, 138
student, 184; art, 59, 65–66, 127, 177n15,
    177n19; female, 70–77, 96, 165
stupa, 25, 140, 152, 160

Tashi Gyatso (*bkra shis rgya mtsho*), 10,
    125–36, 155, *162*, 170nn14–15, *plate 9*
teacher (*dge rgan*): of art, 8, 9, 14, 27, 30,
    70, 105, 177n11, 180n14; of religion,
    10, 58, 93, 121–23, 139, 141, 152–53. See
    also *ge gen*